OLD ST STEPHEN'S CHURCH, a mile from the village, uphill all the way is an unusual building on an ancient site. Here rest most of the Bay mariners who ended their time ashore together with memorials to some of the large company who were lost at sea, or died abroad.

STORM AND COMPANY

Alan Storm

Illustrated by the author

CAEDMON OF WHITBY
Publishers

Edited, researched and compiled by Alan Storm,
Plow house, Little Casterton, Stamford, Lincs.

© Alan Storm 1993
ISBN O 905355 41 5

Typesetting by PROPRINT,
27 Esk Terrace, Whitby, North Yorkshire.

Published by CAEDMON OF WHITBY,
128 Upgang Lane, Whitby. North Yorkshire.

Printed by SMITH SETTLE,
Otley, West Yorkshire.

Dedicated to the memory of
Raymond Storm, Master Mariner
(1892-1971)

ACKNOWLEDGEMENTS

With gratitude I record the great assistance of my cousin Jacob Francis ("Fran") of Whitby, my brother Roy, of Ramsbury, Wiltshire, and of Margaret Denham, the indefatigable archivist of the Whitby Literary and Philosophical Society.

I am also much indebted to Frank Storm of Durban and Eric Storm of Sydney, N.S.W.

My warm thanks for advice, practical help or information over the last twenty years are due to the following, a few of whom have regrettably not lived to see this work to which they contributed:

Mark Adlard, Hartlepool
James Storm Bedlington, York
Major Robert W.Bedlington, M.C., Matlock
Gloria Bagge, Bexley
Lizzie Edith Bye, Bay
Marie Y.Bourdas, Sandsend, Whitby
George Bennion, Leics.
David Burrell of Lloyd's
Edith Chandler, Ruislip
Derek Storm Copeland, Middlesbro.
Janet E.Cook, Wickford, Essex
Dennis Crosby, Thorpe
Elizabeth S.Davies, Pudsey
Ann Dear, Croydon
Mr. and Mrs.Eric Doran, Whitby
Colin Storm Evers, Gloucs.
Capt. Wm.Emmerson, Sleights, Whitby
Adrian Storm Frank, Whitby
Cedric Thompson Frank, Whitby
Capt. Godfrey Storm Frank, Whitby
Robert Dunn Frank, Whitby
Gwendoline Ferguson, Dorking
John Gaskin, Whitby
Capt and Mrs. Arthur Gibson, Bay
Mr. and Mrs. Ronald Storm Gillings, Bay
Major Jack Gillings, M.B.E., B.Sc., Scalby
Ann Gilman, Powys
Rev. Robin C.Greenland
Capt. James Granger, Thorpe
Margaret Granger, Walmer
Susan Halliwell, Norwich
Mary A.Harrison, Hartlepool
Michael Harrison, Whitby
Eliza T.Hunter, Hartlepool
Margaret Storm Jameson, Hon.D.Litt.
Ann Knightley-Smith, London
Richard Knightley-Smith, B.D.S.
Edward T.Kennaugh, Farnham
Mr. and Mrs.L.Labistour, Bay
Dr.J.R.Lamb, Leamington Spa
Alan Leng, Godalming
Philip Marchington, Corfe Mullen, Dorset
Mary McMahon, Deal

Dr.W.R.McLean, Middlesbro.
Lillian Mills, Thornton Dale
Norman Moorsom, Middlesbro.
Alan Morrison, B.Sc.
Alan Neesam, Northallerton
Mary M.Parker, Egton, Whitby
Richard Peene Pennock, Bay
Heather Perkins, York
Gwendoline Randall, Bay
David Richardson, Scalby
Marjorie Robson, Doncaster
Edward Russell, Bath
Beryl Ryan, Upminster
Mr. and Mrs. C.Spence, Bay
Mr. & Mrs. Alan Storm, Hartlepool
Andrew Storm, B.A.
Arthur Storm, Wallsend
Charles V.Storm, F.R.T.P.I.
George M.Storm, Hartlepool
Capt. Leonard Storm, Whitby
Dr.Marion Storm, Stockport
Michael Storm, B.A., Berks
Michael J.A.Storm, I.S.M.
Rachel Storm, M.A., London
Capt. and Mrs.Richard Storm, Whitby
Trevor Storm, B.Sc., Bristol
Eleanor Tennent, Thorpe
Elizabeth Estill Thompson, Thorpe
Bent Trier, California
M.T.Turnbull, Hants.
Edward Theaker Weatherill, Wendover
Sophie Weston, G.R.S.M.
Ruth Wilcock, Brentwood
Peter White, Whitby
Eileen Whittingham, Solihull
May Young, York
Janet Storm, Northants
Maurice Edmund Storm, Hull
Dr.Roger Dale Pyrah, Settle

CONTENTS

Foreword		6
Introduction		7

JACOB STORM'S MEMOIRS

Chapter 1	Family	8
Chapter 2	Ships and the Sea	22
Chapter 3	Master Mariner	45
Postscript	A voyage in the Fylingdales	65

PART 2	TABLES OF DESCENT	73
Chapter 4	No Male Issue	83
Chapter 5	William and Elizabeth	101
Chapter 6	Jacob and Ruth	143
Chapter 7	Matthew and Martha	171
Chapter 8	Mainly Edwards	179

Appendix 1	189
Appendix 2	191

FOREWORD

The decision to continue the admirable genealogical work of Jacob Storm and his grandson Raymond, my father, first bore fruit in the form of the *Storm Book* of 1982. There had been many encouraging - even eager - reponses to my enquiries about the current state of the family, and when the book appeared it was so quickly taken up that I had to think almost at once about satisfying the unexpected demand. Many of those who sought copies were not Storms, but nevertheless sent information about connections, their own roots in Robin Hood's Bay and Whitby, and involvement with the sea.

The great interest displayed prompted further research, and that eventually offered a new, broader perspective. This present work accordingly represents an attempt to use a representative family and its kin to depict a remarkably entrepreneurial and self-reliant small community of some significance at a point where English local history and maritime history overlap.

There is no end to the history of a family and its interconnections, and because information comes in continuously and often in small quantities there are many loose ends here. But one has to stop somewhere, hoping that others will recognise where they might add to the picture, especially where the other typical Bay names are concerned. Experience so far suggests the larger canvas will support the old local saying, "Speak of one family and you speak of them all". Hence *Storm and Company*.

In a work involving the collection and presentation of so much detail it would be unwise to pretend that there are no mistakes or omissions, but it is hoped that readers will concede in mitigation of error that the underlying account of the Bay community rings true.

PART 1

THE MEMOIRS OF JACOB STORM (1837-1926), MASTER MARINER

Introduction

Robin Hood's Bay is a coastal village in the parish of Fylingdales in the North Riding of Yorkshire, between the towns of Whitby and Scarborough. The parish is backed by high moors and shaped like a theatre facing the sea, with the great headlands of Peak and Ness for wings. Many writers have commented on the magnificent scenery of the bay, and as for the village, Whellan's directory of 1859 called it "singularly romantic".
In the middle of the bay a beach gives easy access to the lower, cultivable land, like an invitation to emigrants or invaders from across the North Sea.

The name of the chief place, Fyling, harks back to Anglo-Saxon times. Nearby is the formerly minor Scandinavian settlement of Fylingthorpe, attributable to later invasion. On the higher ground around there are numerous Scandinavian names, examples of which are Ravenscar, Stoupe Brow, Wragby, Saxby, Hawsker and Normanby. Remote from all is the old church of St Stephen, but its proximity to Cross Keld, a spring, suggests an ancient gathering place for early Christians from scattered settlements.

Robin Hood's Bay, a mile from the old church, emerges mysteriously as a fishing settlement in the first half of the sixteenth century. With the expanse of sea before and miles of moorland behind, it is remote, but the people could fish, and make use of the harbour at Whitby, a similarly isolated place. Most aspirations on this strip of the coast backed by relatively unproductive countryside were increasingly focused on the carriage of the goods of others by sea. On such a foundation the village was to become the scene of great activity. Much that is essential to the understanding of this somewhat enigmatic place can be gained from the histories of the inhabitants, one of whom, Jacob Storm, left the valuable record that follows.

CHAPTER ONE

FAMILY

I am writing this account of my family and my life at sea for the interests of my descendants and for anyone else who might be inclined to read it.

My family story begins with the survey of Whitby Abbey properties at the time of the Dissolution in 1539 when John, Matthew, Peter, William, Robert and Bartholomew Storm were named as tenants of the Abbey of Whitby in Robin Hood's Bay. The same names, perhaps their sons' , occurred again in 1565 when Queen Elizabeth sold the Abbey's possessions to the Cholmleys; and other names that have stayed in Bay Town down to modern times are Staincliff, Huntrowes, Richardson, Hewetson, Morsonne, Allatson and Cockerill. About the time I was born there were over a hundred of people of the old names living down in Bay itself and quite a lot more scattered around Fylingdales parish. How we have clung to 't' awd spot'!

Our origins before that are obscure, Robin Hood's Bay comes into history late. John Leland mentioned it about the time of the survey I mentioned, and he said it was a fishing place with a 'dok'. My guess is that it was a sort of growth that attached itself to Fylingdales, having more to do with the sea than the land; and the sea made it pretty well self sufficient and independent, and so it remained. The parish books show that not many Bay men took part in the public life of Fylingdales parish, compared with the farmers and others, and after all for much of the time a seafaring place doesn't have many men about.

A most interesting feature of the population of Robin Hood's Bay, time and again, is the excess of women and girls over men and boys. As well as the sea voyages there has also to be taken into account the great loss of life at sea, as revealed in our 'Register of Missing Seamen' [1] and on the tombstones in the old churchyard. It would often be said in the old days of a man who had been away for some time that he came back to find a wife.

The name Storm before Queen Elizabeth's time occurred quite often in eastern Yorkshire, and occasionally in East Anglia, but hardly anywhere else in England as far as I have been able to ascertain in collaboration with Mr.Philip Lawson and other genealogists. Mr. Lawson is an antiquary and a relation by marriage who became interested in Bay families. [2] I believe the earliest mention of the name in our district occurs in a document of 1332 concerning the outlawing of John Storm for the taking of deer in the Forest of Pickering. His kinsmen who put up money for him lived at Levisham. In the fifteenth century there are wills of Nicholas Storm, clerk of Greenhammerton (1405), and William Storm of Ellerburn (1496). Robert Storm, skinner, was registered as a freeman of York in 1535 and his namesake of the same trade, of 'Flamburg', appears in the York registry in 1441. I think we know whereabouts we belong!

In fact, the only other place in Britain where the name is common, to the best of my knowledge, is Findhorn in the North of Scotland, and it is a remarkable coincidence that the bearers of the name there follow the sea like ourselves. Fifty or so years ago when the Whitby schooner 'Oak' got into trouble in a gale off the Farnes a difficult rescue was carried out by the 'Elsie', Captain John Storm of Findhorn, and the crew were landed at that place.

It is commonly believed among us, and it has been said by some writers, that we are of Scandinavian origin; the main explanation being the strong connection with the sea and the frequency with which the name is met in Demark. I have met Storms in Norway who told me their forebears came from Demark, and I have seen 'Jacob Storm' on a shop in Sleswick.

It has been a source of much frustration to me that the parish of Fylingdales start late, that is to say in 1658, but I have nevertheless been able to compile tables of genealogy for my own and related families from the seventeenth century which show descents and also reveal a complicated

1. *The Genealogical Society has a copy of this work by William Conyers and Capt. Streeting in its collection in London. After its publication a record was kept by Capt. Arthur Gibson of Trongate, Robin Hood's Bay.*
2. *Philip Lawson, R.R.I.B.A., F.S.A., brother-in-law of Rebecca Storm on page 123.*

collection of cousins tying together the strands of Bay life down the years in a pattern that defies unravelling

Perhaps it seems strange that a fishing village without a harbour should have thriven as Bay did on shipping, for fishing cobles can work from beaches but cargo vessels can not, unless they are very small. The explanation is that the menfolk were used to making a living from the deep and when Whitby became an important seaport Bay men took to the trading vessels and Bay Town provided a stock of experienced mariners (a very handy one for the press-gang), who knew the rest of the world better than they knew the old country.

The women were a noble breed. They shouldered great responsibility during long absences of their men at sea, and suffered great sorrow when ships went down. I was only a child at the time but I remember the awful day in 1846 when the news arrived that the three Granger brothers had been lost on their way home from the fishing ground. They were related to most families, my own especially; but if the sorrow was widespread so was the

THE COBLE The design is said to be traceable to Scandinavia. It is well suited to working from a beach, being able to approach stern first while the deep forefoot keeps a firm 'hold' of the water. Robin Hood's Bay had no landing facility other than an approach to the beach between long 'scars' of rock; so the coble was basic to the local fishing.

support for the afflicted. After Mr. Walter White visited the 'King's Head' he wrote in his book 'A Month in Yorkshire', with some astonishment, that there had been over two hundred mourners at the funeral of the late husband of his hostess, my cousin Martha, but anyone who knew anything about local customs and above all about the meaning of family in Bay need not have been at all surprised.

Sometimes the women shared the dangers of the sea with their husbands. In the fishing days there was more than enough hard work for them helping to keep gear in good order, repairing nets, tanning sails, finding bait and so on. Hardworking, thrifty women, good managers as they say, made good wives, not only for Bay men but for strangers who came to stay, like the Officers of Customs (who were long present in strength, regrettably), coastguards, schoolmasters and clergymen. In any case it was necessary for many women to find husbands from elsewhere because of the shortage of men to which I have made reference. That is why, I theorise, typical Bay names like my own stayed here so well represented, while connections beyond our remote parish have most often been established through the distaff side. I have tried to pursue these connections as well as those nearer home and they have often proved interesting, linking our isolated commmunity with events in other worlds.

There is . . . my great-aunt Elizabeth, She was first married to Capt. Andrew Harrison of Robin Hood's Bay but he died, leaving her with a young son who grew up to be a sea captain. In 1808 this son was in command of the 'Nautilus' when she was taken by a French privateer and he remained a prisoner until 1814. This Harrison branch settled in Sunderland and through Andrew's descendants we have many connections (alas now tending to be forgotten) with the shipowning, commercial and professional life of that town.[1] My further interest in Elizabeth, however, is that she next married John Spink of H.M.Customs in 1769 and through them there is a maze of relationships with the 'outside world'. Their son John became a general with an adventurous career in India and other parts. [2] His nephew,

---

1. *One of Andrew's descendants, Capt.Squance of the P&O Line, was co-founder of the Hindoostan Steam Shipping Co. of Sunderland.*
2. *General John Spink, Knight of Hanover.*

Robert Danby, a bank official but son of a shipmaster, used to visit us in my young days. Elizabeth's daughter Esther had a daughter who married Thomas Jackson, Prebend of St Paul's. This clergyman was son of the famous Wesleyan minister, also Thomas, who came of a blacksmith's family, Scarborough way, and was chosen President of the Wesleyan Conference in 1839 and Centenary President in 1849. [1] I believe he preached in the Bay Chapel. One of the younger Thomas's sons became an admiral and for the time directed naval intelligence. [2] He called on me at 'Leeside' in 1914, introducing himself as a cousin. During the war one his sons commanded battleships and was also director of operations at the battle of Jutland. [3] Another son was master in the merchant service.

I have mentioned the subject and so I will say more about the local strong connections with the Wesleyans. It is, of course, well known that John Wesley himself paid no fewer than eleven visits to Bay, which lay on the road from Whitby to Scarborough . . . and many families maintained a strong Chapel tradition. When I was a boy I knew Thomas Newton and his wife who lived in the Low Street, and Thomas's brother Francis who lived at Thorpe, and these were brothers of the renowned preacher Robert Newton, chosen conference president on four occasions. The grandfather of my cousin Jane Ireland took for his second wife Anne, Rev. Robert Newton's sister. Jane was a benefactress of the Thorpe Chapel . . . and her grandfather, Samuel Ireland, who was clerk of the Peak alum works, often figures in documents as a leading trustee of the Bay Chapel.

1. *The Centenary Presidency was the earlier of the two.*
2.. *Admiral Sir Thomas Sturges Jackson, K.C.V.O.*
3. *Admiral Sir Thomas Jackson, K.C.B.*

John Ireland, his son, was a sea captain who ran the Bay Indemnity with Ben Granger - too well known for words of mine. [1] Some of the Newton information comes first-hand from the family and some from the family Bible, bought by Robert's mother Anne on a visit to York, which starts with her husband's birth in 1732 and is still kept in local hands by Mrs. Harding (nee Isabella Anne Newton) of Holgate, Thorpe Lane.

The Bay Chapel was built in 1778 on plots of land bought from Matthew Storm, who may have been the Matthew who built Prospect House, although he died in 1787 and I have seen nothing in the parish books before that. I believe it was the first house on the Bank Top, after the ancient farms. At that time, that is to say towards the end of the eighteenth century, the shipping was beginning to pay off and it is said that the timber used in Prospect House was brought from Scandinavia in the family's own ships. I should think timber from the Baltic was the normal trade for them, and in reasonable weather cargoes could brought ashore from ships lying off. Matthew's daughter Dorothy married John Moorsom, descendant of one of the oldest Bay families, which prompts me to remark that speak of one Bay family and you speak of them all. John, to cap it, had Francis Storm as a brother-in-law. The Moorsoms did well out of Whitby whaling; and John and Dorothy had a son, Richard, who became a Whitby magistrate, and built Airy Hill in 1790. His leading whaling captain was one of our Bedlington kin, and it was Richard's son Robert who commanded the 'Revenge' at Trafalgar. [2].

---

1. *This was one of the village's two ship insurance association.*
2. *The builder of Airy Hill was in fact the nephew and ward of John and Dorothy. His son was Admiral Sir Robert Moorsom, K.C.B.*

Another lady who married away and whose descendants I have been able to follow was my great-grandfather's sister Frances (1713 to 1798) who first married Robert Richardson, Master Mariner of Robin Hood's Bay, and one of another family with which we have links too numerous to record. Two years after their marriage Robert was drowned and Frances took her infant son Robert to Sunderland on her remarriage to Captain Joseph Wright, of a family with longstanding interest in Bay shipping. The Wright fortunes were followed in Sunderland shipping, and young Robert became a shipowner there and married Isabella Atmar, daughter and heiress of Gerard Atmar, a prosperous innkeeper with a lot of property in the town. Research into this branch . . .led me to Mrs. Leighton, Frances's great-great-great-grandchild whose husband happily turned out to be a pedigree agent in London. Together we found Gerard Atmar Richardson, M.D. of Plantation Enterprise, Demerara, and Robert, master Mariner, son of Robert and Isabella, prisoner-of-war in the fortress of Vedun in 1811. Frances's male descendants on the Wright side became lawyers in Sunderland for several generations. [1] Through Frances too there is a link with the ancient Northumbrian name of Shaftoe, and it is time and time alone that calls a halt to these explorations.

Not all the men stayed in Bay in the old days, and even if they did most of them travelled the world's seas a good deal. My grandfather's cousin Edward had an interesting career far from his boyhood haunts and the fishing, although he remained a sailor. He ran off to sea on his mother's

---

1. *Jon Joseph Wright was a Deputy Lieutenant of Durham and Solicitor to the Sunderland Dock Company and the Sunderland Improvement Commissioners.*

Jacob Storm's Memoir

remarriage and for the rest of his life went by her maiden name of Hall. In 1776 he married in New York the daughter of the master of a West India packet. He commanded the transport 'Empress of Russia' before entering the Navy as master in 1777, and went on to see considerable fighting in HM Ships *'Vigilant'*, *'Cornwall'* and *'Sandwich'*, and aboard the last he was Admiral Rodney's Navigator. The Admiral stood godfather to one of his sons, George Rodney, who died while still a midshipman. Edward became Master Intendant at Antigua, and died there of yellow fever. His eldest son, another Edward Storm, alias Hall, had an active and adventurous career which is related in O'Byrne's 'Dictionary of Naval Biography'. [The extract is on page 186.]

This last Edward's son was a lawyer in the employ of the Post Office and he visited me at Bay to look up his kinsfolk and became a frequent visitor and correspondent.[1] We shared an interest in carpentry and woodcarving.

There was a mystery that he and I could not for certain resolve. The mother of the runaway Edward remarried and her second husband was John Granger. Her youngest son was called Reuben and in the crew list of the 'Empress of Russia' there is one Reuben Granger. Whether he was Edward's brother or half-brother I do not know for sure. What is sure is that Reuben was lost when the 'Ville de Paris', a prize, foundered in 1782 in a Caribbean storm, and there is a tradition in that branch of the family that Reuben followed Edward's fortunes and went to sea.

---

1 *'Grandson' is meant here.*

Of the men who stayed with local vessels, not all were entirely concerned with the fishing, and some at least found part of their livelihood in trading. My great-grandfather Andrew Storm once took a cargo of cloth, hundreds of yards of stuff, to Yarmouth in an open boat. That was in 1767, and the event was recalled in the 'Whitby Gazette's' 'Old Time Diary' some years ago. There are still those who will remember how before the days of the railway when a family wanted to move to Middlesbrough, or Shields, as many did eventually, it was usual for the household goods to go by sea, it being easier that way.

A look at Mr. Weatherill's excellent compilation pages 42 and 48 will show how Taylor and Isaac Storm were owners of the ships 'Constant Matthew' and 'Matthews' early as 1747 and 1749 respectively.[1] I dont't think they were involved in the alum trade which depended on the sea transport (the Peak alum works being more or less inaccessible otherwise) because the large amount of ship rates they paid to the parish, in accordance with local custom, indicates vessels too big for that sort of work on our rocky shores.

Issac made a will in 1763 and it gives the impression that shipping had made him fairly comfortably off. The witnesses to Isaac's will were Edward Cayley and William Hauxwell. The latter had succeeded Arthur Cayley, deceased, as curate. Isaac also mentioned a Benjamin Chapman, Mary Storm's husband, who was a master mariner and came of the Whitby

---

1. *Richard Weatherill, The Ancient Port of Whitby and its Shipping, 1908.*

banking family which was to provide. the Bank of England with a director and Whitby with a member of Parliament. Aaron, the infant son of Benjamin and Mary, is buried in the old churchyard.

These people were mixed up with the shipping business. Very interesting to me too was the will of Isaac's grandfather, Thomas, because there went with it a list of his goods at the time of his death, and these possessions help a reader to build a picture in his mind of how a Bay fisherman lived about two hundred and fifty years ago. Thomas, with Robert and Bartholomew Storm, James Helme and Robert Staincliffe, was drowned near Filey Brig in 1690, and this number of crew shows they must have been in one of the bigger Bay boats.

There is no doubt that over the years the fishing paid, if the awful cost in life and limb is not taken into account, and there followed a movement into shipping and trading. In either business the risks of many kinds were high.

The earliest parish record I could find of our local shipping was in the Constable Book for 1751, when the rate to be paid by owners to parish funds was a penny in the pound.

Owners, some of whom were masters, paid as follows:

	s	d		£	s	d
Isaac Storm	1	6	Henry Frank			4
Robt. Storm		6	John Cockerill		1	2
Taylor Storm	2	4	Wm. Watson		2	4
Thomas Richmond	1	6	John Moorsom			4
Phatuel Harrison	1	4	Andrew Rickinson		1	2
Thos. Cropton	1	6	Charles Gray			7
John Hill		7	Isaac Hornby			10
Wm. Richardson	1	6	Wm. Newton		1	10
Dan Huntrods		9	Joseph Wright		1	0
Geo. Richardson		4	" " old ship			6
Rd. Tindale		9	Matthew Wright			6
John Tindale		9	Total	1	5	1

This rating system was absent from any parish books I saw dated after 1818.

The payment in poor rates alone of £33 on fifteen ships seems to have been the finishing touch.

More has been written and said about illicit than about lawful trade on the coast, and in my opinion it is only reasonable to suppose that those who had boats or ships mixed fishing and trading with a little smuggling. It was only too easy when Dutch and English fishing fleets met in the middle of the North Sea. The career of William Storm (1783-1851) illustrates what could happen, because his gear was confiscated and he saw the inside of Morpeth or Durham Gaol (I don't remember which) and he died poor. He is to be found listed among the inmates of Whitby Seamen's Hospital, towards the end of his days, about the time I was bound apprentice. Poor William traded around a bit in his father's brigantine 'Juno' which was chiefly employed in the Hamburg trade, but in 1815 when William and his younger brother James were master and mate of her she brought Louis Philippe of France over from Ostend to Harwich and into exile. It is a little amusing, after the passage of years, to recall that William's uncle by marriage was Officer of Customs John Spink.

My grandmother Storm's cousin, John Pearson, was another offender I knew in my young days, and he lost his holdings in Staintondale.

My readers so far, if any, will surely have realised by now what a great source of interest Robin Hood's Bay and its people have been for me, and how great my affection is for the place. But some may well want to know how I came by some of my information, which is not from historical books and documents.

The answer is that the collection of information was one of my interests long before my retirement from sea. It must be remembered that I was born in 1837, and that as three-score and ten is no great age among Bay folk I knew many old people who had tales to tell of a hundred and fifty years ago. When I first went to sea my grandfather, Andrew, was still living and the parish register shows he was baptised in 1778. Then there was Israel Allison of one our "original" Bay families. He was baptised in 1744 and I remember him slightly. He was a kinsman, and he followed the usual path which led to the sea and became master. When he was commanding a transport in the French wars, with his son as mate, he was captured by the enemy and he remained in their hands for many years, but Israel made up for lost time by living on at Bay till he was nearly one hundred years old. Another long in French hands was Matthew Storm.

Letters of my own family and of my mother's have been another useful source. Among them I have kept those of my great uncle William

Richardson who was pressed into the navy in 1794 and wrote with great affection to his parents from several of H.M. Ships. I think some extracts from these would not be out of place. He wrote from London in July, 1790, saying,"I have no protection now. My master cannot get any for me but he has put me and John Castles ashore to a very good house until our ship be out . . We are at Mrs. Kennedy's, grocer, in Wapping. They pressed three of our boys last night . .but the master expects to get them clear again'. It would seem that William avoided the pressgang then, but in 1794 he reported from Spithead, "I have been pressed aboard the 'Saturn' . . .which is very hard after coming off a long tedious voyage from India after a passage of eight months from China. I was in great hopes. . .of seeing you. I dont't know when I shall have the opportunity. . .as there is no expectation of the war being over soon". A year later William's letter came from H.M.S."Brunswick" at Spithead, "fitting out with all our might", and in August 1796 the vessel was at Spithead "not as yet sailed". By the end of the year she was in the West Indies and William sent from there news of the death by yellow fever of "my old friend and playmate and much lamented Martin Pearson. . .He died in Port Royal Hospital and earnestly begged me to write to you. . .I am sorry to acquaint you that the West Indies is very sickly at present. We have lost one hundred hands since we left England".

Martin Pearson I can best identify through his mother Mary (nee Storm) who had a house in Bay Quarter and rented Moorsom's Ground or Goose Gates, now held by Wm. Wood of Croft Farm, Thorpe. Mary's brother was John Storm or 'Auld Stormy' who kept a public house in Long Entry where they brewed strong ale. Edward Storm, late of Thorpe, once tried it as a boy and was intoxicated for the first and last time in his life.

As well as Martin there was also at Port Royal in 1796 Joseph Tindale whom William once visited aboard the frigate 'Lubeck'. I wonder how many others of our people were in that dreadful place then. Joseph was lucky, for he survived, and if my memory serves me right he commanded the locally owned brig 'Mercury' many years after he got out of the Navy.

The last letter from H.M.S. Brunswick is to my Richardson great-grandparents from one William Rushmore informing them of the 'Miserable News of your son W.Richardson who was drowned on the 20May. I thought proper to write to you my being shipmates of him seven years and Messmates with him so long. . .'. that was in June and in October another letter shows how my great-grandfather, whose ship was in the Wear, called on his relative Joseph Wright, the lawyer in Sunderland, to see about son William's affairs. In a sad letter he wrote home to Bay that there was no word from the Admiralty about the dead men and that he was to put to sea. 'We are are all loaded ready for sea', he says. 'John Bedlington is in and will be loaded tomorrow. Give my love to all our family'. I hope I shall be forgiven a little pride when I say these people were cast in a stoic mould.

Whilst on subjects connected with the pressgang I recall the rule of the Unanimous Benefit Society of Robin Hood's Bay, whose meetings started at the King's head, kept at that time by Isaac Barnard, who was related in one way or another to most of those present, including my grandfather. That was in 1784, and the rule book in those far off hard times said that any member who was pressed into the Navy would be entitled to 'benefit on return to 'Robin Hood Town' - provided he paid off arrears of subscriptions.

Mention of the benefit Society reminds me that there was an attempt to run such a society for the young men of Bay. James Storm, the aforementioned mate of the 'Juno' was one of the last members of this, and from his daughter Rebecca (Mrs. Wm. Bedlington) I learnt how he used his share of the funds at the winding up to buy a grandfather clock.

Putting all my gleanings together gives me such pleasure that I have to confess that I am writing for my own amusement as well as to satisfy the curiosity of my descendants, but they will be unusual people if they are not inquisitive enough to want to know the sort of folk they came from.

Now I am coming nearer to the point where I can give an account of my own career, one typical of the mariners of Bay Town.

VIEW NORTHWARD OVER THE VILLAGE which was described by John Leland about 1540 as 'a fishing place with a dok'. The great headland gave shelter from the north-west gales, once a rare facility on a dangerous coast. In time of Queen Elizabeth there was a recommendation concerning a pier, but there is no further evidence of such a development.

CHAPTER TWO

SHIPS AND THE SEA

In the year 1850 when I first went to sea for a living our people did not value formal schooling in the way they do today. Nor was it easily obtained especially above the elementary level.

The boys had every reason and encouragement to go to sea. Their parents and relatives were all more or less interested in their future, and the fishing had become less remunerative than it had been. There were even at one time teachers of navigation in business in Bay. Walker Tindale is one I remember.

It is true that there were seventeen cobles, two luggers and a yawl in the fishing, but numbers of the adult fishermen had already become merchant seamen and the boys almost without exception were beginning to be trained in the growing fleet of cargo vessels belonging to the place, with the same object in view.

All fisherlads, and indeed nearly all men and boys in Bay, could row and steer, box the compass and knot and splice before they became apprenticed to shipmasters or owners to learn the craft of the mariner. I had my first steering and swimming lessons from an old whaling harpooner, a giant of a man, a real old sea-dog, who told us boys many hair-raising and wonderful tales about hunting whales in Arctic seas.

Before I continue my personal story it is necessary, as will I hope be apparent, that I say something about the fishing and how it led the way to the deep sea voyaging that was to be the living of so many local men.

The parish register shows that Robert Moorsom, Thomas Robson, John Skerry, Thomas Storm and his son Thomas were all lost in their five-man boat in 1686, and that James Helme, Robert Staincliffe and Thomas, Robert and Bartholomew Storm suffered the same fate in 1690. This is sad but clear evidence of fishing from big boats. Such larger boats were rated, like houses, for parish funds. In 1762 the parish books give fourteen boats paying poor, church and constable rates.

Jacob Storm's Memoir

In Fisherhead Quarter the boat-ratepayers were Thomas Bedlington, James Helme, John Richardson, Israel Huntrods, Zachariah Granger, William Prodam and Matthew, James and Edward Storm. Those in Bay Quarter were William Moorsom, Thomas Bedlington, John Nightingale and Andrew and William Storm. How familiar these names are, and what a nightmare for the genealogist! I have had to sort out more that twenty Isaac Storms over the years.

The cobles on which these fishermen paid their rates were found winter quarters up the cliff at Bay and the yawls and luggers went to Whitby.

The Reverend Mr. Young writing at Whitby in 1817 gave the number of cobles fishing there winter and summer as thirtyfive. The catches were disposed of locally or to panniersmen and he said each large boat dealt with thirty tons of fish annually. Incidentally William Storm, panniersman, became a freeman of York in 1551, so the city's register says. Mr. Hinderwell the Scarborough historian states that two Bay boats did so well in 1796 that each man's share was over fifty pounds, and that was without counting the great annual expedition to the Yarmouth herring fishing. I would say that the well cut stonework of the houses and the cottages of Bay is proof sufficient that in the eighteenth century and well into the nineteenth prosperity was the rule here.

The larger boats were nearly fifty feet in length and over fifty tons. They were decked and lugger rigged, and they were swift sailers. Each carried two of the smaller cobles, and there were seven hands as a rule. They sailed out towards the Dogger Bank and in the chosen spot three men in each coble took lines away from each side of the anchored boat, leaving one man on watch, each line having hundreds of baited hooks and being held across the stream by the coble.

Line fishing began with Lent and in August came the Yarmouth herring season, when nets were used. The womenfolk often went along to help the men take care of their effects.

When they came back after a good season they brought new furniture and ornaments for their houses and many of these remain as heirlooms with their descendants today. Clocks, especially the grandfather variety, were favourites.

Weather permitting, they landed gear and stores at Bay. Otherwise they went to Whitby, laid up for the winter and carted their effects home by road. After the return a great supper was made.

The cobles from which the winter fishing was done were only twenty-six feet long, with flat bottom, deep forefoot, sharp stern and carrying capacity of about a ton. Their fishing grounds extended to deep water, about three or four miles out, positions being determined by weather an checked by reference to distant landmarks such as 'Swallow', t'stick', 'Farside's Out', 'Minster', 'Ower Robin a Trum', 'Weapons Ower t'castle', 'Humber Head' and others.

During the summer months when the larger boats were still fishing locally they folded their wings on Sundays and rested like monster gannets on Grunwick Deep in the shelter of North Cheek. They delivered some catches on weekdays from there, and weather allowing took on store and more baite lines. I remember talk of longer periods of steady weather in those days, with moderate land and sea breezes.

During the fine season fishermen and sailors who from age or infirmity were unable to go deep sea augmented the coble fishing with two-man craft and fished near the shore with trunk 'hoop nets' for crabs and lobster, nets for salmon and handlines for such small fish as haddock, whiting, flounders and rockfish, all of which could be caught in abundance. Bait was plentiful. Mussels were brought from Boston deeps and the Tees and stored between the scars. Fishermen's wives and daughters picked flithers from the rocks at various places between Maw Wyke and Hayburn Wyke and they also baited the lines, and twenty or thirty men digging sandworms in the Landing was a common sight. Large catches of cod, ling, sole, halibut. skate. haddock and others were landed.

The Panniersmen's route was over the moors, with packhorses, by May Beck, Lilla Rig, Ellerbeck and Saltergate to Thornton Dale, Pickering, Malton and York. When carts came into use they took an extra horse to get them up to the Saltersgate Brow and sent it back from there by man or boy.

All the unsold cod, ling, sole and skate were cleaned, salted and dried in the sun, and all except the skate were sold by the ton to the northern seaports for ship use. The haddock were cut up and used for baiting the haaver lines hooks for the big boats. [1] Cod sounds were taken from the bones, cleaned, salted and bleached and packed in small cases for market, and the fish livers were converted into oil for domestic use.

It was the women who did most of the shore work, such as gathering bait, baiting lines, barking sails and nets and spreading them in the fields and so on, they were noted for their methodical house-keeping and the stately gait which much exercise and carrying of burdens on the head gave them.

1 *The haavers were long, deep-sea lines: the term is of Scandinavian origin.*

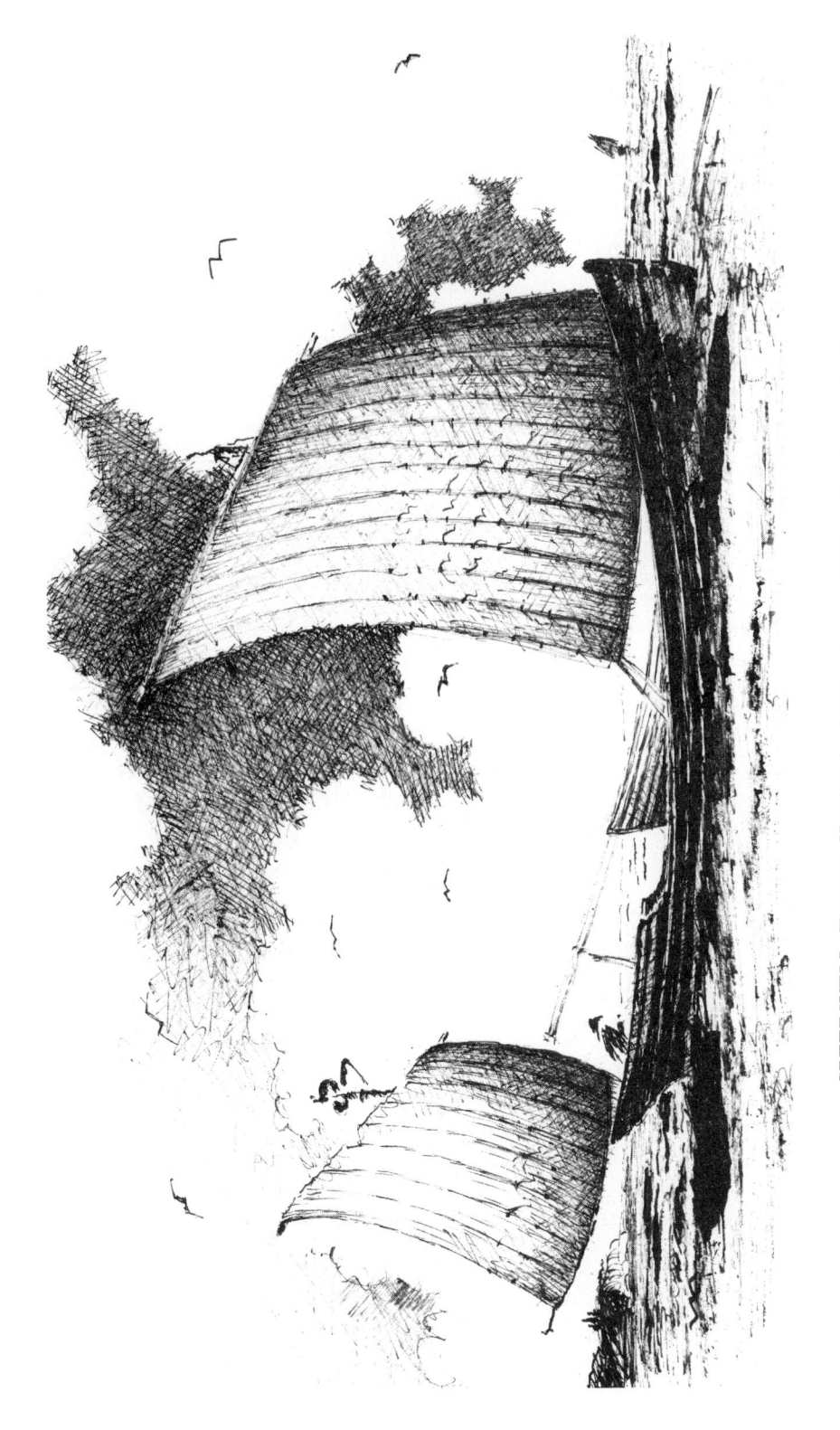

SPEEDWELL Thomas Harrison's fishing lugger. "When the larger boats were fishing locally, they folded their wings on Sundays and rested like monster gannets on Grunwick Deep in the shelter of North Cheek.

Notwithstanding the drain on the ranks of the fishermen made by merchant shipping the work was prosecuted with vigour until the middle of the last century, when there were seventeen cobles and three large boats, that is to say the luggers 'Speedwell' and 'Isaac and Isabella' and the yawl 'Providence Protector'. But the young fishermen, almost to a man, came to be apprenticed in the Mercantile Marine, so that towards the end of the century the fishing was a small fraction of what it had been and the native fishermen were represented by one family of Storms, William, Thomas, Reuben and Oliver the sons of Thomas Smith Storm (still going strong at ninety-odd years) and his wife Rebecca (nee Moorsom).

They combined their fishing with lifeboat work as coxswains and crew, and among them saved many live. They descend from my great-great-uncle Isaac who went whaling with Scoresby.

At last the inhabitants of Robin Hood's bay had to learn to be contented with stale fish imported from Scarborough and Whitby and even places further afield.

It goes without saying that the fisherfolk were tough, hardy and not lacking in courage. Many suffered death in their calling, but the rest were undeterred. The reasons for their disappearance, other than the merchant shipping, were the extension of the railway transport of fish, which interfered with local markets, and, from what I remember of local experience, great and prolonged deterioration in weather conditions which made the Bay unusable by the improved vessels that came along.

I have written about the fishing because it brings me to the subject of my grandfather, Thomas Harrison, some of whose notes I have. In 1841 he went to Yarmouth in the lugger 'Speedwell', 59 tons, and his account was as follows:

Disbursements at Yarmouth

	£	s	d		£	s	d
Thomas Pinkney		15	6	Oct 9th 100 herrings at Yarmouth		4	6
Boyce Harrison	9	0	0	Oct 16th 700 herrings at Yarmouth @ 4/-	1	8	0
Wm Storm	7	0	0	Oct 23rd 800 herrings at Cromer @5/-	2	0	0
Geo Pinkney	5	0	0	Oct 25th 5000 herrings at Whorlton at £24 a last	12	0	0
Robert Pratt		18	0	Oct 27th 5000 herrings at Whorlton at £25 a last	12	0	0
Henry Cayley		18	0	Nov 12th 7 lasts at Whorlton at £13 10s a last	94	10	0
John Pinkney	5	0	0	Nov 15th 7 lasts to a Frenchman	6	15	0
Balance	110	1	6				
	128	17	6		128	17	6

If you consider the wages of my great-uncle Boyce and my cousin William, the master's return on the venture was good, because he got the usual 'one for the boat'. The fishing was once even more lucrative that this. I should explain that the low pay went to the boys, who had no sort of financial share in the venture.

Even in 1859 Whitby fish dealers paid out £26,262 for herrings, and Rev. Mr. Young said in 1817 that Whitby fishing was worth £25,000 to £30,000 a year.

At all events my Harrison grandparents saved and bought a brand new trading vessel, a brigantine, in 1844, for £1,104.13.2, and they called her 'Harrisons'.

This was a culmination of many years of hard work. Thomas's grandfather (also Thomas) had also been a fisherman. He lived from 1721 to

1795 and he became the owner of the square-sterned lugger 'Speedwell', an open boat, in 1787, and later boats in the family kept the same name. My grandfather's 'Speedwell' carried six men and a boy, and ten men all told when the bounty was paid. The older Thomas had two sons who were lost at sea. One of them, John, also had two sons lost, and the circumstances of the loss of one of them, John junior, are recorded on his tombstone. He went to help a vessel off the rocks and his coble was overwhelmed by the sea.

My Harrison connections were close, the reason being, in part, that my grandmother Harrison was born Mercy Storm. She was sister of the venturesome contrabandist William. When I was very young and my parents were away at sea it was with my Harrison grandparents that I stayed often. My indomitable grandmother played an active part with her sailor sons in the running of the Harrison vessels after my grandfather died in 1860, and she lived until 1880, when she was 93.

The 'Harrisons' was my first ship when I went away to sea. She had six busy years before I joined her. Thomas and Mercy put her in the care of their son John in July, 1844, on his leaving the 'Rusco Castle'. John was twenty-eight and stayed with her for nine years. I can give a little more information about costs because seventeen years before this Mercy's brother James, former mate of his father's vessel 'Juno' bought a new ship in partnership with John Smith of Bay from Messrs. Spearman and Rowntree of Ayres Quay, Sunderland. I have inherited rather more details about this purchase.

The agreement was made 26th January, 1827 and it was for the payment of £1,260 for the hull. This was later changed for the addition of a break at a charge of £17.10.0 The money was to be paid as follows:

- £100 at the signing of the agreement
- £100 when the bends are sound
- £150 when the hull is all timbered
- £150 when the decks are laid
- £160 when the vessel is launched into the water
- £600, the remainder, after the launching, in approved bills for equal sums at three and four months intervals.

Andrew Storm's schooner 'Crosby'

ANDREW STORM'S SCHOONER CROSBY which the nineteen-years-old Jacob brought home unaided when his father was taken ill in Rouen.

HARRISONS "was my first ship when I went away to sea. I was to serve on her for six years." She was built at Whitby by Barrick, a name respected in the town for quality of work.

When the 'John and James' was fully rigged and fitted out the final cost was £1757 and she was about 170 tons. She cleared the Sunderland customs house on her maiden voyage with twelve keels of coal for London on 3rd May, 1827, fourteen weeks from the date of agreement. On sailing, James, her master, paid £3.8s.2d. harbour dues, two guineas to the trimmers and £1.5.0d. for foying out. [1] The master was entitled to £9.10s. per voyage. Her carrying capacity was 1800 quarters for oats, 1352 for barley and 1245 for wheat, which meant she was getting on for half as big again as the 'Harrisons'. Some idea of the cost of sails I give from details of replacements in the 'Harrisons'.

Mainsail, made by Mr.Joss of West Hartlepool	131	sq. yds.
Top sail made by Andrews of Whitby	111	"
T'gallent made in London	50	"
Main Royal made by E.Watson of Rochester of no.7 Coker canvas (at 1/6 per sq. yard)	22	"
Top sail made in London	90	"
Fore Top sail made in London	111	"
Fore T'gallant made in London	50	"
Top mast staysail made in London	40	"
Jib made by Andrews of Whitby	73	"
" " " Day and Butterwick in November, 1854 for £5.12.11d.	75	"

Canvas worked out at about 1/6 a yard and this vessel carried over 750 square yards of sail, bringing the cost of a suit of canvas to over £56. This is only a rough idea, however, because the rig of the 'Harrisons', like that of many ships, was changed from time to time to suit her owner's or her master's needs. The sails were no small item if the lot were carried away in foul weather, a not infrequent occurrence.

---

1. *Foymen are the boatmen who seek work on the river, assisting ships into and out of the harbour.*

Jacob Storm's Memoir

The 'Harrisons' sailed on her maiden voyage in July 1844, for the Baltic and thence for London. In Dantzic she loaded 951 quarters of barley at 3s 5d a quarter and proceeded to the Thames, spending in all one month and twenty three days on the voyage. She sailed again in ballast, for Dantzic, and took on 845 quarters of wheat at 4/- a quarter, for Jersey, a trip of two months and one day. There followed that year two voyages between Middlesbrough and London. For the second of these crew and pay were: John Harrison, master, £8 a voyage; Thomas Harrison, mate, £5. 10s; William Barnard and Geo Robinson, A.Bs, £4. 10s a month each; two apprentices, Edward Harrison and George Shafe, received about 7s 6d a month each.

The next year's trading began in February with a trip in ballast to Archangel and it hardly needs stating that she ran into bad weather! Next she went to Elisinore and Landskrona with 1099 quarters of oats at 2s 3d a quarter. She took a month and eleven days over this and A,Bs' wages were down to £3.5s a month. In this month Thomas Harrison left to take over the brig 'Fortitude', My grandparents had given John Mennel of Robin Hood's Bay £600 for her. Edward Storm now became mate of the 'Harrisons'. In 1846 she made a voyage to Riga and the rest of that year was spent in the coal trade and coasting. For that year I have a record of a mate's pay at £4 and an A.B's at £3 a month.

My records for 1847 are fairly complete. There were ten voyages and I list them because they give a fair idea of the work.

1. Middlesbrough-Rochester with 183 tons of coal at 9.0d a ton, in February;
2. Whitby, Landskrona, Helsingborg and Leith with 1090 quarters of oats at 3s. 0; she took one month and eighteen days over this;
3. Pilau and London - no freight recorded;
4. Middlesbrough and Guernsey with eight keels and four waggons of coal at two guineas a keel;
6. St Peter Port, Guernsey, to London with 185 tons of stone at 6s. 3d;
7. Middlesbrough and London with coal;
8. Middlesbrough and Ipswich;
9. Middlesbrough and London;
10. Middlesbrough and Rochester, carrying 180 tons of coal at 8s.6d.

In 1848 the 'Harrisons' called at Middlesbrough, Plymouth, Guernsey, London, Stockton, Rochester, Whitby, Hartlepool, Whitstable, Traelleborg, Leith, Hartemunde, Riga, Aberdeen and Hamburg. Her cargoes were mainly coal, wheat, barley and timber.

Her profits for the years of which I have given some details were: 1844, £150; 1845, £150; 1846, £5.16s.4d; 1847, £195.16s.4d; 1848, £46.16s.2d. In the last-mentioned year rerigging as a brig was an expense, undertaken in the hope of increasing her profitability in the long run, but as can be seen freights were variable.

It was much the same with 1849, in which year Edward Harrison, now nineteen, was promoted mate. This brings me to the point where I joined her. I was twelve years and four months old when I was bound apprentice at the Whitby Custom House on the fourteenth day of February, 1850. I was to serve Thomas Harrison, shipowner and master mariner of Robin Hood's Bay for six years. My remuneration over the whole period was to be £40 and washing was provided. In lieu of board when the ship was laid up (which well it might be in winter in the North Sea) I was entitled to four shillings a week, and my first winter was spent at home whether the ship was laid up or not.

We sailed from Whitby on or about the 20th February with a part cargo of ironstone for Middlesbrough and a crew of six: John Harrison, master, the mate, an A.B. and three apprentices. We arrived all well, discharged our stone and loaded eight keels of coal and coke for Hamburg. The crossing took us to about 1st March and we discharged at Altona. After taking in ballast we sailed from the Elbe on 8th March for Randers in Jutland.

Ice and foul wind brought delay on this passage. I remember particularly being at anchor at Hertshalls because we lost an anchor and in the attempts to recover it I received my first pair of Yarmouth mittens. [1]

At last we made Randers Fjord, moored in the stream at Hudbyhoy, discharged our ballast, washed ship inboard and out, and made all ready to take in grain cargo. The royal yard was rigged aloft, jobs and staysails stowed in cloths, all yards squared by lifts and braces, and everything made

---

1. *Yarmouth mittens are hands made raw by rough work in cold water.*

clean and smart for Sunday. It comes back to me so very clearly because we tested the vessel for stability that Sunday morning by rushing to and fro across the foredeck till we got such a move on her that she rolled the fresh water casks out of their beds and caused such a commotion that the master ran on deck to see what had happened.

Our cargo of barley was loaded from lighters and we had to move further out to finish, because of our draught. This meant the master had a long pull back to the ship after a trip ashore to encourage the lightermen to speed up with the loading. He rowed back in a lighter's boat, called a 'laurky', a craft with broad stern, round bottom and long snout and one very difficult to keep on course at the best of times, and especially when being pulled against wind and sea. John Harrison was a powerful man but was much exhausted when he got aboard, and angry at having given a demonstration of bad seamanship before his crew, whose eyes he could read well. However, he managed to get the last of the lighters to come alongside, and so we were complete, with 958 quarters of barley for Bristol.

Before sailing we laid in a good stock of eggs, cheese and butter. The cheese and butter surprised me, for they were white like lard. All were cheap and the master allowed 3 eggs per man per meal in lieu of beef.

We experienced fine weather on passage and were in Bristol by mid-June. I remember vividly how the wire rope and basket which crossed the gorge of Avon at Clifton two hundred and fifty feet above us claimed our attention as we approached the city. Still a child, I appreciated the scenery more than the hazards of the crooked reaches of the river, about which I was to learn more in later life.

After discharge a tug towed us to Glamorgan canal, Cardiff, where we loaded iron bars which had to be stowed diagonally or in grating fashion to make the vessel sea-kindly.

My recollection of the Cardiff of 1850 was that the people were foreigners living in a wilderness of mud.

Our destination was London and the weather was fine all the way to our berth in Cherry Garden tier, where we got rid of the iron and took in ballast from a Paddy's lighter to get us to West Hartlepool. From there we continued trading with various places in the south until November, when I was transferred to the brigantine 'Brothers' in Dartford Creek. This was to get me home for the winter, according to agreement.

John Harrison was a good captain under whom to start a life at sea. He was enormously strong, physically, and indeed I saw him set his little crew a challenge by lifting all the coal meter's weights of about a quarter of a ton from the gunwhale to the deck and back again. I have also seen him knock the heels of both masts aft a few inches to set them more upright, but it also set him more cantankerous when they weren't exactly right and so he kicked them back again.

I have even seen him repeatedly trim the ballast and drag cable chains fore and aft to alter the trim of the brig while under way. By energy and sheer pluck he gave his little craft a name for sailing among the coastal community that she would never otherwise have deserved. He drove crew and ship almost aggressively and never lingered in port. He never overslept a tide, and his crew were given plenty of food and little time to digest it. Of course the laws regarding adulteration were not so strict then and you couldn't be sure of the quality of a ship's provisions. Once when we were discharging in the Regent Canal, London, I was told by the captains's wife to set the evening milk up to cream, but when she asked for it in the morning the cream was plainly to be seen lying at the bottom of the basin. John's wife was Sarah, daughter of William Keld who used to keep the 'Robin Hood', and her sister married Coultas Storm, master of the brig 'Nymph' and part owner. John and Sarah had a home in the Square.

Years after this time - in 1862 in fact - John was in command of the Harrison's brig 'Daring', and his conduct in one of the Autumn storms of that year was related to me by his leading hand. He was on his way from Riga to London and when the sky and sea began to look forbidding he made for the quieter waters of the Norfolk shore. Unfortunately the storm broke violently from W.S.W. Driven seaward again, he was east of Outer Dowsing Bank when a heavy sea stove in the fresh water tank and carried away the deck cargo of timber. His decision, when the wind reached hurricane force, was to run for the shelter of the Elbe. Great waves roared onthe quarter, threatening all the time to break aboard. When his dead reckoning told him he should be nearing safety there was no sign of land or stars and so he hove to until he decided he must feel his way to the north. Eventually he found seven fathoms off Amrum Bank, off the North Frisian Islands, and then he wore ship to avoid running aground, while the wind urged her eastward to the shore all the time. The master led the fight to take in sail, but to shorten the struggle he struck savagely at the foremast, to bring down all the canvas. Then he cut away this wreckage on the deck to clear the hawse, and let go both anchors. So they rode out the rest of the night and in the morning there were signs of better weather.

The 'Daring' made Cuxhaven under jury rig after heaving up one anchor and having to cut away the other. Captain Harrison battled on thus almost to the end of his days in 1890 at the age of seventy-four, one of the most persevering men of his time. his one son died aboard the brig 'Daring' at Rye, aged fourteen. Thomas, John's brother, former mate of the 'Harrisons', died at Arendal, Norway, in 1872, in harness, but I suspect heavy drinking shortened his days. His son died at Yokohama and his grandson died in an explosion aboard the steamship 'Abaris' at the age of eighteen. My uncle, James, the third of the five sons of Thomas and Mercy, had two sons who commanded ships: Thomas Harrison and all his crew went down in the brig 'Naiad' and Storm Harrison was lost in the 'Joseph'.

I have digressed, in my desire to show that they were men of great tenacity of purpose to say the least, amongst whom it was my great good fortune to spend my early days at sea. Theirs was the ability and the determination that made Robin Hood's Bay allegedly once the most prosperous community on the coast.

My next ship after the 'Harrisons' was the 'Brothers', 120 tons, a brigantine re-rigged from a schooner. My father, Andrew, had been her master, but now James Harrison was in command. My father and my grandfather were her owners. She lay in Dartford Creek laden with coal, until four of her crew in the waterman's boat towed her nearly all the way to Cherry Garden tier whence, after discharge and ballasting, we proceeded downstream under the guidance of waterman George Parkinson and made a good passage to Whitby. The 'Brother' was moored at the Bell side, with cable chains fore and aft, then unrigged, and the sails and the running gear went to Sam Andrew's sail loft.

The ship was washed down, locked up and left to the mercy of the Esk. She was a solid job of oak, built well by Campion of Whitby. There was no gilded figurehead, but she was a good sea-boat and the master was kind and liberal to a fault. The carrier took our effects to Robin Hood's Bay. For many years the well-known carrier was John Thompson of the 'King's Head inn, a brother-in-law of my grandmother, Mercy.

How glad I was to be back home, to see my mother, the old place and some of my playmates again!

A boy may not be expected to remember much of the many strange and varied sights presented to him during his first year's apprenticeship, and it would be better to forget some that I do recall.

At the beginning of March 1851, after tramping to and fro the six miles between home and Whitby daily (Sundays excepted) for three weeks, to rig the vessel out, I sailed in the brig 'Fortitude', 160 tons, William Harrison master. Yet another of the brothers, my uncle! She had been bought from John Mennel for £600 in 1845 and her work was in the coal trade between the North and London and Rochester and the small rivers about the Thames estuary. She carried eight keels. We usually worked our own cargo, except at London, and sometimes we took in ballast ourselves. When bound for the Tyne we usually threw the ballast overboard ourselves before entering port.

We had windlass worked by handspikes to shouts of 'Yo heave ho' with interludes of rhythmic profanity in the mate's most choice vocabulary and musical dialect. My duty was to see the chain did not ride on the windlass, flet it down when the claws were on, put dollies on when necessary and flake the chain clear of kinks alongside the forehatch coaming in even numbers, or be damned.

She was an old-fashioned craft, built at Sunderland over thirty years earlier. She had a narrow stern, round bows, sides and bottom, low bulwarks and scuppers before the fore-rigging, and a fore pump that was frequently jogged with an old-fashioned pump brake.

Her foremast was before the windlass, with the topmast overlooking the knightheads. The forecastle, right in the eyes of her, accommodated an A.B. and the two oldest apprentices, who slept in hammocks. The scuttle hatch was between the heels of the bowsprit and the foremast, an arrangement that provided a shower bath to keep the forecastle sweet when meeting a head sea.

The cable tier abaft the forecastle was used as a store for hawsers, stunsails, old shakings, and fresh water casks in which rats sometimes drowned themselves. One of the old rope cables still remained in the tier, but chain cables were now in use, the chain locker being below the fore hatchway.

The master's stateroom was on the starboard side of the cabin space, and the mate and I slept steerage, I in the lower bunk. We had sliding shutters to keep our breath in, and I had to creep in like a rabbit, sitting upright being impossible.

An open hearth where we cooked our food was placed just before the mainmast. It was indeed an improved sort of range with oven, coppers and so forth, and I have a very clear recollection of it because in December 1851, we were blown off the land in a heavy gale and had our Christmas dinner washed overboard.

The longboat was lashed in chocks over the main hatchway and inside that the jollyboat was stowed.

Thirty years was no great age for a vessel in the trades we knew, for many worked twice as long as that. The 'Harrisons' was run by the family for twenty-one years, until 1865 and then someone else found her useful until she was wrecked at Hartlepool in 1880. I would say that even then she was only middle-aged. Naturally there was every inducement to take care of a craft, not the least being that we not only owned it but manned it ourselves.

Crew all told of the 'Fortitude' consisted of master, mate, A.B> and three apprentices. One apprentice served as cook and for this received an allowance of 2s 6d. extra per voyage. All of us had an allowance of 2s. 6d. a voyage for small items such as tea, coffee and sugar. If an A.B. took on cook's duties he had an extra 5s 0d. a voyage and the small extra stores allowance for A.B. was 3s 0d. If a voyage was unexpectedly prolonged there were demands, from apprentices especially, for extra stores. There was no trouble over the other provisions. They were good and sufficient unless the master supplied condemned pork or 'London pantiles' which generally found their way over the bows.

There was a change in the usual run of pay in 1853 and 1854 when the collier sailors held their first strike. An A.B. had a voyage in the beginning of the latter year and a mate earned as much as a master. The portage account of the 'Harrisons' at that time showed John Harrison, master, £8. 10s., Isaac Storm, mate £8. 10s., Wm. Harrison, A.B. £8., , John Cooper, Ordinary seaman, £6. The apprentices were of course bound by their agreements to £40 over six years. plus washing, etc.

Every winter of my service with the 'Fortitude' we put into Whitby. My new captain, William Harrison, was tall and spare but strong. He seldom became alarmed and never swore. He had learnt his seamanship under the deep tan sails of fishing vessels and in the five years I sailed with him I never knew his judgment to be wrong or his nerve to give before the threats of sand, rock and shoal. He neither sought nor boasted of daring exploits. A man of little schooling, he was a mariner of rare aptitude. More than that, he had a dauntless heart and the respect of all his crew.

Ned Storm, one time mate of the 'Harrisons' joined the 'Fortitude' in

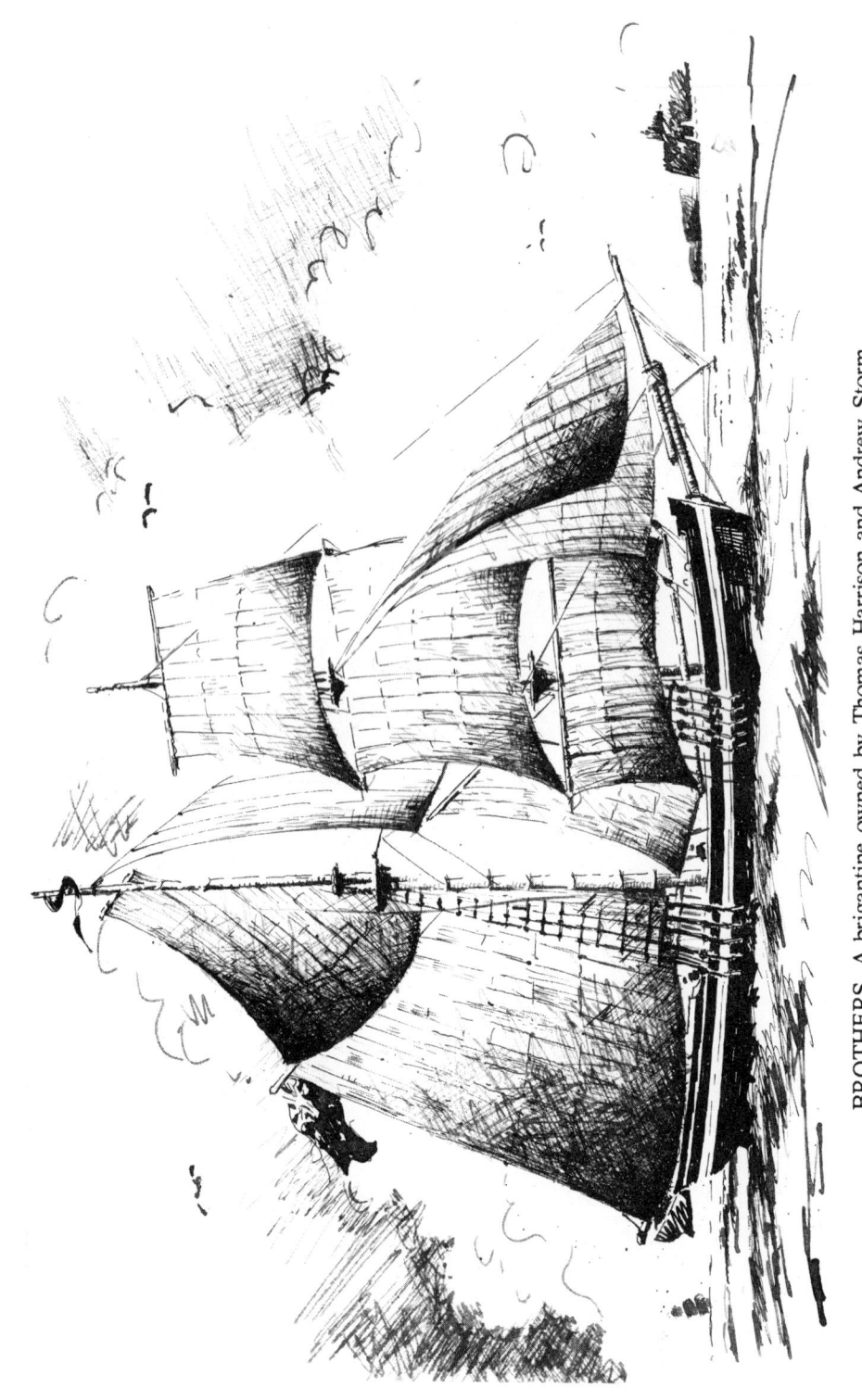

BROTHERS. A brigantine owned by Thomas Harrison and Andrew Storm, for whom she was built at Whitby by the Campions, a related family.

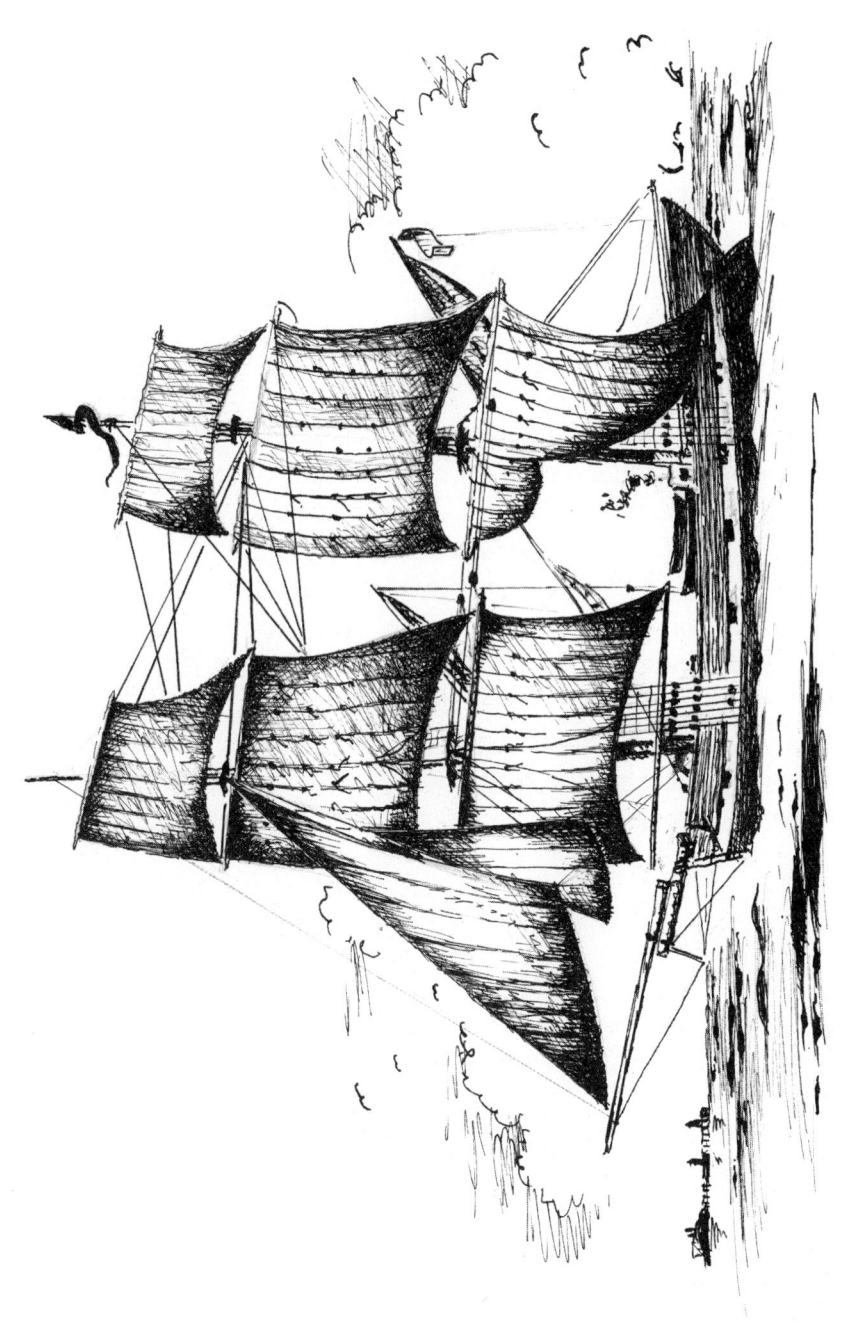

FORTITUDE was commanded by William Harrison, Jacob Storm's uncle. "He seldom became alarmed and never swore . . . I never knew his judgment to be wrong or his nerve to give . . . More than that, he had a dauntless heart and the respect of all his crew."

1852 as A.B., waiting for a master's berth. He was nephew of William and James of the 'Juno' family, but kinsman or not he bustled all hands and me especially. When he left after a short stay to take over the brig 'Gazelle' belonging to John Mennel, everyone from master down to myself was very glad. On Christmas Day of that year we got into Filey bay after being driven off the land, and there rode out a very heavy gale until on the following Monday we were able to make Scarborough for better shelter. In the same storm Ned Storm our recent shipmate and his command the 'Gazelle' disappeared on passage from Seaham to London. Ned's father was also lost at sea, and in 1883 his son followed him in the brig 'Emily', without trace.

I have reflected a great deal upon the hazard that attended our calling. We were not reckless, but it was a risky occupation. However, risks apart, it was a free and healthy life, ashore as well as at sea, and for many of us it was a prosperous one. Our native place was for me one of great beauty where the ties were strong and there was little want. Throughout my life at sea I have seen at home and abroad many places where life was attended by poverty and oppression too, as well as danger.

I had many rough trips in the 'Fortitude' between Tyne, Wear, Blyth, Warkworth, the Tees and the South. On one of these we took chalk aboard before leaving the Thames on a fine, southerly breeze. Then at nine at night a fierce change of wind caught us off the Spurn. There was a cry of 'All hands on deck'. Then came 'She's sprung a leak'. The chalk choked the pumps and when we looked in the hold it was like a huge milking pail. For the rest of the night we bailed with buckets as the ship scudded south again before the wind. We won the fight by early morning and the pumps were working again just as the gale stopped shrieking. Eventually it became possible to anchor off Yarmouth, and after a rest we got under way again hugging land by Flamborough and Whitby and so to Hartlepool. No pilot boat braved the approaches and when we went ashore we learnt that many ships and men had been lost during the night.

There were certain ways of setting about the business side of the coal trade in those days. Owners liked full holds and as many voyages as possible per year before the laying up for the winter, and masters were well aware of this in the days when there were literally hundreds of vessels competing in the trade. A successful owner-master was necessarily a self-reliant man. To be sure of a quick turn-around at the coaling staithes on the Tyne he had to know how to deal with the trimmers and with the tug skippers who drew the ships down to the sea to start them on the race with scores of others on the same tide, for the Thames. At the London end the ship might make an exhausting haul up the estuary in the face of a westerly and wait for days with a fleet of rivals before being assigned a berth for discharging. We once arrived in Gravesend with five hundred vessels in one day. Speeding up the transactions often involved expert diplomacy with officials, like the coal meters, or showing hospitality to the basket man and the whippers to keep the operation going well, although the Coal Exchange had strict rules about bribery and the like. Whether hospitality could be afforded depended on the price the master obtained at the Coal Exchange. I was fortunate to learn my trade under experienced and energetic masters.

At last my six years of servitude expired and I began to earn my living as A.B. until some owner should decide to offer me a mate's berth. The all-important recommendations of masters under whom one had served usually told all that was necessary in few words. I have by me now this handwritten note:

> 'This is to certify that Jacob Storm, seaman, served
> with me one year, 1856, on board the brig 'Harrisons'
> of Whitby, 116 tons, he being a sober, steady man.
> James Harrison,
> Master'

So, for the time being, I was back at the age of nineteen aboard my first ship. The mate was Reuben Storm, another who had started in the fishing, and although he was an agreeable shipmate the only real seamanship I learnt from him was how to tune my old fiddle.

For six years after my apprenticeship ended I gave my parents my earnings, receiving back a very modest sum with which to begin married life. Such was our way. My wages when I became mate averaged five pounds a month, supplemented by the chance of one or two winter voyages in the coal trade at £9 a voyage.

After the usual tramping between home and Whitby to fit out we sailed in March, 1856, but we received no remuneration either for the fitting out or for getting the ship to the loading port.

That year we traded not very profitably until December when we dismantled and laid up again in the Esk. This is probably the place to give some idea of how profits went in this sort of work.

Profits of the brig 'Harrisons'

	£	s	d		£	s	d
1844 bought for	1104	13	2	1855	187	17	0
	150	0	0	1856	50	0	0
1845	150	0	0	1857	30	0	0
1846	55	16	4	1858	nil		
1847	195	0	0	1859	52	9	11
1848	46	16	2	1860	114	10	5
1849	71	1	8	1861	16	3	2
1850	14	8	1	1862	nil		
1851	79	9	6	1863	nil		
1852	74	17	2	Sold in 1864	484	10	4

Thus over the years she earned nearly £600 over her cost, and this was lifted by her sale price to well over £1,000, equivalent to just over £1 a week income for her owners. In addition to this she had paid the wages of one or two members of the immediate family and indeed some of the wider family of cousins. However profits were so variable that the owners always had to be ready for a poor year.

The Harrison family fortunately had several ships at any one time, as a rule. The Robin Hood's Bay Ship Insurance Association (alias the Bay Club) list for 1867 shows Mercy Harrison and Sons owing the vessels 'Arica', 'North of Scotland', 'Spectator' and 'Lucy', and John with his own 'Daring', and each was commanded by one of the brothers.
Their total value was £6,360

James was good-hearted and easy-going. Sometimes we took advantage of him aboard the 'Harrisons', yet he always kept a good ship as regards stores and provisions and we lads and men worked hard for him without a growl.

I joined my next ship also as A.B. She was the schooner 'Crosby', 89 tons, getting on in years but well built. She was flush-decked from stem to stern, soundly caulked and copper-fastened from her keel. She didn't feel her age and her lines were beautiful, and the way she romped over the waves like a pleasure yacht haunts my memory to this day. My father bought her in 1850 for £400 and in March, 1857, he commanded her, taking with him as well as myself my brother-in-law and cousin removed Andrew Storm, who had married my sister Damaris the previous year.

We worked in the coastal trade until December, by which time my brother-in-law had taken over the 'Fortitude'. This meant there was a mate's berth, and in the following spring my father employed me in that august capacity. William Pearson, whose sister was to be my wife, was 'out of his time' and came as A.B. in my place.

THE WAYFOOT is where the main thoroughfare meets the water. Just above this access to the sea lies The Dock, were on a May evening in 1753 John Wesley preached 'to a multitude of people', most of whom turned out at 4.30 on the following morning to see him on his way.

BAY BANK. This notoriously steep road was the replacement of the old approach which fell into the sea two centuries ago. The name 'new road' is still in use.

CHAPTER THREE

MASTER MARINER

Trading began from Hartlepool and on the year's last trip to the south my father handed her [the 'Crosby'] over to me at Ipswich and I brought her back to Whitby without mishap.

The next March brought only one crew change and trade followed the usual routes until June when we sailed from the Tyne to Rouen. Here my father became ill and was found to be suffering from smallpox. He had to be taken to a house on the South Quay. My mother was with us on that voyage and she nursed him through a severe illness. I remember the doctor, who spoke no English, presenting my mother with an opening rosebud as a sign that the crisis had passed.

I got the schooner chartered through Betancourt the broker to load burr stones for Hull, and started for home the day my mother and father were able to start their own journey home. This event was a never-to-be-forgotten experience, as was the kindness of the people, French and English, who helped us in our time of need.

I shipped no extra hand, and so we numbered only four aboard. A pilot took us down the Seine to Havre Roads and thence we made for Hull where we arrived all well and discharged our cargo to Mr .Child, a manufacturer of millstones. From there I found a handy cargo of coal in Goole for Le Havre, but before we could sail we had to be towed above Blacktoft Sands and left there to encounter the stress of the bore and the shifting sands, which the pilot assured us could easily wreck us. He was mistaken however, for the little craft floated like a duck when the bore came. At high water the tug picked us up again and towed us to Hull Roads. To please the mate I went ashore for another hand, but a Good Samaritan told me we should do better without the man I found and so we went as we were.

The passage to Le Havre was fine and we proceeded next to

Sunderland where the 'Crosby' was sold, for what my father had paid for her, to Mr. Candlish for his bottle trade. We all joined the brig 'Coquette' at Bill Quay, I carting our effects over to Pelaw Main.

Father was master when we made three voyages with coal to Rochester in what was left of the year.

I have a note of profits we made with the 'Coquette'. Three voyages in three months was not bad going. Some masters, and more owners, used to say a ship in the east coast coal trade should make twelve trips a year, but nine or ten was nearer the fact. So each voyage in the last three months of 1859 produced a profit of over £26. As a master earned £8 a voyage my father was earning about £10 a week as long as the freights kept up. This was very good indeed for the times, especially as competition from railways and steamships was looming up. The fuller account of the 'Coquette's' profits I now give:

Year	£	s	d	Year	£	s	d	Year	£	s	d
1859	79	0	0	1866	147	2	0	1873	200	2	9
1860	124	17	5	1867	165	19	6	1874	214	18	3
1861	137	16	7	1868	80	19	11	1875	107	9	5
1862	203	4	0	1869	153	19	11	1876 carried to 1877			
1863	247	4	7	1870	122	10	0	1877	22	11	2
1864	154	12	1	1871	148	17	4	1878	170	10	8
1865	115	17	6	1872	48	14	3	1879	32	1	3
								Total	2687	19	8

As she cost £830 and was sold for £300 in April 1880, she brought in £2237. 19s. 8d. all together, or an average of just under £112 a year over the twenty years, or £2. 3s. a week. So the run of three voyages at the end of 1859 had been exceptional, but an income of £4 to £5 a week, wages and profits, was far from unsatisfactory in those days. From time to time, also, several of my family had more than one vessel. The biggest owners in Bay in those days were Matthew Storm and Ben Granger, another cousin, each with six vessels much of the time. There were usually about twenty Storm-owned ships at any one time, and close kin like the Bedlingtons, Moorsoms, Hewsons, Skerrys and so on brought the total near a hundred. All sorts of trades and professions were drawn into share-holding in the fleet, like Matthew Storm's son-in-law the Rev. Thomas Phillips and John Rickinson the grocer. In any one of the many reasonably good years thousands of pounds of profit came back to Bay, and it is not surprising that it was well provided with shops, trades and inns. There were two doctors.

THE SQUARE in Bay Town. It was here that John Wesley preached on some of his many visits to the place, 'and many families maintained a strong Chapel tradition'.

every space was built upon, and older houses were enlarged. Most of them were held on ancient or very long leases, granted by the Cholmleys in the seventeenth century. Prosperity and a lot of independence made the appearance of Bay Town, for which I and many more have so great affection, and for which now the summer visitors express so much admiration.

I have kept some accounts of local shopkeepers who supplied the ships as well as the inhabitants. Captain Phatuel Granger in 1819 bought for the brig 'Mercury' these provisions:

				£	s	d
Feb 13 to	Potatoes	*1 Bushel*			3	4
20 "	Beef	*2 Stone @ 6d*			13	4
Mar 2 "	"	*2 cwt. 2st. 22 @ 56/-*	7	11	0
6 "	Potatoes	*2 Bushels*			6	8
13 "		*1 Bushel*			3	4
Sept 11 "	Beef	*1 stone 2lb at 7/-*			8	0
18 "	leg mutton	*12 @ 6d*			6	0
Oct 2 "	Beef	*8st. 12 lb @ 7/-*	3	2	0
	Salt				5	0
	1 Bushel Potatoes				2	4
		Total	13	1	2

This account was rendered by butcher Stephen Crosby, whose family was also in farming and moved into shipping and seafaring. Business like this with scores of locally-owned ships was an important part of local trade, and the Crosbys bought a lot of property, in Stephen's time, and his son after him.

By 1880 times had turned against the sailing ships on the coast and colliers in particular.

Returning to my seafaring narrative, I must tell of an experience in one of the most disastrous gales ever known on the coast.

In the great gale of 28th May. 1860 I was still mate of the 'Coquette', and we got our anchors down in Hartlepool Bay, with Hastie the pilot on board. Our chains held and we got towed into W. Hartlepool Basin when the weather moderated. In this gale the 'Fortitude' was caught in the wold.

Andrew had Damaris and child on board and he ran up by the beach through the Hemsby Hole and thus saved the lives of all on board. The Cockle Gat was a death trap. Ships could not carry sail enough to fetch into the roads and the Scroby Sand got many victims.

On 8th February, 1861, I sailed in command of the 'Coquette', having at the age of twenty-three some experience of ships and their affairs. The cargo was nut coals from Hartlepool for Rochester and we caught the last of the tide. The morning was fine with a light breeze from the west which lasted until we were off Huntcliff Foot, when a freshening gale came up from the south, testing the close-hauled sailing qualities of the fleet, amongst which the 'Coquette' was not to be despised.

We beat to southward under all sail until about 4 p.m., when off Whitby the wind increased with the ship on the port tack. North Cheek was well on the lee bow and I debated in my mind whether to signal to our people at Bay before dark or take advantage of the flood and seek a good offing ready for the fight with the cantankerous North Sea which outlook and glass foretold. Thanks to Providence and my early training among fishermen, skippers and shellbacks, who taught me to dread a lee shore, I adopted the right course, which is to say I tacked, single-reefed the topsails, set main t'gallant and sailed her hard for two hours , in which time we reached a very safe position twenty miles east of High Whitby and were able to close reef and make all snug.

During the night the wind backed to the eastward and became of hurricane force. Towards midnight we had put our vessel before the wind to cross the hawse of a craft that seemed bent on running us down. When we brought her to the wind again I put her on the port tack and well up to her course but the heavy sea prevented her making much headway. It was now really bad weather with rain, wind and sea all exceedingly heavy, but we rode the surges buoyantly.

Towards noon on the 9th the sea came more abeam and heavier than ever, causing the 'Coquette' to labour now, and very heavily at that. The weather fore-topsail sheet carried away and so we furled it and set foresail, which in the trough of huge seas was almost in calm. But towards evening, the weather improved and our speed increased, and in the early morning light of Sunday 10th we saw Flamborough Head, still well to leeward. By full daylight the wind was moderate north-east which allowed us to set course and sail for the Wold, and, thank God and a good sea boat, we were among the favoured few that made port safely after a night that had taken many

THE REVENGE was commanded by Richard Moorsom's son Robert at Trafalgar, in which action her casualties were 28 killed and 51 including the captain wounded.

THE BLACK PRINCE "She was tight, staunch, shapely and strong and steered like a fish as well as being a splendid sea boat . . . I have seen her pass all kinds of ships and dance her way through a large fleet."

fine ships, including the tea-clipper 'Kelso'. The Whitby lifeboat capsized, and drowned all but one of her crew, and the loss of ships and lives in Tees Bay and on the adjacent coasts was appalling. Nearly eighty vessels went in that storm. The Harrison's good little brig 'Claret' was stranded at Hartlepool and sold as a wreck, although she was later refloated and lengthened. Allison Crosby, the master, and Boyes Cooper were lost at Hartlepool in Isaac Shadforth's 'George Andreas', and ten of the ships that went down took all hands with them.

My crew were a fair sample of the coasting seamen. They went steadily about their work of reefing, steering, keeping look-out and the rest of it and they won through.

A little after these events, on 27th May, 1861, Miss Isabel Pearson, daughter of Captain and Mrs. William Pearson, and I were married. Mrs. Pearson was one of the daughters of Mr and Mrs. William Robinson of the Bay Mill, and Capt. Pearson's ancestor came from Ebberston to Bay in the seventeenth century.

At the beginning of 1862 my wife and I kept ship at West Hartlepool, without remuneration, except for victuals, to give me time to obtain my certificate for mate.

Any of my family who read this may think we had good heart to marry in such circumstances. I can only say that we counted the cost before doing so and that I have known many people marry under more favourable circumstances whose married lives have been less happy. With strict economy and hard work on the part of my helpmate we rubbed along without getting into debt but, to use an Americanism, we lifted our bottom dollar several times, and I was able to return my father a Roland for his Oliver when he spoke of the hard times in his generation.

Two years later while I was still master of the 'Coquette' we took a cargo of gas coal to Erith gasworks, but the coal whippers made an attempt to boycott me and make their own price. However I fairly surprised both meters and whippers by proving myself an able basketman and the crew well able to follow. We discharged the ship in four days and made an extra 25/- each. When I visited the local barber he said we had become the talk of Erith. This, 1863, was the 'Coquette's' most profitable year.

In June of the same year we went to the Baltic with a cargo from Seaham Harbour, and it is an indication of the competitive times that before we left port we had the topsails fitted with Colling and Pinkney's patent reefing apparatus.

I stayed with the 'Coquette' for another eighteen months or so, by which time I had been at sea for fifteen years, and I decided it was high time I took my master's ticket. In January 1865 we were discharging in Dover, and frequently leaving the mate to keep an eye on operations, I gave all the time I could to revising my studies and navigation. We sailed up to Hartlepool where my wife came to keep ship with me again while I studied, including four days of cramming at Marine School, I passed before Captain Gillies and Armstrong in Sunderland. My certificate is dated 8th February, 1865.

That same month I moved across to the barque 'Hallyards', to make room for my brother-in-law, Andrew. My father bought her in Birkenhead for £1,015, with another £308. 15s. 1d. for stores and some new decking. Her register tonnage was 299.

There was a trend to bigger vessels, and a need to run them more cheaply as the steamers with their huge holds and tiny crews entered the race. The 'Jon Bowes', the first screw collier, took 650 tons of coal to the Thames and reappeared in the Tyne five days later, which meant she could comfortably make three or four times more voyages than a sailing vessel, and far more cargo. About the time my father was contemplating buying the 'Coquette', the steamer 'Lifeguard' made the voyage from the Thames to the Tyne in just over twenty-eight hours. Nevertheless the steamers too were vulnerable, for in December of 1867 the 'Lifeguard' disappeared with all hands and passengers off Scarborough in a fierce storm.

The 'Hallyards' was a bad bargain. Nearly all her profits in ten years went on repairs and insurance, and she cleared at the end of our ownership £113. But for my father's sake I stuck to her for seven years. Indeed I had much for which to thank God, for while I was her master she helped me to weather storms which overwhelmed many of her contemporaries.

I eventually got out of her without much discredit or loss, physical or moral, and with the valuable experience that only an unhandy vessel can give a master. That same year of purchase brought one lesson almost at once. We were in the North Sea bound for London from Memel with staves and sleepers, making three inches of water in moderate weather, when we got down to the last piece of pump leather. I reduced the pump box, increased the thickness of the leather by pegging a slice of my leather boot-top theron and thus effectually stopped the scour in the pump chamber caused by the coarse Memel sand ballast. This contrivance enabled us to make London.

Around this time conditions of trade meant that sailing ships on the coast had to face more of the winters, and insurances were naturally affected. It was in the winter of 1869-70 that the 'Hallyards' was bound for Soderhamm in company with the brigs 'Levant', 'John and Jane' and 'La Belle'. The first was owned by Smith Stainthorpe and the second by the Bedlingtons, of Robin Hood's Bay. The weather caused us to take refuge in a small roadstead on the coast of Sweden until the wind changed and we were able to get under way, each taking an Oregrund pilot. Unfortunately my 'Hallyards' was drawing two feet more water than the others and I found myself trapped by a barrier of rocks. Attempts to beat to windward failed, wherupon I had to persuade my pilot that my vessel would jump a two-foot barrage and follow my friends through the channel. The feat was accomplished in grand style, to the satisfaction of all.

It was less than a year after this escapade that Capt. Jenkins of Robin Hood's Bay died of exposure aboard the barque 'Canopus', having been caught in the baltic winter. He lies buried in Dantsic.

When I left the 'Hallyards' in 1871 I had a brief spell ashore, and having nothing much to do I offered to relieve my brother-in-law, Richard Knightly Smith for a day or two to take the brig 'Laura', 274 tons, to the Forth, A fierce wind intervened and we put into the Tyne, where I was relieved. That was all I saw of the 'Laura', although my father, R.K. Smith and I owned her for nine years, paying £563 in cash and £562 in six month bills for her, and taking a good profit over that time of £1,264. 6s. 10d.

My next command was the barque 'Maggie', 305 tons, lying in Northumberland Dock in the Tyne when I joined her in May of 1872. Almost at once we sailed from Shields with coal for Alexandria. Her owner was George Russel of Thorpe, Fylingdales, of the family best known today by the Bay Post Office. The voyage out, and the return trip with cottonseed to Yarmouth and the Tyne went well. The only trouble I would record was the dispute between the crew and the rats to determine who should have the provisions. We had to make safe lockers and invent traps. Richardson Dixon, second mate, and I had some success by baiting the store room itself with one bag of oatmeal and nothing else and stopping all holes but one, over which we contrived a sliding shutter. Before we reached Alexandria we had placed sixty-one vermin *hors de combat* and the rest were in a timid condition with no relish for further conflict.

In October, 1872, we loaded a full cargo of steam coal in Northumberland Dock for Alexandria at £25 a keel, and sailed into a favouring gale. Off the Goodwins the wind dropped and beyond Dover we didn't even have steering way. The ominous calm stayed with us until night, when rain warned us to prepare for a squall. Although the wind rose at last from the west and we tacked many times, we fairly danced down the Channel. It was when the Lizard light dipped that we got into the cyclone's track, began to ship water and heard the first awful howling as the storm burst on our starboard bow. The night had become pitch dark, and it was not long before the bulwarks and stanchions were smashed. About eight bells the wind increased from the west, the 'Maggie' heeled heavily and the cargo was flung to port. The situation was chaotic and the crew clung to the rigging for dear life whenever she went under.

Amazingly she rose each time, shaken but free, but we lost helm and compass. Luckily there was no trouble with the pumps, which sucked well each time we got to them when our ship rose from the water. Nevertheless it was one night I shall not forget.

At daybreak we were able to refit the wheel and I decided to make for shelter. this meant that the shifting cargo now kept the vessel heeled into the oncoming seas, and although the young helmsman stood firm and kept a good course I felt at heart that our fate was sealed, until at last we closed with the land. It was into Dartmouth that we eventually limped, and our thoughts were of thanks to God rather than dwelling on the damage we had suffered.

Every Channel Port had been crowded with sheltering ships that night and there were many latecomers with damaged masts and yards, lost boats and shattered hulls. Repairs and refitting kept us seven weeks in Dartmouth, and there was also a cargo to retrim.

When we sailed again it was in company with the 'Laura', master R.K. Smith, my brother-in-law. We were into 1873 and on 3rd January we were caught in a hurricane from the SSE which threw the cargo to starboard. Once again bulwarks and stanchions went and the only sail we had set was blown out of the boltropes, leaving us helpless. First light on the 4th brought clearer weather but the wind was still hard. I mustered all hands to deal with our dangerous list and after cutting a manhole in the after bulkhead into the hold we went to trim the cargo to port. Without this steering a course was impossible. Then the 'Laura' came bearing down and spoke to us, but as we didn't need assistance she proceeded on her course and toward noon we were able to follow her under all sail.

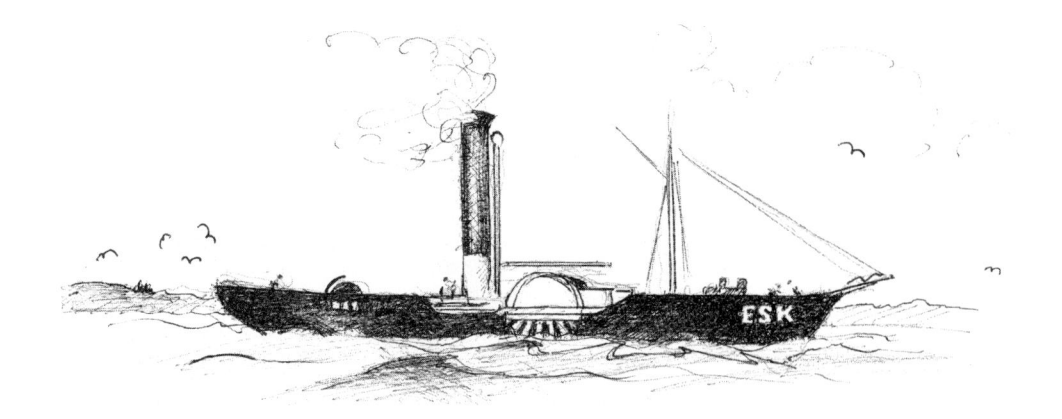

ESK One of three vessels of the Whitby and Robin Hood's Bay Steam packet Company. She was bought in 1857 for rescue and towing work, scheduled passenger services to Hartlepool and occasional excursions to Scarborough and Sunderland. Among the many Bay shareholders was the company trustee Sampson Storm.

S.S. KILDALE of the Rowland and Marwood fleet of Whitby, in which Raymond (1892-1971) first went to sea in 1909 as a premium apprentice. He joined her in Barry dock and many years later recalled that after the peace of a moorland farm he thought he had arrived in hell. The Kildale was typical of the ocean-going traders manned by hundreds of men of Whitby and the neighbouring villages.

We had fine, favourable weather for the rest of the passage and arrived all well at Alexandria where we repaired our damaged bulwarks while discharging cargo. Our next calls, Scalanueva, Smyrna and Mytilene, where we loaded bones for Leith. With such a cargo, the most detestable I ever had charge of, it was a blessing that we had a good passage, because the ship was overrun with insect life from keel to truck. I have never wanted another cargo of bones. Before loading again we had to smoke the ship and then we were off to Kronstadt with coal. I escaped a severe dressing in the Gulf of Finland by seeking anchorage under Nargan Island when the glass told me the storm was close. In the Russian port we loaded wheat for London, arrived all well, discharged and were taken by John Brain's tugs to Northfleet for chalk, for the Tyne. From there I went home. In 1873 the 'Maggie' cleared £400. She had proved herself a good ship in some of the worst gales of 1872-3, but I would not consider her the best of seaboats because the lack of bulkheads meant an insecure cargo. When needs must the Devil drives.

In 1874 I took over the brig 'Black Prince', 272 tons, in the Wear. I owned 32/64ths of her and had a navigation bond which gave me liberty to trade where I thought fit but compelled me to keep her in repair and work her for the benefit of myself and my partners. She cost £1,425.

I must say she was a delightful vessel to command and sailed well in any wind, but close-hauled or beating to windward she was unsurpassed by square-rigged ships in the home trade. She was tight, staunch, shapely and strong and steered like a fish as well as being a splendid seaboat. There was plenty of bright metal on display, but the prince had vanished from her head and had been replaced with the plainest gammon knee. I have seen her pass all kinds of ships and dance her way through a large fleet.

When bound for London with a cargo and deck load of deals, in the year I joined her, we were caught on the tail of the Dogger Bank in a heavy SW gale that kept us under a close-reefed or lower main topsail for three days. Many ships were caught in the North Sea, some lost and most damaged, while the 'Black Prince' not only weathered the storm but got her deck cargo to London intact. Thirty shillings made good all the damage sustained.

In November 1875, we made a record passage from Kronstadt to Leith, 1,284 miles in seven days and two hours. The daily average was 183 miles and the round voyage from Troon had occupied only forty-four days.

In December we sailed out of Leith for Boulogne with pig-iron and coal. From St Abb's head to Farnes a heavy NE gale tested her sailing and seagoing qualities severely, but after clearing the Long-stone she simply flew before the gale and the snow showers like a seabird. We arrived at Boulogne before the word that we had left Leith reached home at Robin Hood's Bay. This was the gale in which Captain Campion of Whitby and all his crew went down in Gideon Smales' 'Aid'.

Notwithstanding the good qualities of the 'Black Prince' she was bought too dear for the times. Her 1874 earnings were carried forward to 1875 and the profit then amounted to £200. It had become impossible to do much more with sailing craft, but I had loved the 'Black Prince' and delighted in navigating her in the narrow seas, until 1879 when, for the sake of my family, now grown to five, I had to leave her and go into steam. After installing my partner, Richardson Dixon, as master, and giving my father my 32/64ths of her I went Chief Officer of the S.S.'Tom Pyman', owned by Geo. Pyman and Co., and I knew the sailing ships no more. [1].

I joined her in Hartlepool in October. She had been built nine years before by Dentons at West Hartlepool. There was a coal cargo to finish discharging before we sailed for the Baltic two days later. At Swartwick in Sweden we loaded 3-inch-by-9-inch deals for Surrey Commercial Docks, London. After discharging there we went up to West Hartlepool to take on coal for Dantzic. From there we went to Libau in Courland and loaded barley for Honfleur. The next call was Cardiff, in ballast, and there we took in coals and while we were loading I relieved Captain King as master on 27th December.

There was a rather uncanny experience on the voyage from Libau to Honfleur. When we sailed there were already signs of northern winter in the still air. Beyond Courland the rigging and yards became encrusted in fantastic moulds of crystal. We rounded the reef of Falsterbo, saw the spires of Copenhagen come up, and approached Saltholm Island before we saw a

---

1. *Richardson Dixon came from the moorland farm of Billera, in Fylingdales. He died in Southampton in 1901.*

feeble glimmer of sun. The spires went down again, and off Taarbeck reef the ice became tough. Frozen wavelets were lit by a pale, silver light. Eventually the awful grinding noise brought the chief engineer on deck in some alarm, but he stayed to stare at the many vessels held fast in the sea in absolute calm. Beyond them to the west we could see country houses set in the sombre Danish woodlands. Many flight of wildfowl passed overhead in the pale sky as we inched our way through thickening ice and Captain King sought weaknesses in the crust. It was hard work for the gang in the stokehold and we were beyond Elsinore before we found clearer water.

Those few days left a deep impression on my memory, but needless to say when a few of us get together at home someone could come up with stranger and more exciting tales from all over the world, and that without exaggeration either. My nephew William Storm's tale of his adventure at Galveston in the hurricane of 1900 would take some beating. When the great storm had died down his ship was lying high and dry and a long way from the sea. [1].

My son Jacob also has many years at sea behind him now, and has his share of tales to tell in retirement. He was Master of the S.S.'Blue Cross' and one of his apprentices was Alfred Church, my great-nephew. By coincidence William was a few miles away at sea, making for Coronel for bunkers, with Laurence, Alfred's brother aboard, when they were suddenly caught by the enormous wave set in motion by the 'quake' and the look-out was nearly washed overboard. Anyone who knew Bay would also know that with so many of us at sea coincidences like this were not infrequent.

William and his S.S.'Roma' were well known. He had the reputation of being a first-rate navigator, which he upheld after the Valparaiso incident. When he had bunkered at Coronel he entered the Penas gulf and took his ship through the hazardous channels of the west coast of Chile to the Magellan Straits, over six hundred miles without once stopping. A small-scale map will help anyone who does not know that coast to understand what a feat that was, especially in a ship drawing over twenty feet.

1.   *The S.S. 'Roma'. (P.164)*

The morning I took over as master of the 'Tom Pyman' we sailed for Port Said, and making our way under the Cornish coast near Trevose Head and St Ives we dodged a heavy gale, the same that brought the Tay Bridge down. On the 29th the weather moderated and the rest of the passage to Port Said was good. Alexandria was our next call and we took a cargo of cottonseed from there to Hull. We next went to the North East for coal and when we had delivered that in the Baltic we went to and from various ports with coal and pig-iron outward and deals and sleepers homeward until the Autumn. During the winter months we were employed in the ore trade between Bilbao and Huelva and other places until the Baltic was open again, when we reverted to coal-out and timber-back trade. I remained master of the 'Tom Pyman' until the end of 1881 when I left to join the S.S. 'Solon'.

I had been most happy aboard my first steam command. She was a good ship to navigate, tight, staunch and strong, but I had some strange experiences on her, notably on a voyage to the Vefsen Fjord, 66 degrees north in Norway, in November. I could not find a pilot and had to take her twenty-five unknown miles from the sea. When we left the pilot wanted to be ashore and so I turned him adrift in his boat and found my way as well as I could the last fifteen miles back to the sea.

She was what was called a weekly boat, the crew having a weekly wage and finding their own provisions, and the master finding the cabin only. After two years drill aboard this vessel in narrow waters I was quite at home on a steamer's bridge and felt fit to take on anything in the shape of a steamer.

The S.S. 'Solon' was built at Messrs Turnbull and Sons' Whitehall Yard, Whitby, for Messrs Rowland, Robinson and Company. I have a note from my brother-in-law, R.K. Smith, who owned 2/64ths of her. His shares cost him £306. 3s. 4d. each and in two years each of them earned him £97. He then sold one for £350 and the remaining one earned £115 in the next two years. It was usual for a master to have a financial interest in his ship, although the vessels involved were no longer truly Bay boats like the old sailing craft.

The sums I mention were not large, but the rates were good enough, and small holdings in several ships brought considerable prosperity to Bay people who were sharp enough to see the future in steam. Several well known steamship companies were founded in Whitby and Robin Hood's Bay money.

The change that was overtaking us was that while Bay Town still produced mariners the ownership of the vessels on the trades we knew now lay elsewhere. Ships were getting bigger and Whitby as a harbour was no match for Tyne, Wear and Tees. But masters with shares who lived at Bay still did pretty well, and the bank top began to look very different from a hundred years before when Matthew Storm took the lead and built Prospect House up there. The new village of terraces and villas appeared. I was responsible for 'Aurora' and 'Leeside' myself, after living at Sleights and Whitby. The old place had a strong pull for us, although some people say now it is without opportunities. Some idea of the prosperity that could be achieved is provided by the case of my brother-in-law, a sailor and owner. I kept the cutting from the 'Yorkshire Post' which reported his estate of £35,000 some years ago.

The Turnbulls of Whitby who built the 'Solon' provided berths for many Bay mariners in their own ships. Following trade, they set up in Cardiff as well, exporting Welsh coal. For many years there was prominent in their counsels Matthew Bedlington, who took over the Secretaryship of the Bay Club from his and my relative, John Estill.

Some bay men went to Cardiff, following the Turnbull move. One of them was Captain John Storm, my father's cousin, who served in the Turnbull ships for many years. I believe one of his sons went into the butchering business there, but another, Matthew, has become a marine engineer. [1].

One who cleared out completely was another cousin, another William, who went out to South Africa. His father, John Harrison Storm, was a much respected figure in Whitby shipping, and once owned several sailing vessels. John Harrison Storm sent his sons away to school but they nonetheless became sailors. James, the youngest, was lost at the age of twenty-one when he was second officer of the S.S. 'Saxon Monarch', which went down with all hands. William, the eldest went on to become a most enterprising master. His wife was the daughter of a sailmaker from Elsinore. In 1873 at the age of twenty-seven, he made a record voyage in his barque 'Teazer' to Port Natal, and was so impressed with the prospects there that he went back a few years later to take up employment in shipping. A year or two later he set up as a shipping agent on his own account. We kept in touch until his recent death. He prospered there, and from some of our people who have put into Durban from time to time news comes back that his name is held in high regard there [2].

1   *The late Matthew Storm, O.B.E., Director of the Turnbull Scott Shipping Co.*
2. *Storm & Co. Durban, Capetown, Port Elizabeth, East London and Johannesburg.*

Jacob Storm's Memoir

Robin Hood's Bay had begun to change before the Great War, and visitors had begun to rent the fisher cottages, but many people came back looking for family information. We find them looking at the tombstone in the old churchyard. Some are becoming difficult to place despite some of the old stocks. the railway kept some families here for a time, because it was possible to get away to Scarborough and Whitby and thence to the ports to join ships. Those were the days when there were Whitby men earning a living carting the gear of whole ships' companies to the trains.

After I ceased to be a shipmaster I became a marine superintendent, husbanding the ships of Messrs Rowland and Marwood of Whitby, and in that work I frequently visited the seaports. This enabled me in my spare time to seek information about Storm and related branches with links in Middlesbrough, Hartlepool, Sunderland and Shields, and further afield. I found a lot of useful information in the cemeteries, finding the later Eskdales and Robinsons at North Shields, and I interviewed Jonathan Eskdale when he was mayor of Shields some years ago, he confirming that he was of the Whitby stock. [1]. On my visits I often came across the old bay names in the directories in the public libraries, particularly in the lists of trades and professions, like pilots. Names in the business of teaching navigating officers in shields were Nellist and Frazer. [2]. Capt. Wm. Nellist of Bay married Martha Storm and Capt. Andrew Frazer married our niece, Isabella Moorsom Pearson. We seem to have established a maze of connections throughout the North East, but at present the links with shipping seem to be strong, and the family is stronger than ever. Yet there are notable breaks with the past. Capt. Wm. Storm Jameson, my cousin Hannah's son, tried

---

1 Although the writer believed the Robinsons of Bay Mill and those of the Stag Line of Steamers, North Shields, proof is inconclusive. One of the North Shields Eskdales was George, "internationally renowned trumpet virtuoso". (Concise Oxford Companion to Music, 1964.)

2. Nellist's Nautical College, South Shields and Newcastle.

VIEW S.E. OVER VILLAGE AND BAY.
The protective arm of the Ravenscar cliffs sweeps round the southern part of the bay. The far headland was the site of important alum works which gave much employment in Fylingdales and which were serviced at some risk by local sailors for two centuries.

A BIT OF NEWS by F.M. Sutcliffe. 'Lomar Will' Storm is on the right in the picture which, like so many of the kind, tells only part of the truth about Bay, for although 'Lomar Will' was a fisherman, he had served on ships and was also owner of several trading brigs. On the left is Harrison Allison, village baker but also a shipowner to be found listed in Appendix I. (By courtesy of the Sutcliffe gallery, Whitby.)

MARGARET STORM JAMESON, M.A., Hon D.Lit., novelist and sometime President of PEN International; great granddaughter of Sampson Storm (1803-65), Master Mariner, and daughter of Captain William Storm Jameson.

CAPTAIN ISAAC STORM (1869-1949) with his wife Annie Lydia (of the Harrison family of Bay sailing ship owners) daughter Lizzie and son Harry in 1913. Isaac learnt his seamanship aboard the brig <u>Black Prince</u> and Harry became Superintendent of the Headlam (formerly Rowland and Marwood) fleet of Whitby steamers.

his son at sea but he did not take to it. At one time we were all moulded to it, but Harold Jameson ventured into a new element in the war, joining the Royal Flying Corps and winning the M.C. and the D.C.M. and the French Medaille Militaire before his death in action. His sister has distinguished herself at university, and another young lady who has broken with tradition is a niece, Florence Storm Taylor, who has studied singing in London. [1]. Isaac Storm, of one of the last fishing families, went away to become a schoolmaster near Lincoln, and his son Ethelbert was ordained recently. I believe his vocation came after seeing the Church Army at work on the Western Front. Richard Knightly Smith, my sister's grandson, served as a Green Howards officer in the war and lost a leg at Paschendale, after which he turned to medicine and qualified at St Bartholomew's in London. Thomas Louis, the son of Rev. Thomas Philipps and his wife Martha (nee Storm) became a solicitor.

In a few generations much may change, and be forgotten. I have seen Sampson Storm recorded simply as an innkeeper in the Whitby of sixty or seventy years ago, but he left Bay about 1832 and I remember him as the master of sailing ships and owner of the brig 'Pet' and the barques 'Mary Ann' and 'Royal Rose'. How much information we have lost because at the time we did not think it important or interesting.

My own family is still very much occupied in seafaring. In my collection of cuttings is a page picture from the Scarborough paper of a little steamer coming alongside. The date is the 8th May, 1924, and the ship is the 'General Havelock', starting up again the London passenger run that the war caused to be interrupted, and her master is my grandson, Raymond, in his first command. His elder brother Wilfred is a master and his younger brother Richard recently passed for second mate at the Nellists' marine school at South Shields. Their sister Isabel's husband is also at sea. I wonder if yet another generation after them will continue in our calling.

On a somewhat unsteady course I return to the shipping to take up again the thread of the story of my time in steam. It was in 1881, in December, that I joined the 'Solon' relieving Capt Miles Burrows. I had been shipmates with him before and we were related through his daughter's marriage. This was a bad time for him as three months earlier his two sons were lost when the barque 'Essex', carrying timber, and commanded by Capt Sayers of Robin Hood's bay, went down in a storm in the Gulf of

1. *Margaret Storm Jameson, Hon.D.Litt.: novelist and author of the acclaimed biography <u>Journey from the North</u>. Florence Storm Taylor married the singing teacher Albert Garcia. (<u>Oxford Companion to Music,</u> 1970).*

Mexico. Stephen Crosby Burrows and Miles junior are among scores in our 'Register of missing Seamen'.

The 'Solon' had a crew of twenty, and I am afraid the chief officer was a wet hand. After discharging we sailed for Cardiff and traded thence between Black sea grain ports and home or Continental ports until December, 1883, when I left her for the new 'Fylingdales', in which a share was held by my wife. The certificate says she paid £40 2s. 6d. for 1/64th, and among other details it says the 'Fylingdales' was schooner rigged and unarmed. As far as I know all had gone well for ship and owners during my command of the 'Solon', but for various reasons I was not too happy and gladly accepted the offer of a new appointment. The pay of a master at that time was £18 a month.

The first crew of the 'Fylingdales' was signed in 1884. For two years we were pretty busy. In 1886 we had a memorable voyage because we carried 12,604 quarters of barley from Taganrog in the Sea of Azov to Bristol. This was nearly 1200 better than our previous best. By contrast my old friend the 'Black Prince' was still sailing the seas and for three consecutive years while I stayed with the 'Fylingdales' the little brig made no profit at all.

I have many reasons for remembering the 'Fylingdales'. One is that later in 1887 I took with me for two voyages my son Richard as my steward. My youngest son, Jake, who was out of his 'time', served as an A.B. after I left her and joined me again later. I kept Richard's two accounts of earnings, showing that at a rate of £5. 10s. a month he earned £27. 17. 4d. Richard went farming but Jacob stuck to the sea and when I took over the 'Enterprise', a bigger vessel, there was a third mate's berth for him. A few years later Jake came second mate with me on the 'Golden Cross' to the east, as far as Shanghai.

In 1889 I had an interesting time in the 'Germania', which carried a crew of 31. The reason for my being there was that Captain Thomas was taking a voyage on shore, his first in fourteen years. At the end of one voyage Captain Sanderson, the 'super', was sick, and I had to attend to the ship until she sailed, under the guidance of Captain Smith. Under the latter's orders I sent down all the ship's yards and gear, about seven tons of useless lumber we agreed; Captain Thomas returned and informed me I had spoilt his ship. I could only reply in such a way as to smoothe his ruffled feelings, and I tried to, but when he would not be pacified I told him I thought he would change his mind. The next time we met I was glad to hear

Jacob Storm's Memoir

him say she really did look better. The removal of yards and rigging from a steamer was for me a step almost as significant as my quitting sail for steam, ten years before.

[Postscript]

I have included some notes I made of a typical voyage in 1887 because there might be some Storm mariner in years to come, or a bearer of another Bay name, whom it will interest to compare his lot with that of his ancestor or kinsman.

A VOYAGE IN THE SS *FYLINGDALES* IN 1887

Saturday, 5th February, 1887. Took on 1913 tons of coal and 392 tons of bunker coal. Draught 17 feet 11 inches foreward and 18 feet 3 inches aft. Proceeded from Newport, Monmouth towards Venice at 3 p.m.

6th February. Dropped pilot off Nash Point. Much coasting traffic. Took departure from Longships. All shipshape. Usual Sunday thoughts of home. High cross seas and a strong breeze by midnight.

7th February. Sea subsided in the morning; clear, cold atmosphere and a rising glass foretold pleasanter weather. South-easterly breeze by evening and Biscay calm.

8th February. A sunny morning and a breeze veering more easterly helping us to make nine knots. Noon course SSW and land hidden by haze. Engines running well and speed up to 9 knots.

9th February. Gentle breezes and long swells. Altered course at 9 a.m. to S. Lisbon abeam at 4 p.m. and saw Cape Espichel light at 6.45; bright moonlight.

10th February. 3.15 off Cape St Vincent, about 2 miles. Course SEE. A fine night with a light breeze from the NE. Thinking of the battle and the ships more lovely than our tank. Beyond Trafalgar at midnight and Spartel in sight.

11th February. 11 a.m. course E. Air keen. Snow on hills of Granada. Passed cape de Gata.

12th February. Course unchanged. Tunny sporting around us. Paint scrubbing in progress and mate complaining about quality of paint. A fine, pleasant afternoon with all hands in good spirits.

Sunday, 13th February. Course still E. Much sacred song from profane throats today.

14th February. Course and speed change for St Vito. Saw light on beam at 11 p.m. Course now E by S and log reset. Night very clear.

15th February. Course still E by S. Glass says storm coming off the land. Volcano abeam at 10.15 and rounded Cape Faro at 1.50. Etna wrapped in cloud. Cape Spartivento at 7.30 right beam. reset Course and Log.

16th February. Cold wind off Italian shore. Steering NE Roaring headwind impedes progress across Gulf of Taranto, but off Otranto at 5 p.m. and into the Adriatic. At 11 p.m. off Cape Gallo with northerly wind in our teeth. Glass far too low.

17th February. Still strong headwind and very cloudy. Gargano Head passed at noon. Glass rising. St Andreas's Isle on starboard beam at 5 p.m.; no light. Weather moderating at midnight. Course NW by N.

18th February. Wind still quite stiff at 5 a.m., with Italian mainland to leeward. Cloud cleared by noon and sea calm. Extra twist out of engines. Pilot alongside at 6 p.m. and moored by 6.30.

19th February. Shore people assured me of good dispatch. The shipper's agent Mr. Pardo. Cleared customs. Just before going ashore to look at the sights hailed by the crack 'Rosehill' just coming in. We have the honours.

Sunday, 20th February. No rest. Sabbath broken - and dirty.

21st February. Took myself sightseeing. Ragged Gondoliers and desolate palaces. A rather ghostly place, once beautiful no doubt. Reloading under way.

22nd February. Saw St Mark's today, Doges' palaces and Bridge of Sighs.

23rd February. Art gallery today - gods, monks and brigands. Heard monks at vespers.

Jacob Storm's Memoir

24th February. Discharge completed and, I hope, fairly weighted. Left the 'city in the mud' hastily to make most of daylight. Passed through the lagoon to the sea and dropped the pilot at 6 p.m.

25th February. Course SE by SS at ten knots. A fine morning., St Andreas again at 1.40, on the port hand now. Palgrossa Island at 5.40 p.m., and Santa Croce abeam at 7.30 Course straight and all clear. Destination Nikolaieff in Russia, for grain.

26th February. Off Cape Gallo 6 miles in the morning. Off Otranto at 10.45 and Ionian Islands in sight to port. Reset log and course now SSE. Making about ten knots. Crew busy clearing up the effects of the coal.

Sunday. A moderate gale came up from the S during the night, but we could see Sapienza, and Matapan was close on the port beam at 5.15 p.m. Malea at ten o'clock. The three southerly extremities of Greece today. Course NE by E now.

28th February. Morning brought a NE gale and a very nasty sea. Wondered about the bearing each time the screw cleared the air.

1st March. Glass climbing again. and spirits rising with it. At 10.30 at night we cleared the Doro Strait and found better weather as we headed towards Sigri. Grateful that engines are still going well.

2nd March. Passed Tenedos at 4.30 a.m. and crossed the bay in smooth water and entered Hellespont. Saw the point where the current slackens and Leander swam. and entered the Sea of Marmora in the afternoon. Anchored off the city of dogs and mosques and kiosks at 9.15.

3rd March. town crowded with people and rubbish. Rags speak of decay. Wondered whether the Sultan was in residence . We were able to proceed, and not without relief, clearing Kavak at 6 p.m.

4th March. Sea in turmoil. An experienced crew, but some stomachs moved. Racing engines made the Chief look thoughtful. Felt none too well myself.

5th March. The weather abated by morning and frost took over, with a cold drizzle. Anchored at Odessa in the evening. The port doctor made a perfunctory call.

Sunday, March 6th. Nikolaieff unapproachable because of ice on the river. Decided to wait for sun, or change of orders from the owners. A Sunday rest for once.

7th March. No news at the agent's. We may have to wait some weeks for the ice to give.

8th March. Mate angry today; everybody is well employed but he is running short of paint. Has some ambitious idiot of a clerk at home clipped our orders?

9th March. Paint chipping; awful row. Chief Mate happy with fresh supply of paint. The skipper has done his best to please.

10th March. Chipping, scraping and painting as usual. It was the Czar's birthday today and there was bunting from every spar in harbour and church bells seemed to be ringing across the water all day.

11th March. Telegram from the owners. We go down the coast to Danube to load at Sulina in Rumania. Health bill obtained and anchor weighed at 4 p.m. Wind a piercing spanker of a north-easter. Twelve hours to Sulina.

12th March. Pilot took us in at dawn. Shore folk less anxious about loading than I am. Much dismal talk of rain spoiling the cargo.

Sunday, 13th March. A day of rest, for which I was not sorry, cargo or no cargo.

14th March. Northerly breeze, clear, cold and dry. Mate kept crew at cleaning every corner, ready for millet seed and barley. Grain started pouring into every hold today.

15th March. Very cold still. Crew scaled a bunker today. Surprised at no mail for us at the agent's today. Grain coming aboard in good style. Very oriental-looking dockers.

16th March. Loading goes well but the continuous cold is most dispiriting.

17th March. We are a sallow, sombre lot, dockers included. The mate is trying hard not to growl. In the afternoon loading began to flag. Is the agent's word worth anything?

18th March. Wind SW, soft and fine, and a glimpse of the sun. Grain dribbling in slowly. A saint would sin if he had a skipper's job to do.

19th March. A calm. still day, with sunshine. It began to look in the afternoon as though we would have to use the Sabbath for loading.

Sunday, 29th March. Loading finished. Sailed at 3 p.m. Course SW from St George.

21st March. Intensely cold, but clear at first. Snow and hail later from the north. Course brought us straight to Kavak by 6 p.m., while there was still light on the hill. Received pratique, but heavy snow and darkness made us anchor.

22nd March. Weighed anchor at 6 a.m. in a strong wind and pushed along to anchor off the city for bunkers. Took a final look at the place, with its veiled women, bearded Jews, Greeks and grim Turks. Glad to be on our way.

23rd March. Off Gallipoli at 5.30 a.m., and Nayra point at 6.30. Passed Tenedos at 10.45. In the afternoon the log was recording ten knots.

24th March. Zea Island light abeam at 2.30 a.m. Very clear and bright. Course SWS. Georgios abeam at 5 a.m. and Belopoulo at 9. The archipelago was smooth off Malea and at 1.30 a.m. we changed course W for Matapan. I remember how the cape once had no light.

25th March. Strong headwind and sea at first light. Took a shaking as we went into the storm on W1/2N. Some moderation by evening.

26th March. A clear day and a fresh breeze and we were into Malta at 6.40 before the weather got up again. I think I reproduce my interrogation by the pilot accurately: From which place you come, sir? Anybody sick on board, sir? Everybody all well, sir? Nobody dead, sir? Hard a starboard, sir! Who's your agent, sir? Want coal, sir? Steady your helm, sir! Got any washing, sir? Let go the anchor, sir!

Sunday, 27th March. The Sabbath again. We left Valletta, but I suspect we were sold short on bunkers by some crafty checkers.

28th March. Steering NW by N Pantellaria. Off Cape Bon at 8.50 a.m., and Carthage just across the bay. Passed Galita Island at 9 p.m., with the sea quite smooth.

29th March Day began clear and fine. Course W by N. Coast became hazy. North wind became angry and we began to rock about until we smelt the bilges.

30th March. We went on deck to an east wind and a deluge of rain. By 6 a.m. it was clear again, and for the first time in weeks we felt the sun, at 8 a.m. Time to hand out paint pots again! Log records 289 (11 knots). Surprised to find tanks and bilges sound. Algerian coast hidden by mist.

31st March. March ended lamb-like. Watchman spotted Cape de Gato right on starboard beam at 9.50.

1st April. In Gibraltar bay at 3.40 a.m. for more coal, but away again at 2.15 p.m. bound for Altona. Tarifa near at 4.40, and saw Spartel, the last of Africa, an hour later.

2nd April. Wind and course both Nw, making a fresh breeze and a slight head sea. Left St Vincent astern at 3.30, but ship labouring hard.

Sunday, 3rd April. Course NE. Wind going down. Cape Roca near at 9.45 a.m., giving us proof of our faster pace. No slackening past Berengas. A good Sunday.

Jacob Storm's Memoir

4th April. Steering NNE now. Sea quiet. Particularly good pea soup today. Still off the coast of Portugal, with north wind coming up again. Saw warships at speed.
Off Finisterre at 9 p.m., but wind now at gale force bringing showers, and squally.

5th April. Gale still blowing. A very white sea. Set fore and afters in the afternoon. Wind NNW now and making only 4 knots. Hard pressed at midnight.

6th April. Barometer rose, hearteningly, but scud still flying past. SS'Mezalah' signalled in the afternoon and asked us to report leaking boilers and loss of speed to her owners.

7th April. Better speed now about 3 a.m. Wind veering E, more steady. In the afternoon saw much outward bound shipping running free.

8th April. Saw Ushant light at 1.40 a.m., bright and red. Set course for Portland into head wind. A howling forenoon with everything sodden. Better towards midnight, when a few stars appeared.

9th April. A grey day in a sulky Channel. In Portland at 10.30. Moored to Collins' hulk for more coal. Bunkering finished and on our way again at 7.30 p.m. Notified the owners.

Sunday, 10th April. Coastline seemed all towers and spires. Thoughts of home.

11th April. Wind against us, but a fine day. Course NEE. A fine afternoon. Even pleasant to take tea. Saw Terschelling light just on dark. and set course N. A meland light to starboard at 10 p.m.

12th April. Borkum SE 1 a.m. A fine night. Steered E and saw Heligolnad at 8 a.m. Dodging Neuerk Sand at 10, and anchored off Cuxhaven at noon. Given pratique at 1.15 and proceeded up the Elbe, reaching Altona at 6.40. to discharge at Dolphins. Good to relax at the end of a voyage. Found my wife waiting for me ashore.

From other notes by Jacob it can be deduced that at one port of call on this voyage he received news of the death of his brother-in-law, Andrew Storm, when the brig Magnet of which he was master went down with all but one hand off the Suffolk coast. He recalled how he and Andrew had often walked the moors together, and wrote that his "dear old shipmate, friend and brother" had been a brave sailor and a successful and respected master who worked hard for his family. (p.165)

PART 2

THE TABLES OF DESCENT OF THE STORM FAMILY

Editor's note: A son who has male descent is shown in capital letters. Other son's and daughters' marriages are indicated by the sign = and the date, where known. The children of first and second marriages are separated by a continuous line.

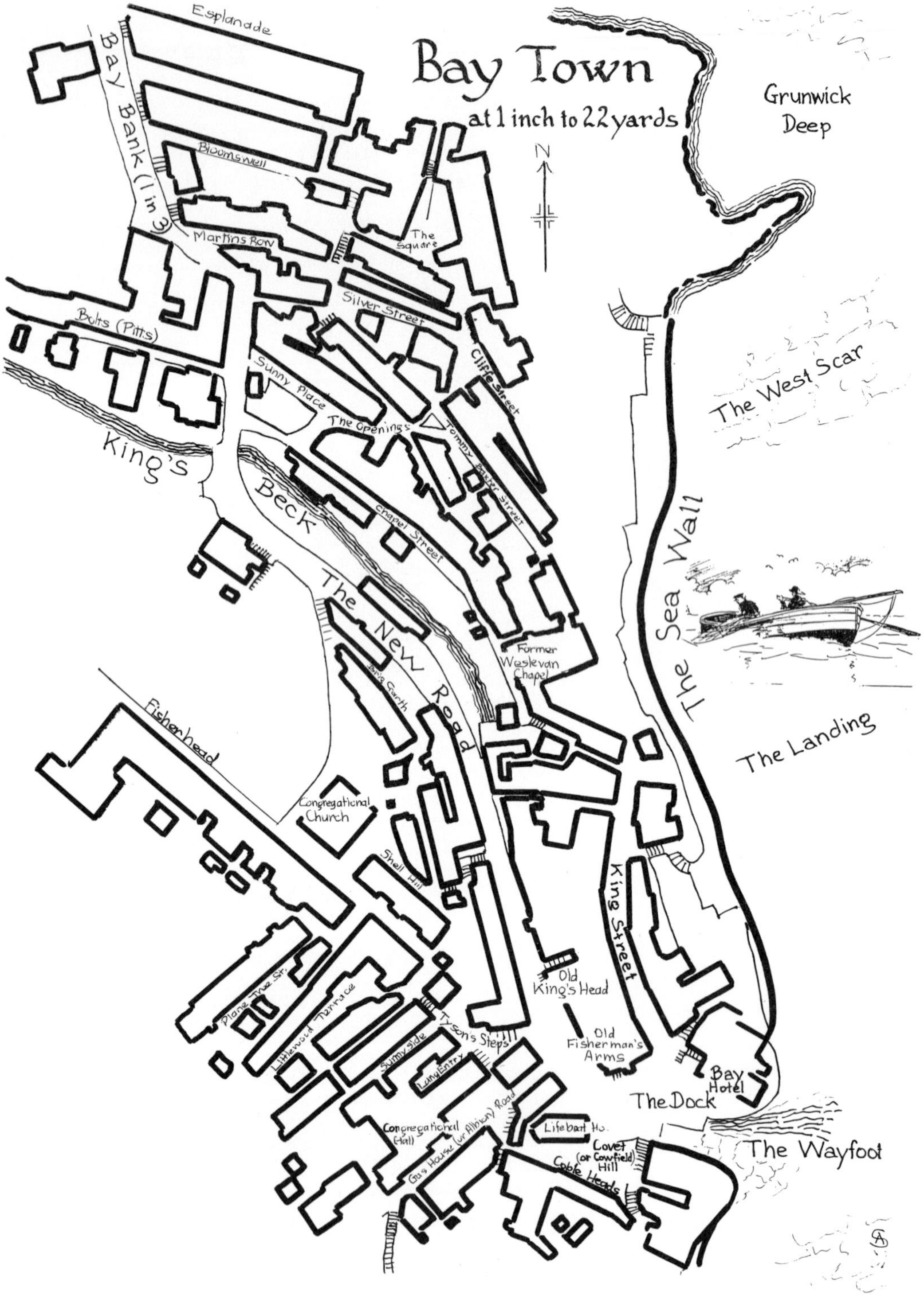

Bay Town
at 1 inch to 22 yards
N
Esplanade
Bay Bank (1 in 3)
Bloomswell
Martins Row
The Square
Silver Street
Bolts (Pitts)
Sunny Place
The Openings
Cliff Street
Tommy Baxter Street
King's Beck
Chapel Street
The New Road
Brig Garth
Former Wesleyan Chapel
Grunwick Deep
The West Scar
The Sea Wall
The Landing
Fisherhead
Congregational Church
Shell Hill
King Street
Old King's Head
Plane Tree St.
Littlewood Terrace
Tyson's Steps
Old Fisherman's Arms
Sunnyside
Long Entry
Bay Hotel
The Dock
Congregational (Hall)
Gas House (or Albion) Road
Lifeboat Ho.
Covet (or Cowfield) Hill
Coble Heads
The Wayfoot

Introduction

Robin Hood's Bay - "Bay" to those who belong - comes into history late. In 1539 the men of Fylingdales parish were mustered, and among them were several Storms. Jacob Storm listed John, Matthew, Peter, William, Robert and Bartholomew who were tenants of Whitby Abbey when it was dissolved at this period, and "Robin Hoode Baye" was their place of residence. The name of the village recurred in 1542 on the occasion of another muster, and among the 82 billmen and archers of "Robynhoyd Bay" and "Fyllyng Dayll" were William, Robert, Peter and John Storm. Descent from Scandinavians was commonly claimed in Bay, and there is some reason to accept this, because it might apply to much of the North Riding stock. Surnames, however, do not take us very far back, and most of the typical Bay names are to be found in the neighbouring countryside as early as they occur in the village. It may be that enclosure of lands to make larger farms drove increasing numbers to seek a living from the sea.

The earliest reference to the name Storm near Fylingdales comes in 1330, when John Storm of Levisham took a hind calf in Pickering Forest; he failed to appear and was outlawed, and his kinsman William lost bail. There may have been some of the family among the fishermen, not of Bay but of Fyling, for whom Whitby Abbey provided a net in 1394. Subsequently there are a few early references at Beverley, Hull, Scarborough and York, and the Ripon area, and many at Howden near Hull until the time of the plague in that city, in the sixteen-thirties. It might be presumed, however, from the number of Storm households in Bay before mid-sixteenth century that the family had been growing in the settlement for some time. In the absence of accurate information about origins, members used to refer to the family cheerfully as "one of the lost tribes of Israel".

The best-known early reference to the village is that made by John Leland who visited the coast about 1540. He called it a "fischer townlet" with a "dok". From this time the Bay people have often been thought of - not very accurately - as fishermen exclusively. Occupations are not often given in the parish register until late in the eighteenth century, but sometimes they can be gleaned from other sources, like wills. Nevertheless, a few mariners and masters are to be found early in the century, and from then on it can safely be said that "fishing village" was an increasingly inadequate description of Bay. Scores of careers can be noted, from apprentice to able seaman or boatswain, and so to mate and master, in the many vessels that belonged to the village households. However, Leland in his day saw twenty boats on the beach, and a document of 1563 concerning Richard Cholmley's application to purchase land and properties in Fylingdales from the Crown reveals that there may have been a sufficient population in the settlement to man this number of craft. There were some fifty households and the boats were more than likely the three-man cobles, the type evolved in working from a beach and thus significant in Bay history.

Many tenancies are listed in 1563, including Matthew Storm's Cow Close, one of the largest holdings in the parish, and the largest in the village, judging by his rent. A large "close" like this tends to support the view that reduction of the number of holdings was forcing people to look seaward for livelihood. Peter Storm had another close, and a cottage, and among the occupiers of 28 other cottages were William, Peter, Bartholomew and two Roberts. This was the most numerous family in Bay. Bartholomew may have been he who died about 1590 leaving a widow Jane and children Edward, Robert, Bartholomew, Joseph and Agnes.

It is probably necessary to accept that in the early years while some Bay people farmed, most fished for a living or mixed the two. The death of Robert Storm, fisherman, not at Bay but inland at Fylingthorpe in 1603 suggests this possibility of secondary occupations. His son had a holding at Bonsidedale on the moor, near Flask, which makes him rather more a farmer than a fisherman. A little before this an Anthony Storm also died at Fylingthorpe.

Among other "Bay" names there were present in 1563 - and before - some of those with which many links were to be forged by marriage and co-operative employment in fishing and trading vessels over the next three centuries. These included, notably, Hewitson, Moorsom and Richardson.

In 1638 the Cholmleys began to dispose of property in Whitby and Fylingdales by means of 1,000-year leases. This may have been to encourage settlement and stimulate the economy; it was certainly an inducement to inhabitants to stay. But there was great social significance in the development because it conferred a great measure of independence on the community, and would seem to explain why so many people appear in the parish register as householders, as though they were freeholders. The inhabitants are subsequently to be found paying a few pence a year for their houses and garths, and a shilling for any dwellings they built on the latter. The "as- good-as-freehold" tenure continued into the twentieth century, and was finally removed by conversions to freehold, long after any payments had ceased. Freedom to build and extend dwellings can be seen as one cause of the romantic appearance of the village, which Professor Pevsner called "delightful", and it may be coupled in effect with the erosion of the cliffs which has compacted the village at the rate of about 90 feet per century.

Social change also arose for other reasons. One was that the Cholmleys, the lords of the manor, removed from Fylingdales to Whitby, and sold their house and demesne lands in the parish to their relatives, the Hothams. Sir John Hotham and his son were both executed after the Civil War engagement at Hull, and around 1660 only Lady Margaret Hotham remained at the hall. From this time the Bay community was increasingly equalitarian in nature - and the more so because it derived its livelihood substantially from the sea rather than from having to labour in an influential landowner's fields. This character persisted, and those who can remember the village before WWII will recall how it was normal and common to meet about the place people of vastly differing economic fortunes but of the same blood.

This circumstance introduces one of the most striking aspects of this family history, which is the retention in Robin Hood's Bay of representatives of most of the branches, with the effect that at the time of the Census in 1841, for example, there were some ninety members present, if those away at sea are included. With the other most numerous families of Bedlington, Granger, Harrison and Moorsom they accounted for nearly half of the population. There was a strong awareness of indentity among these people, if the handing down of baptismal names and the use in baptism of one another's surnmames be taken as evidence. The combined effect of these two factors - the large size of the family and the common family names - is to create a tangle of ancestors, a situation many family researchers would envy, up to the point where the numerous Annes, Elizabeths, Jacobs, Janes, Isaacs, Matthews, and the rest, have to be sorted out. As Jacob Storm of the memoirs remarked, nearly a century ago, "The Storm's pedigree has been the toughest hunt I ever had, and had it not been for the traditional information, for which I am beholden to my Mother and Grandmother, I should have been out of the hunt long since....and you must take the book [i.e. his record of the family, the first such effort] as we took the old wooden sailing vessels, viz, with all faults". Despite much work on the records since his time, notably by his grandson Raymond, the researcher can still sympathise with his exasperation. A major difficulty at the outset is that the parish register begins late, in 1653. There is a transcript for only half of the years between 1600 and 1640, and the decade 1691-1700 is incomplete. However, although many of the people in the scattered entries cannot be built into a continuous history, intermarriage must secure them as ancestors, sometimes in a female line but direct rather than collateral, for most of the family living at the present time, despite the continuing lack of some detail.

Vital events concerning several of the family are recorded in, or to be inferred from documents, other than the parish register, of the early seventeenth century, and these might be starting points for descents if more evidence is discovered. Robert Storm, possibly one of the children of Bartholomew who has been mentioned, married Ellena Poskett in 1606. "Poskett" was a prominent farming name in Fylingdales neighbourhood. Its most famous holder was Father Nicholas Postgate of Egton, who was executed at York in 1679. Robert and Ellena had a son, Edward, whose wife Agneta bore a daughter Hellen, (or "Hellinor") who married Richard of the important Hewitson family, but there is no record of children. Joseph (probably another of Bartholomew's sons) lost his wife in 1633, a few months after the death of their son, Thomas. The children of Robert, the Fylingthorpe fisherman who died in 1603, leave little trace: Henry disappears after his holding at Bonsidedale is listed in 1638, and William died in 1634; their sister Elizabeth's marriage to William Huntrods is worth noting, because her husband's family was one of the best known in the parish - and so well represented by Williams that it defies sorting out for much of the time. Sometimes one might be guided by the recurrence of Christian names. There were in the seventeenth century several Thomas Storms, and these may descend from one whose daughter Elizabeth was born in 1617. Again, searching the registers of neighbouring parishes produces yet another Robert, who married Isabel Chapman at Egton in 1632/3, but he cannot be safely connected to the other bearers of the name, and experience of the problem of identity in these years gives early warning that it would be unwise to link him too confidently with the Robert, mariner of Whitby, who was buried in 1638 at Bishopwearmouth.

There is difficulty with one marriage of the eighteenth century, concerning a William who married Anna Nightingale in 1714. He was probably born in the incomplete decade, 1691-1700, and although one or two guesses might be made about his parentage, there are no children who can safely be assigned to the couple. He has therefore been omitted from the tables, but he has not been forgotten. The same century produces a few interesting "strays": for example it would be good to know more about the Thomas Storm of Bay who at the age of thirty in 1755 was a shipmate of James Cook in the Whitby vessel Friendship .

On such fragments much might be built, if new evidence appears. Meanwhile it is proposed to start here with rather more substantial evidence, the first item of which concerns the household of Joshua. The record for his children begins in 1617, after a gap in the transcript of the parish register of nine years (which means that he may have been married for some time before that). The transcript of the register begins in 1600 and shows no marriage; therefore Joshua who starts the "family tree" on page 83 may have been born before 1580 and thus have been the son of one of the men of 1563, and perhaps grandson of Bartholomew of 1539. The fifteenth century, however, remains below the horizon.

Descent from many of the daughters' marriages has been pursued; those with Bedlington, Granger, Harrison, Helm, Hewitson, Moorsom, Peacock, Pinkney, Richardson, Rickinson, Robson, Skerry, Tindale, Todd, Trueman and - naturally - Storm, are of particular note since they created over a long period of time a highly integrated group at the heart of society and economy. An effort has been made to find a place for the names mentioned: no picture of Bay would be complete without them. Most of them occur among the owners and masters listed with the vessels in the Appendix. Not all the inter-relationships can possibly be given, but the repetition of names in the tables will make the point about complexity. The intention in respect of the formidable-looking detail in text and footnotes which this sort of research can produce has been to give enough information to help descendants of the group - probably hundreds of them - to see where they fit in, and to take the matter further if they wish, but greater importance has been attached to presenting concisely and readably an impression of the triumphs and tragedies of a doggedly persistent community of ordinary people.

One of the most engaging and important aspects of the history of Robin Hood's Bay is the inhabitants' talent for survival as their own masters. Having little land, they turned to the sea, and by the middle of the nineteenth century about a thousand people living there, in what more than one writer recognised as great prosperity. There still survive some of those who remember the retired shipmasters of Bay who liked to recall how "this was once the richest place on the coast for its size" before the steamers drew people away to Tyne, Wear and Tees. The spirit of indepencence is well represented by the words of Henry Matthew Storm, a member of the Massachussetts Senate, knownin Boston as the honest selectman, who has not been found a proper place in the ensuing pages, but who undoubtedly belongs there, somewhere. His son Henry Hallgate Storm of Cambridge, Massachussetts knew that his father's people hailed from Bay but had moved away, and told how he liked to say that one day he would go back to "a village in Yorkshire" - not Robin Hood's Bay - and stand covered in the street while the locals doffed their caps to the lord of the manor, and declare, "I am a citizen-of the United States of America". Anyone who wishes to further the research work might consider the placing of Henry Matthew (1853-1917), son of Thomas and Mary Storm, a worthwhile undertaking. *

But independence is not the whole story. The customary business arrangement in the fishing was a co-operative one: the master - the person described in this work as "Master Fisherman" - provided the boat and his crew were responsible for the gear. When

---

* *Henry Hallgate Storm's daughter, Mrs Carey Bok, devoted much interesrt to the Curtis Institute of Music, Philadelphia [1924], endowed and presided over by Mrs Marie Louise Bok [nee Curtis], wife of the publisher and music patron Edward William Bok.*
[See Bok in <u>The New Grove Dictionary of Music & Musicians, 1980</u>]

ISAAC STORM AND SONS THOMAS, REUBEN AND MATTHEW photographed by F.M. Sutcliffe near the Wayfoot with their coble Gratitude and their dog 'Spy' c.1895. At the time of his death Isaac was about 97. (By courtesy of the Sutcliffe gallery, Whitby.)

THOMAS SMITH ('Argy') STORM (1833-1928), fisherman, (in well known unique costume) with his more conventionally attired sons Oliver, Thomas, William and Reuben, all of whom served as Coxwain of the Bay lifeboat. 'Argy' lived to be 95. This is believed to have been the 'Fosdyk' family of Leo Walmsley's Bay novel *Three Fevers*, filmed by J. Arthur Rank as Turn of the Tide in 1935.

WILLIAM STORM (1860-1936), fisherman, Lifeboat coxwain and church man, returning from a fishing trip.

profits were divided everyone got a share but the master took an extra "one for the boat". Thus co-operation was familiar, and it is to be seen in the shipowning days when kinsmen and friends put their money together, and a leading master mariner among them would head the company. Young men served apprenticeships with relatives, experienced men made their way to become boatswains and mates of vessels owned by familiar groups, and then worked to secure masters' berths which would allow them to earn the means of continuing the cycle of co-operative involvement. Thus the community kept itself going, in a way quite different from that in, say, a manufacturing town.

One cost of the chosen way of life was danger. Any reader of the pages that follow is likely to be impressed by the frequent reference to loss of life at sea. Jacob Storm of *Leeside* left a note that helps to put the matter in perspective. Without quoting his source, he stated that from the beginning of 1873 to mid-May, 1880, 1,965 British ships were lost, of which 1,171 were sailing vessels, and 10,827 lives went with them. Freak weather in the first six-and-a-half months of 1881 accounted for 919 wrecks on the British coast; in the previous year there had been 700. The Bay experience was thus not unusual: the training and the subsequent life were rigorous and hazardous, and difficult for both men and dependants. Storm Jameson in *Journey from the North* wondered about its effect in his youth on her seemingly unfeeling and unapproachable father - a shipmaster who had served his time in sail - when she unexpectedly received from him in his last years a post-card view of the moors, on the back of which he had written, "A place of dreams". Perhaps a good word to apply to these people is that chosen by Jacob to describe John Harrison, the shipmaster uncle whom he admired and whom he placed among "the most persevering men of his time".

A necessary note is that since dates of birth are not available from the register until late in the eighteenth century, those of baptism have generally been used, but the two are seldom more than five months apart. The local taste for whimsey used to have it that children were not presented for baptism until their parents need not carry them up the long hill to the church, which leaves the village with a one-in-three gradient. A more realistic but unhappily more prosaic controlling factor was that in the sailing- ship days men came ashore at the beginning of winter, and many births occurred in the following autumn, to be followed by baptisms before sailing was resumed at the approach of the next spring. Insurers could obviously influence the length of the working season: 1st March was a popular starting date, and many family occsions had to be celebrated by then.

Mention must be made of a few Storm households at Lythe, a little north of Whitby, in the later seventeenth, eighteenth and early nineteenth centuries. There is no reason to suppose these did not spring from the Bay stock, and that impression is strengthened by the popularity of similar names, notably Matthew and William, and involvement with the sea. It may be that these people were drawn there by employment in shipping serving the alum industry, of which there were branches at Peak and Brow near Bay. Many Bay sailors and vessels brought materials there and took away the finished product, but the most successful operations in this North Riding industry were those carried out at Sandsend, only a mile from Lythe.

Most of the historic trends that have been detected in the village and its neighbourhood will be discernible in the chapters that follow. Chapter 4 consists of lines - mostly short - that no longer have Storm male representatives, but it ends with a descent that survives to enter the twentieth century with male representatives. Even in the short descents there is evidence of much that will be seen in subsequent chapters to be characteristic of the community. The main lines - that is to say those which have been and still are best represented - provide the content of Chapters 5 and 6. The former consists almost entirely of the descent of William Storm and his wife, Elizabeth Reachey, and their eldest son, William. Chapter 6 explores the branches that follow from William and Elizabeth's son Jacob, and Chapter 7 presents another branch, in which the name has only recently died out, that exemplifies the familiar long-term developments and serves to emphasise the great continuity. Besides offering evidence of the pattern of trends, each chapter adds to the accumulation of personal experiences from which it is hoped there will emerge not only a picture of a way of life that has all but vanished, but also reflections of wider themes, one of these being, for example, the North East's three centuries of obsession with merchant shipping. It would be unnatural if complete uniformity prevailed, and Chapter 8 deals with another, separate branch which contains the example of a rare, deliberate association with the Royal Navy, serving to emphasise by contrast the great concentration on trading vessels in previous chapters.

The reader of the notes that accompany the descents may well consider it a matter of regret that only one of the long processionof mariners of Robin Hood's Bay thought fit to leave a record like that of Jacob of Leeside .

THE OPENINGS It shows very clearly how closely the houses were built where building space was restricted and also giving protection from the strong winds which prevail on the East coast.

The marriage of Bartholomew to his kinswoman Elizabeth is the first of several links that bind the various branches of the family together.

Four years before the loss of her husband Bartholomew in 1690, Elizabeth's father, Thomas, had also been drowned on a fishing voyage. (p.89) Each had been with four other men, and the loss of so many suggests that the five-man boat, a vessel of some fifty tons, was in use. As well as the cost in lives, there is the economic effect to consider, because the price of a fishing craft of this size was in the region of 500 at the time. Although the masters found most of this money, the responsibilty of their crews - i.e. the partners - for the rest meant that in the days of many large boats, the capital they raised ran into thousands. The community has to be seen as one characterised by entrepreneurship and partnership. For the inshore work there were three-man cobles. On the subject of cost it is interesting that when a French privateer seized two local boats in the bay in 1705 the fishermen were able to pay the large ransom of 50 for them. The fishing in the bigger boats was on a weekly basis, far out on the North Sea, until the autumn, when more men were taken on and several weeks were spent at the Yarmouth herring fishing.

The family of Francis' wife Jane Moorsom is found in the earliest village records, in the sixteenth century. Francis in his will disposed of two houses, a garth, and a close with a barn. These went to Jane and then to his surviving children. It would appear that like many, probably, he combined fishing and shipping with farming. His son Isaac got "the cellar wherein my drink standeth together with the garth above my mother's house". The involvement with land as well as sea is observable in the case of Jane's kinsman, Robert Moorsom, a fishermen, who in 1672 owned two closes on the moorland side of the parish, namely Kirk and Foulsike, the latter being one won from the moor in the previous century. These names are still to be found on the map of the parish. In the eighteenth century there are in the Fylingdales rate books frequent references to charges on Storm's Ground (and also Moorsom's, Granger's and Harrison's), not in Bay but in a country part of the parish, the Thorpe Quarter.

The sons and son-in-law of Francis, who were pressed into the Navy (together with Christopher Storm (p.87) served in the Mediterranean campaign of the time, against Spain. Richard Rolt's history of the war, written just after hostilities ended, says that before the fleet sailed there was a "vigorous press" on the Thames, seizing 2,370 men in 36 hours. Kinsmen worked together in Bay, and so it is likely that these men were at sea together when they were taken. The oldest, Matthew, had a son with descendants, among them some of the village's prominent owners and masters of ships in the nineteenth century. (p.169)

James Morrow was master of the Whitby vessel *Free Love* in 1765.

CHAPTER 4:

No Male Issue

All but one of the branches where the Storm surname has died out form the content of this chapter.

Joshua's line is important for the links it provides with other parts of the family, and brief though it is it can be used with other descents that follow to show collectively the movement from fishing to seafaring, and thence to shipowning in sail and ultimately command of steamships. The intensity and variety of maritime experience are evident almost at once.

JOSHUA (-1638) m. ?
Elizabeth (-1617)
BARTHOLOMEW (1617-)

    BARTHOLOMEW (1617-) m. ? (-1658)
        BARTHOLOMEW (1656-1690), Fisherman

BARTHOLOMEW, (1656-1690), Fisherman
    Lost off Filey with Thomas (p.91)
    and Robert Storm (p.65), James
    Helm and Robert Staincliffe.
	m.1678 Elizabeth Storm
	(c.1662-1733) dau. of
	Thomas and Margaret.
	(p.89)

FRANCIS, (1679-1737), Householder	
FRANCIS, Householder (1679-1737)	m.1708 Jane Moorsom, householder (1686-1744), dau. of Richard and Jane.

       Francis (-1709)
       Elizabeth (1711-1776)
=1732 MATTHEW STORM (1705-42). (p.171).
       Pressed into the Navy.
=1744 John Peacock, M.Mariner.
       Isaac (1712-1742). Pressed, and died aboard H.M.S. Lenox.
       Bartholomew (1714-1744). Pressed, and died aboard H.M.S. Lenox.
       Francis (1714-1724)
       Damaris (1716-1721)
       Anne (1718-1721)
       Richard (1720-)
       Isaiah (1722-1743). Paid off from H.M.S. Lenox in 1741.
       Rebecca (1725-1776)
=1747 John Dobson (1720-)
       Jane (1728-1785)
       =James Morrow, M.Mariner.

No Male Issue

The Bedlington family first appears in Fylingdales in 1607. The name is that of a village in the Northumberland coalfield and, appropriately, as early as 1394/5 a Robert Bedlington was paid for delivering fuel to Whitby Abbey.

George Storm was lost in the "King's ship" *Sunderland*. Timothy is mentioned in the document concerning his property. This is an early example of a Bay man not fishing but serving at sea. Another was John Storm (of Bay, but one of our "strays"), lost in the vessel *Industry* some time before 1694, and owing money to a widow in Wapping. The place is of greater interest than the debt, because it is next to the Pool of London, where colliers from the North East moored in great numbers, and a small colony of Whitby and Bay people came into existence.

The parentage of Robert who married Ann Bedlington is unknown, but would probably take the story back in one generation into the sixteenth century, before even the transcripts of the parish registers are available. Three generations can be traced, in which both fishing and seafaring are represented. There may be surviving descent from John and Jane Morrow, and there are certainly connections via the families of Ann Bedlington, Ursula Robinson and Jane Moorsom.

ROBERT (-1658) m.1639 Ann Bedlington (-1681?)

        ROBERT (1640-90), Fisherman
1680   Jane (1654-1690)?
        =John Morrow

| ROBERT (1640-1690), Fisherman | m.1665 Ursula Robinson (1637- |
| Lost off Filey. (p.83) | 1688) dau. of Edward and Anna. |

Ann (1666-)
Elizabeth (1669-1671)
TIMOTHY (1672-1708+)
Ann (1677-)
George, mariner (1680-c.1707). Lost at sea.

| TIMOTHY (1672-1708+), Mariner | m.1697 Isabel Moorsom(1676- |
| Died, or lost, at sea. | 1705), dau. of Robert and Elisse, nee Huntrods. |

John (1698-)

The parents of the next Robert, who might have died at about 40, probably married between 1641 and 1652, when there is no help from parish registers; therefore they are not identifiable. There is little or no doubt, however, that if no further evidence emerges there will at least be a link with one or more of the main Storm lines through Robert's daughter-in-law, Elizabeth Bedlington.

ROBERT (lost at sea in 1690) m.1672 Elizabeth Temple (-1682?)

Elizabeth (1672-78)) twins
Robert (1672-))
=Jane (1674-)

Elizabeth died in infancy, 1678
THOMAS (1679-)

No Male Issue

Coverdales and Milburns (the spelling varies) are among the families that moved in and out of Fylingdales. They are to be found working on the land, at the alum works, following the sea and owning ships. The principal interest of Coverdales in Bay was their cooperage, which earned two of them, Nicholas and William (both of whom had Storm wives) an independence sufficient to qualify them for the title 'Gent.' (p.103)

After Mercy's death Bartholomew joined his son Johnson in Whitby, but as with many others who had moved away his body was brought home for burial at St.Stephen's, Fylingdales..

THOMAS (1679-)   m.1705 Elizabeth Bedlington (1680-),
    dau. of Thomas and Jane.

John (1706-)
Robert (1708-1714)
Thomas died in infancy, 1711
Rebecca (1711-)
Elizabeth died in infancy, 1715
Jemima (1716-80)
Dinah (1717-)
Sarah (1719)

John who introduces the fourth short branch may have been a son of Robert and Ann who married in 1639, but again, there are no parish register entries to help around the probable years of his baptism and burial.

JOHN   m.1663 Barbara Lockwood (1636-)

   Elizabeth (1664-)
=1698 Robert Milburne
   Jane (1669-?1764)
=1704 1 .Robert Jobling
=1716 2. Richard Coverdale
   JOHN (1670-1697), Householder
   Dolora (1673-)
   Robert (1678-)

JOHN (1670-1697), m. Jane Harrison (-1731)

BARTHOLOMEW (1690-1775)

(There follow several years of gaps in the register)

BARTHOLOMEW (1690-1775) m.1716 Mercy Johnson (1694-1748)
    at Danby

Helen (1718-1739)
Elizabeth (1719-1721)
Christopher (1722-41). Pressed, and died aboard H.M.S. Lenox .
Elizabeth (1723-1797)
=MATTHEW STORM (1714-1804) (p.113)
JOHNSON (1727-1759), Carpenter, Whitby
Mary (1729-85)
John (1734-)

No Male Issue

Carpenter was a good trade for Johnson at a time when Whitby's shipbuilding had achieved great fame - something that Daniel Defoe remarked upon - but another reason for abandoning the fishing or seafaring tradition may have been that he was of age to be apprenticed in the year when his brother Christopher died in the Navy, into which he had been pressed. With Johnson's line there may connect John Storm, cooper in Haggersgate, Whitby, in 1823, and also in 1841 when he was 75; he married Jane Atkins in Whitby in 1815, when he was described as 'gent.' in the register. With cargoes and ships' stores to be packed, a cooperage was a sound investment. Jane died in 1850, at Haggersgate, aged 72. John was a member of the Whitby Lion Lodge of Freemasons at its foundation in 1797, and held office several times.

Ursula and Will Shepherd were grandparents of Rachel who married William Robinson (c.1728-1793), mason and innkeeper in Bay, and Parish Clerk of Fylingdales, who combined these occupations with work for the Customs, metering the coal delivered in great quantities to the alum works of Peak and Brow, near the southern edge of the parish. Their son, William (1761-1815), succeeded his father in his many duties. The Robinsons were traditionally keepers of the Mason's Arms in Bay: thus, for example, one can read of a special occasion in the churchwardens' accounts: "dinner at William Robinson's" on Ascension Eve. It is from William and Rachel Robinson that there stems a line of shipmasters and shipowners, starting with son Richard who married Jane Mennel, daughter of George, M.Mariner of Bay, and eventually entering the age of steam with Messrs.Robinson, Rowland & Co. of Whitby.

JOHNSON (1727-1759), Carpenter, Whitby   m.

Jane (1750-52)
John (1752-)
William (1754-)
Eleanor (1755-)

Yet another John married around the time that John on page .. married Barbara Lockwood. He and his family look somewhat isolated here, but there is known descent - an important one in Fylingdales history - from daughter Ursula.

        JOHN (-1704)   m.1657 Katheren Richardson (-1704)

        Dorothy (1658-1660)
        Jane (1661-1662)
        Ursula (1663-)
=1691 Will Shepherd
        Deborah (1685-1687)
        Thomas (1666-1672)
        A son died in infancy, 1667
        Dorothy (-1668)
=1705 Catherine (1669-)
        John Thompson
        Anne (1671-)
        Jane (1675-1676)

The line of Thomas and Margaret has only two generations but it is important because its first household produces not only the marriage with Joshua's grandson that has already been recorded, but also that with the William to whose numerous descendants Chapter 5 is largely devoted.

        THOMAS, fisherman (-1686)   m.1660 Margaret Marrinde or
        This may have been his second   Marriner
        marriage. Thomas was lost at sea
        with his son Thomas, Robert Moorsom,
        Thomas Robson and John Skerry.

        Thomas (1661-1686)
        Elizabeth (c.1662-1733)
=1678 BARTHOLOMEW STORM (p.83)
        WILLIAM (1664-1703)
        John died in infancy, 1666
        Margaret (1667-)
        Mary (1671-1750)
=1695 WILLIAM STORM (p.101)

No Male Issue

The illustration facing page 92 is an inventory, made in 1692, of the property of Thomas who was lost in 1690. It gives some idea of how the master of a fishing vessel lived. The haavres among the fishing gear were the long deep-sea lines. The large boats carried two of the smaller cobles to sea, and used them, one on each side, to draw the lines away and hold them across the current. For this arduous work an extra hand might be carried, to be rewarded with a half-share of the proceeds. By Thomas's will there was money for each son, a house for Matthew, two stables in Bay for Isaac, and Ings Close above the village, together with its barn, for Taylor. There was thus a continuing interest in the land, but all three sons served their time to the sea. (Ings House early in the present century was owned by Thomas's descendant William Andrew Smith, nephew of Jacob Storm, postmaster and creator of a valuable photographic record of the village).

Harrisons are to be found in Bay early in the seventeenth century. It is difficult and perhaps invidious to make categories, but on account of their large numbers these people, with Moorsom, Granger, Bedlington and Storm, might be called the inner core which most effectively characterises Bay in history.

Matthew (1676-1757) first appears in the parish register as a sailor, and eventually as "merchant" and "Mr.", a style usually restricted in Fylingdales to the more substantial landholders. He was owner of the *Matthew and Joseph*, whose activities under command of his son Isaac can be followed in the crew lists or "Musters" at the Whitby "Lit. and Phil.". Taylor was master of the *Constant Matthew*. There were voyages to America, Scandinavia and the Baltic. Their brother-in-law, John Moorsom, was the son of a fisherman who at his death was owner of six dwellings in Bay. John and his brothers Richard and Robert, all shipmasters with financial interest in their ships, can also be traced in shipping records, trading between Tyne, Wear and Thames in 1727 with the *Two Brothers, Richard and Jane* (their parents' names), and *John and Ann* respectively. Benjamin Chapman's kinsmen Aaron, Abel and Ingram were active in the same trade at the time. Benjamin and Mary had a child Abel, who did not live long, and was buried at Fylingdales. These names in Matthew's family circle take one straight to the heart of the Whitby shipping interest. Another of them, Holt, was associated with shipping, sailmaking and ropemaking, and both Holts and Chapmans became involved in banking, which is to say in Whitby at that time the financing of shipping.

Martha, wife of John Holt, receives special mention in the Rev.Dr.Young's *History of Whitby*, her survival to the age of 97 being quoted as a particular example of longevity in the town. The names of her descendants and their spouses recall much of Whitby's economic life: a son-in-law, Joseph Atty, had an interest in the whaling ships, and another, Nathaniel Campion of a well-known family of shipbuilders, was one of the town's bankers. Jacob Storm stated that it was Robert Campion, son of Nathaniel, who in 1824 erected the obelisk on Easby Hill, overlooking Marton in Cleveland, in memory of Captain Cook. George Buchanan, the lawyer, came of parents who died young, and on his way to making a name eminent in the legal life of Whitby and Fylingdales married into the shipping circle of Martha's descendants. There is an element of Nonconformity among these people; the Chapmans for instance were Quakers, and Matthew Storm and Joseph Holt, parents of Martha and John respectively, were trustees of the bequest (a property in Upgang Lane) that provided a Congregational minister's salary in Whitby. Matthew and his brothers Isaac and Taylor were absent from the list of those who paid for pews when the parish church of Fylingdales was rebuilt in 1709.

WILLIAM (1664-1703) m.c.1690 Dorothy Hodgson (1664-1725)

Thomas (c.1690-1710)
Jane (-1694)

Philip Lawson, F.S.A., a genealogist and relative by marriage (i.e. brother-in-law of Rebecca Storm (p.121)) thought that the head of the next household was a son of Thomas who was drowned in 1686, and - what is perhaps more likely - grandson of Thomas known to be living in 1617. (p.3) Another theory was that Thomas married the widowed daughter of Richard Taylor of Temple Hirst, near Selby, and this accounted for the subsequent popularity of "Taylor" as a baptismal name in the family. Her first husband's name was Johnson and the marriage at York is verifiable.

This is the first line so far seen that comes into the twentieth century with male descent. For convenient reference researchers call it the Prospect House line. There are known living descendants in female lines, and probably many more yet to be found.

THOMAS, (-1690), Master Fisherman   m.1676 Dorothy Johnson
Lost at sea with Robert   (-1689)
and Bartholomew Storm, James Helm
and Robert Staincliffe. (p.83)

MATTHEW (1676-1757), M.Mariner and Shipowner
Isaac (1679-1720), M.Mariner
=1706 Mary Harrison (1684-1778), prob. dau. of Leonard and Margaret.
TAYLOR (1684-1715), M.Mariner. (p.99)

MATTHEW (1676-1757), M.Mariner   m.1701 Joanna Moorsom (1676-
and Shipowner   1748), dau. of John
    and Margaret.

Dorothy (1702-1787)
=1728 John Moorsom, M.Mariner and Shipowner
John (1704-)
THOMAS (1706-1745), M.Mariner
Jane (1710-1794)
=1737 Robert Baker, M.Mariner
(Mary (1711-)
=1738 Thomas Rickinson, M.Mariner
=17.. Benjamin Chapman, M.Mariner and Shipowner of Whitby
Martha (1713-1811)
=1740 John Holt, M.Mariner of Whitby
Isaac, (1717-1765), M.Mariner, Shipowner and "gent".
TAYLOR (1719-), M.Mariner living in 1763, at
        Ilfracombe. (p.97)

No Male Issue

In 1738/9 John and Dorothy Moorsom were entrusted with the care of their nephews and nieces, Richard Moorsom's children. It is to be presumed that Richard was lost at sea. One of these children, another Richard, became Whitby's leading whaling magnate, and builder of the town's Georgian mansion, Airy Hill. The interest in Arctic whaling explains Cape Moorsom on the east coast of Greenland. It was Richard's son, Robert, who commanded the *Revenge* at Trafalgar, and became an admiral. Robert was given a place of special honour at Nelson's funeral. He settled in Northamptonshire, but preserved a Whitby connection by serving as Master of the Lion Lodge of Freemasons. The nautical connection extends to the present to include the naval officer who married the Princess Royal in 1992, Commander T. Laurence being a great-grandson of Isabella Moorsom, Robert's grand-daughter.

Mary and Thomas Rickinson had a son, Thomas, who also became a master mariner.

Matthew's younger brother, Isaac (1679-1720) "master and mariner", had no children. Among his dispositions in his will was 30 for the poor of the parish and 150 for "my nephew Taylor Storm son of my brother Taylor Storm late of Whitby deceased". Young Taylor was living in 1716, but was to have no descendants, and his heirs were therefore his uncles Matthew and Isaac.

In 1764 Lionel Charlton, Whitby historian, schoolmaster and surveyor, made a plan of "closes adjoining to Robin Hood's Bay, belonging to Mr.M.Storm, deceased". Matthew and Mary were buried in the old churchyard on the north side of the path, midway between the east gate and the church. Whether they had intended to build a new house is unknown, and the plan indicated only where Mr.Isaac Storm proposed to place a dwelling, in "Taylor's Field". This was to be *Prospect House*, now *The Bay Tree*. It was the first move out of the old village, to where there are now so many shipmasters' villas. The tradition is that the timber used in the house was brought to Bay in a family vessel, which is not surprising considering the number of voyages made to the Baltic. The timber could easily have been floated ashore, and such practice was not unknown: a few years later, in 1773, rafts of timber were floated from Scarborough to Peak, where Captain Child (son-in-law of George III's doctor, Francis Willis) was building Ravenhall. With Prospect House Isaac marked the success in shipping ventures of the descendants of fishermen. When his will was made 1n 1763 he was still living down in the village, where he seems to have been comfortably-off. The document, abstracted, mentions "my new mahogany bedstead with hangings, two of my best feather beds, with blankets and quilts, six of my best chairs with covers and my large easy chair with covers, also my mahogany escritoire and bookcase on it, with all my books, also my clock-case and my set of casters, also my two mahogany dining tables, my two looking glasses in mahogany frames, also my set of china with large china teapot and punch bowl, and two large silver spoons, also all the liquor or drink in the house at the time of my decease with the bottles and vessels, also all my ranges and grates, with togs, pokers and fire shovels, together with my horse, saddles and bridles". The household contents that did not go to brother Matthew were assigned to "my maid servant Aggy Day", who also got the milk cows, calves and hay, an annuity of £10 a year and £4 for mourning. Isaac's friend, the Rev.William Hauxwell of Fylingdales, was left a silver watch and a gold ring, and John Dale, son of Peter, a friend in Shields, was bequeathed £20. In a codicil Isaac specified that Aggy Day should have some linen, all the line spun and unspun, and the provisions - with the exception of the strong drink. The Dales in Shields

A true and perfect Inventory of all and singular the Goods Chattells and Creditts of Thomas Storm late of Robin Hood Bay deceased taken and apprised the twenty fourth day of August 1692 by us whose names are hereto written viz. Matthew Browne, William Storme, Thomas Skirry

Imprimis his purse and Apparell — 00: 15: 06

Item Plate of Two silver Cupps and a dram Cup A thimble — 01: 10: 00

Item two Guineas and two halfe guineas — 03: 04: 06

Item A Cow sold to William Stanicliffe for — 02: 15: 00

Item an other Cow delivered to Elizabeth Storme for the Children worth — 02: 05: 00

Item a fishing sacks viz.
netts, Lines &c valued to — 04: 00: 00

Item Debts owing to thereof as desperate viz.
Francis Meinte — 03: 00: 00
James Holme — 01: 10: 00
Richard Codlington — 0: 15: 0
Thomas Codlington — 0: 12: 0   11: 19: 00
John Dickinson — 07: 10: 0
John Johnson — 00: 12: 00

Item in the Low house one table & frame A long Table, Chaire, two turn'd Wood Chaires, A forme, A Buffett stoole, A Long Settle and A Cupboard Herbon and A Salt Kitt and two Iron potts — 05: 10: 00

Item in the ploor A Bedsteed, two fillin Tables, one Jooll stool and A Gillburt — 00: 10: 00

Item in the Chamb: three Bedsteeds A table and frame, A forme, two Jool stooles, two stoole Chests, A turn'd Chaire — 01: 10: 00

Item in the Color pa other dishes tin doshes and other smale things valued at — 02: 00: 00

Item more pigons and other smale things valued att — 00: 02: 00

More two paire of Tongs A fendor A warming pan and other bast things — 00: 10: 00

Item A Kose of Linnen valued att — 01: 10: 00

Item In the Garrett one Kettle A Cinder Chane, A Kimlin, A frying pan, &c — 01: 00: 00

Item three feather beds and other Bedding and bed Cloathes valued att — 05: 00: 00

Item Bonds viz.
William Yeoman debt att — 10:
James Tho: Corkhill — 10:   22: 11: 00
Chr: Brinson — 2: 11

Totall is — 162: 001: 00

came from Fylingdales, and they were still in business as shipbrokers in Howard Street, North Shields, in 1857, represented by a Peter Dale.

There succeeded to Prospect House Matthew (1741-1819), the son of the childless Isaac's brother Thomas. He was active as master and owner in Whitby shipping. From time to time he had shares in the *Achilles,* the *Benjamin and Mary* (Israel Allison of Bay, Master), *the Martha* and the 300-ton *Venus*, which last Matthew himself commanded. Among his partners were Chapmans, Holts, Richard Moorsom, Nathaniel Campion, Taylor Storm and William Linskill. The last was a ropemaker who went to North Shields, where his grandson became first mayor of the new County Borough of Tynemouth and a member of the Tyne Improvement Commission; several streets in North Shields bear the name Linskill.

In 1778 Matthew sold a building site to the Methodists and in 1779 John Wesley was able to celebrate his interest in Bay - he paid in all eleven visits to the village - by preaching in the new chapel (the modern Exhibition Centre), instead of in the Square, or down by the sea.

Matthew was known in shipping circles in the North East: his death in 1819 was reported by the *Durham Advertiser*.

Jacob Storm took down details of the family of Matthew and Mary from their Bible. Few of the children survived. There is some doubt about Matthew (1785-). Taylor was unmarried and Robert married but died at thirty, and his son Matthew remained a bachelor. Robert received - posthumously it would seem - an award of land when the Raw Pasture was enclosed in 1807, and this is presumably the land referred to in his brother Taylor's will, at Smales Moor in the north of the parish. Taylor and his sister-in-law are mentioned in a note in the parish register: in 1822 the church was rebuilt (to create its present unusual form) and Mr.Taylor Storm and Mrs.Christmas Storm paid £7 15s.11«d for the front pew on the north side of the aisle leading up through the west gallery. Christmas was buried at Pickering where many Kitchens have lived, and "Taylor Storm, Gent." is inscribed on his tombstone beside the church porch at Thornton-le-Dale.

If Matthew (1741-1819) was the father of Matthew (1785-), as supposed here, it is strange that he should not have been mentioned in the parent's will. Some of his children were baptised in Fylingdales, and during his long absence in France Ann his wife was living there, in Bay. They were married at Wapping in London. Perhaps a family dispute is to be suspected. From their daughter Margaret Brown, who married at St.Mary's, Whitby, there descends Marjorie Robson of Doncaster who also has the distinction of representing an unusual line, Mary Harwood of Scarborough, daughter of Henry Storm (1688-), being a direct ancestress.

REBECCA STORM (1813-1904), daughter of Thomas and Mercy Harrison, shipowners, who married Andrew Storm (1810-97) in 1834. She is seen here in the traditional dress of a widow, about 1900.

ANDREW STORM (1810-97), Master Mariner and owner of sailing vessels, who lived in *Wavecrest* in Cowfield Hill. The photograph, of about 1880, is by F.M. Sutcliffe.

CAPTAIN JOHN HARRISON STORM (1819-1888)
One of the enterprising master/owners at the time of the village's greatest prosperity, the 1860's. He was among the first shipmasters to leave the old village for the bank top before the modern township of sea captains' villas was created up there.

RICHARD KNIGHTLY SMITH, Master Mariner and Marine Superintendent, who in 1869 married Fanny Storm, daughter of Andrew and Rebecca of *Wavecrest*. The Knightly-Smiths lived at Ings House and Richard was proprietor of the gasworks and donor of the village's reading room.

THOMAS (1706-1745), M.Mariner   m.1737 Ann Robson (1717-1741),
                                                                      dau. of Robert and Rebecca.

    Rebecca died in infancy, 1739
MATTHEW (1741-1819), M.Mariner and Shipowner.

MATTHEW (1741-1819), M.Mariner   m.1765 Mary Hunter (-1822)
                                                                   of Whitby; died aged 77.

    Ann died in infancy, 1767
    Elizabeth (1768-72)
    Thomas died in infancy, 1770
    Benjamin (1772-)
    Matthew died in infancy, 1775
    ROBERT (1776-1806), Gent.
    Elizabeth (1779-1781)
    Mary Ann died in infancy, 1781
    John Robson (1782-1784)
    *MATTHEW (1785-)
    Thomas (1786-)
    Taylor (1789-1850), Gent.

*This is not yet verified: there was a Matthew of this household baptised in 1785, but by one account he died in 1807. According to Jacob Storm he was a prisoner-of-war of the French from that time for eight years, which could account for a presumed death and the long interval between the births of his first and second children. He is believed to have been lost at sea. Descent from him has been entered below, after Robert's family.

    ROBERT (1776-1806), Gent.   m. Christmas Kitchen (1775-1837).
                                                           Buried at Pickering

    Matthew (1804-1850)
    This Matthew is always distinguished
    by Jacob Storm as "Doctor Storm")

    MATTHEW (1785-), M.Mariner   m.1805 at Wapping Ann Brown
                                                         (1783-1867), dau. of
                                                         William and Margaret
                                                         (nee Postgate). William
                                                         was Master and owner of
                                                         the Peggy of Whitby.

    Margaret Brown (1805-)
=1825 Joseph Shaw of Huddersfield
    Mary (1814-)
=1836 William Weatherill, Whitby
    WILLIAM BROWN (1817-), M.Mariner
    Ann (1819-)
    =Robert Mills, M.Mariner, Whitby

No Male Issue

William Brown Storm lived for a time on *The Esplanade*, Whitby, a part of the seaside development intiated by "Railway King" George Hudson, and Mary in 1861 was taking advantage of the reviving interest in Whitby as a resort by letting rooms to visitors. In Whitby Musters William is recorded in 1842 following the familiar trades, with voyages to Riga and Leith, in the *John Barker*, owned by Turnbulls of Whitby. His son-in-law, J. Alderson, was master in 1875 of the *Othello*, another Whitby vessel belonging to the same fleet, trading in Black Sea grain until 1880 when she was broken up. She was the last Turnbull venture in sail. The *Esplanade* house was later occupied by Robert Tate Gaskin, the Whitby historian.

John Matthew and Elizabeth Ann lived in Park Terrace, Whitby, the home of many shipmasters. Elizabeth Ann's father farmed at South House, Fylingdales. One of her brothers, John Baxter, was a Thames pilot, and another, Harrison, M.Mariner, was owner of Whitby steamers. Harrison Baxter represents a Methodist tradition: he was a great-nephew of the Bay smith William Cobb, a pioneer of the Bay chapel of 1779, and in 1890 he presided over the celebrations when a new chapel was founded at Fylingthorpe. A source of inspiration is perhaps detectable, for William Cobb's daughter-in-law was Mary Newton, whose father settled and farmed in Fylingdales, and her brother was a Methodist celebrity, the Rev.Dr.Robert Newton, four times President of the Methodist Conference. The picture is not a uniform one of piety: information was laid against Mr. and Mrs.Wm.Cobb in 1772, and a search of their premises revealed a large quantity of contraband.

This line is represented by Derek Storm Copeland of Middlesbrough, grandson of Dr. and Mrs.John Arthur Kilvington.

In 1881 Harry was master of the Whitby steamer *Ouse*, when she was lying at Bilboa. The home in Whitby was Esk Terrace, another location favoured by shipmasters. Trade out of South Wales and especially to South America - "coal out and corn and nitrates in" - took Harry and family to the Cardiff area, and they are buried at Llandaff cathedral. Many Whitby ships and crews came to work in and out of Cardiff. Men who stayed in Whitby could catch a night train from Cardiff and arrive in Whitby at 6 a.m. The train whistle used to sound at Sleights, three miles up the Esk valley, letting families know that a crew would soon be home. The Milburn family of shipmasters, descendants of William and Elizabeth Robinson of Bay Mill (the Boggle Hole Youth Hostel now), became occupants of Harry's Esk Terrace house. The Robinson's grandson, John William Milburn, M.Mariner, went to Tyneside, eventually to become superintendent of the well-known Prince Line founded by Sir James Knott, Bart., son of a pie-maker in Howdon-on-Tyne. In numbers of ships the Prince Line was the largest on the coast around 1900.

Presumably trade first took Taylor (1719-) to Devon, but he retained shares in Whitby-registered ships, as did Benjamin Storm of Ilfracombe, whose date of birth has not been ascertained. They were fellow shareholders of Matthew Storm of Prospect House, Benjamin Chapman and others. Two years after Taylor's son Matthew died his widow, Mary, married Nicholas Vye at Ilfracombe. Matthew and Mary's son- in-law, John Pomeroy Gilbert, Fellow of Exeter College, Oxford, Vicar of St.Wenn, Cornwall, and Prebendary of Exeter Cathedral, was a descendant of the mother of Humphrey Gilbert and (by her second marriage) Walter Raleigh. He was the son of the Rev.Edmund Gilbert. John Pomeroy Gilbert junior was General Manager of the West of England and South Wales District Bank. The prominent obelisk at Bodmin im Cornwall is in memory of the India general Sir Walter Raleigh Gilbert, the Rev.John Pomeroy's brother.

WILLIAM BROWN, M.Mariner (1817-after 1869)

                                                                   m.1842 Mary Brown
                                                                       (c.1820- 1869)

        Isabel (1843-)
        Ann (1845-)
=1869 J.Alderson, M.Mariner; married at Middlesbrough.
        JOHN MATTHEW, M.Mariner
        HARRY, M.Mariner
        William Brown (1853-1862)

JOHN MATTHEW, M.Mariner   m.1871 Elizabeth Ann Baxter
                                                                      (1850-1902)
                                                  dau. of David, M.Mariner, and
                                                  Elizabeth, of South House,
                                                  Fylingdales; sister of John,
                                                  Thames pilot, and
                                                  Harrison, M.Mariner, owner of
                                                  Whitby steamers.

        Elizabeth Mary (1875-1954)
        =Dr.John Arthur Kilvington
        William (-1944), M.Mariner

HARRY (1815-1917), M.Mariner   m.1876 Laura, dau. of Isaac,
                                                  farmer of Hawsker, Whitby.
        Lillian Laura (1892-1919)

Continued from page.91:

TAYLOR, M.Mariner (1719-)   m. 1754 Mrs.Joan Bowen, at
                                                    Ilfracombe.
        MATTHEW (-1787), M.Mariner and Shipowner

MATTHEW (-1787), M.Mariner and Shipowner   m. 1781 Mary Vye,
                                                              at Ilfracombe.

        Mary   ) married at Constantine,
=1807 Rev.John Pomeroy Gilbert (1779-1853))   Cornwall

No Male Issue

Taylor (1684-1715) "master and mariner", left Ings Close and its barn to his son, and instructed that his own ship and all his shares in other vessels should be sold to educate and maintain the boy, with Elizabeth having the benefit of half of the proceeds in her lifetime and all the residue of the estate.

PROSPECT HOUSE, now a retirement home called The Bay Tree was planned by Isaac Storm, Master Mariner, 200 years ago. For more than a century the house stood virtually alone, overlooking the sea; a hundred years later the Bank Top began to be developed as the site of villas of many shipmasters.

Continued from page 91:

    TAYLOR (1684-1715), M.Mariner m.1713 Elizabeth Granger,
                                                    dau. of
                                                    Edward and Mary,
                                                    nee Robson.

Taylor (1714-)

AIRY HILL Isaac's cousin, Richard Moorsom was the builder of this most lavish of Whitby's Georgian houses. Money in whaling ships founded the fortune of this grandson of bay fishermen.

William and Elizabeth

There is no known male descent from William and his first wife, after their son Henry. With William and his second wife, Elizabeth Reachey, there begin the families which include most of those people belonging to male lines, but it will be seen that with the marriage of their son William to Mary Storm the links with other parts of the family are resumed very quickly.

John Todd belonged to a second generation of his family in Fylingdales. By a previous marriage he had a daughter Mary who married Benjamin Granger. Seafaring Grangers are still represented in Bay, by Capt.James Granger, a master in marine services to the offshore oil industry in the Arabian Gulf. Their numerous Benjamins have frequently been among the most prominent people in local maritime occupations. The Todds remained in the village, the descendants of John and Isabel in particular becoming very much a part of fishing, seafaring and shipowning circles over the next 150 years. The broad movement already illustrated from fishing towards seafaring, command, and then ownership of vessels will be recognised in the tables that follow.

Isaac's wife Ann died in childbirth

CHAPTER 5:

William and Elizabeth

The main content of this chapter is the descent of William Storm and his wife Elizabeth Reachey via their son William, his elder brother Isaac having had no sons who survived. Jacob's descent belongs to Chapter 6, somewhere at the end of which the youngest brother, Henry, would be in remote isolation if the normal sort of sequence were followed, but it makes sense to deal with Henry quickly and so he follows Isaac. The traditional changes in occupation are illustrated, and almost from the start the interest in shipping produces an inclination to look north, towards Whitby, Tees, Wear and Tyne, which determines the direction of most outward migration. Prosperity creates a new village above the old, but some descendants preserve a strand of continuity with the immemorial fishing and this retains the name in old "Bay Town" until 1983.

WILLIAM   m. (1) ?
                                         (2) 1670, Elizabeth Reachey (-1698)

        Henry (1663-1728)
        Elizabeth (1665-)
=1697 Richard Clarkson
        Jane (1668-1674)
        Isabel (1671-1749)
=1705 John Todd
        ISAAC (1672-1701)
        WILLIAM (1673-1711), Mariner and Fisherman.
        Mary (1675-1681)
        Jane (1676-)
        Margaret (1677-1683)
        JACOB (or JAMES) (1680-1750). Continued in Chapter 6.
        William)
        Ann   ) Twins died in infancy, 1681
        John (1684-)
        Mary died in infancy, 1686
        HENRY (1688-). (p.103)
        Edward (1690-)

ISAAC (1672-1701)   m.1701 Ann Moorsom (1679-1702) dau. of Richard
                                                        and Jane

        Isaac died in infancy, 1703)
        Ann died in infancy, 1702) Probably twins

William and Elizabeth

There is at least one descendant of Henry (1688-) - and in Yorkshire still - through his daughter, Mary Harwood of Scarborough; this is Marjorie Robson of Doncaster, another of whose forebears was Margaret Brown Storm (Mrs.Shaw) on page 94.

Thomas and Grace Granger were the parents of Zachariah, Master Fisherman, one of whose sons, Zachariah, became a sailor and another, John, a master mariner. The ties were strengthened, and they endured, for Peace, daughter of Thomas and Peace Marshall became by intermarriage the great-grandmother of the Benjamin Granger who managed one of the Bay shipping insurance businesses of mid-nineteenth century, a time when the village owned scores of vessels. The mesh of the network becomes finer with Peace's second marriage, to William Moorsom, Master Fisherman. Thomas Marshall was of the Fylingdales family that produced John, who was chosen by the people to be their "register" during Cromwell's Commonwealth.

"Allotson" is an ancient - and variously spelt - Fylingdales name. It occurs in the well-known legend, of medieval origin, that lies behind Whitby's annual "Penny Hedge" ceremony, and "Allison Head Wood" is still to be found on the map of the parish. Anthony and Margaret Allotson were grandparents of Israel Allison, M.Mariner (1744-1841) who commanded an Admiralty transport (owned by Chapmans of Whitby) in the Napoleonic Wars and spent some time as a prisoner-of-war, as did his son William.

Jonathan and Dorothy Skerry had a son Thomas, a fisherman who married Esther, daughter of James Storm, Master Fisherman (p.186). Esther was widowed in 1783 when Thomas was lost with his brother-in-law Jacob Storm and kinsman Jacob Peacock, but they had a long-lived son, Jonathan, M.Mariner (1771-1860), commander of the Whitby transport *Ceres* in 1809 and one of the principal shipowners in the village at the height of its nineteenth century prosperity.

The commercial importance of the Coverdale coopers' involvement in the circle of kin in which they found themselves might reasonably be presumed.

John and Isabel Smith had a son, John, who is variously described as a fisherman or master mariner. The change to "fisherman" frequently occurs with elderly men who no longer go off to sea but remain at home, keep or share a boat and "do a bit of fishing". The situation can still be observed late in the nineteenth century, and a retired shipmaster with a boat is still a feature of village life today. In 1827 John Smith bought a newly-built Sunderland brig the *John and James* with James Storm (p.123), his nephew by marriage, for £1,277 and an additional £480 for fitting out. John Smith had served in Whitby whalers, as harpooner, and either this James Storm or his contemporary, namesake and kinsman (p.145) was he of that name who sailed to the Arctic with with William Scoresby in 1812 and was boatswain of the specksioneer's watch on the whaler *Esk* in 1814.

Martin Pearson (1773-1796), son of Martin and Mary, died of yellow fever at Port Royal in the West Indies during naval service, into which Jacob of *Leeside* says he was pressed. This death was reported (in a letter which survives) by William Richardson of Robin Hood's Bay, who had himself been pressed at the end of a long voyage from the Far East and sent to the same place. William was drowned at Port Royal.

Mary and Martin Pearson lived in William and Isabella's family home in Bay Quarter, and when the parents died in 1774 Martin Pearson succeeded as the householder, and tenant of Moorsom's Ground, known as Goose Geats (above Greenhills, in the north of the parish) and according to Jacob Storm of Leeside part of Wm.Wood's Croft Farm, Thorpe, in 1921.

HENRY (1688-)　　　m.

        Mary (1715-), baptised and Married at Scarborough
= 1735　Richard Harwood
        William (1719-), baptised at Scarborough
        Johannah (1723-)

WILLIAM (1673-1711), Mariner　　　　m. 1695 Mary Storm (1671-1750)
      and Fisherman　　　　　　dau. of Thomas who was lost in 1686. (p.89)

       Grace (c.1696-)) parents of Zachariah, Master
=1717　Thomas Granger)　　Fisherman
       Peace (1697-1728)) parents-in-law of Williamm Moorsom,
=1716　Thomas Marshall)　　Master Fisherman.
       Ellen (1697-1784)
=1732　Nicholas Coverdale, Gent. and Cooper
       WILLIAM (1699-c.1774), Master Fisherman.
       Margaret (1699-1772)
=1718　Anthony Allotson
       NATHANIEL (1702-1749), Victualler. (p.113)
       Elizabeth (1704-1771)
=1725　John Hodgson
       Marion (1705-1788)
=1747　William Coverdale, Gent. and Cooper
       John died in infancy, 1708
       Dorothy (1708-1788)
       1732(Jonathan Skerry
       Isaac, fisherman (1710-1791)
       MATTHEW (1714-1804), Master Fisherman. (p.113)

WILLIAM (1699-c.1774), Master　　　m.1726 Isabella Harrison (1702-
      Fisherman　　　　　　　　　1774), dau. of John and Elizabeth.

       Timothy (1727-1730)
       Isabel (1729-1823)
=1748　1. John Hays
=1766　2. John Smith
       Mary　　(1732-1801)
=1766　Martin Pearson
       Timothy (1734-); probably died in infancy
       Elizabeth died in infancy 1739
       JOHN (1740-1813), Master Fisherman
       Elizabeth died in infancy 1744

William and Elizabeth

John (1740-1813) lived at no.2, Langentry from 1765 until his death.

Richard Marshall was a fisherman and sailor. A daughter, Anne ("Nancy") went to Scarborough, where it is likely Mary ended her days.

In 1791 Elizabeth, daughter of John and Mary gave birth to a son, John Hodgson Storm, five months after the Bay fisherman John Hodgson had been found "drowned or killed" in the harbour at Whitby. He was 21 years of age. She eventually married John Garforth who had formerly been in H.M. service, but he died in 1817, and Elizabeth is to be found in 1851, in her eighties, staying with her granddaughter in Bay. Illegitimacy is a rare condition in this work. That and pre-marital conceptions were infrequent among the long-term families, so much so that even if some allowance has been made for possible concealment it would seem that there was a will and a capacity to protect the family.

Although he is known to have been at one time a fisherman, Lancelot Moorsom is described as a retired mariner in 1851, when he and Margaret had their son John living with them. He was a tailor employing two men, one of them called Fishburn, which was the name of the builder of James Cook's famous *Endeavour* at Whitby. Another son, Thomas, a mariner, had been lost at sea in 1829.

The fisherman John Hodgson Storm was always known as Hodgson, rather than John. In 1861 his daughter, Elizabeth Wickham, a widow, was living in Bay and taking care of two young sons of her widowed brother-in-law, James Storm Harrison, who was absent at sea. The relationship is not apparent from the Census, in which "servant" or "housekeeper" are very frequently applied to women who on investigation are found to be close relatives of the household. One of the boys in 1861 was Storm Harrison who became a master mariner. He was lost in the brig *Joseph*, and left a son, William Storm Harrison who spent 52 years at sea. A.G.Course in *The Deep Sea Tramp* listed the variety of cargoes that Capt.W.Storm Harrison carried: tea from China and Ceylon, rice and teak from Burma, gingelly seed, rape seed, linseed and manganese ore from India, raw cotton from Egypt and the United States, grain from Russia, the United States, Canada and Argentina, iron pyrites and wool from Australia, wool and provisions from New Zealand, live cattle from Canada, nitrates from Chile, softwood from New Brunswick, Nova Scotia and the White Sea, Oregon pine from the United States, lignum vitae from Argentina, iron ore from Sweden, Spain and North Africa, wine and olive oil from Portugal, esparto grass from Oran, peanuts, coffee beans, palm oil and kernels from Nigeria, Gold Coast and Ivory Coast, coffee from Brazil, fish from Norway, and marble from Italy.

Thomas (1818-33) was lost in a fishing coble with Thomas Storm (son of Isaac and Elizabeth (p.125)) and William Harrison. Mary Ann and Isaac Storm continued to live in Bay, but Ann and John Pinkney moved to the growing industrial town and port of Middlesbrough. Tindale Avery, husband of Margaret, was the descendant of a fisherman married in Fylingdales in 1770, and his baptismal name came from intermarriage with the Tindales, who came into the parish from neighbouring Hackness, across the moor, around 1750, and became much intermarried with the maritime community. In 1867 Tindale Avery was master of the brig *Emma* owned by Ben.Granger and Co. of Bay. His brother-in-law, John Hodgson Storm, M.Mariner, disappeared from the shipping lists in that year; the *Whitby Repository* of the time tells of "a terrific storm on the North East Coast" in December, and the loss of Capt.J.Hodgson Storm and his vessel *Iddo*. A son was working as a carrier in the Bay area in 1871. Isabella, the youngest of the family, kept house for her sister and brother-in-law, the Averys, and in the Census is "housekeeper".

JOHN (1740-1813), Master   m.1762 Mary Moor (1739-1811), dau.
   Fisherman   of George and Margaret.

   Mary died in infancy 1763
   Mary (1764-1848)
=1790 Richard Marshall, Sailor and Fisherman
   Elizabeth (1766-1769)
   JOHN (1769-1845), Fisherman.
   Elizabeth (1771-after 1851), mother of JOHN HODGSON STORM.
   =John Garforth, of the Coastguard
   Isabella died in infancy 1774
   Isabella (1774-)
   =Isaac Harrison (1776-1799); lost at sea.
   Margaret (1776-1856)
=1807 Lancelot Moorsom (1777-1851)
   William died in infancy 1780
   Thomas (1781-)) twins
   William (1781-1795), Fisherman)
   George (1784-)

JOHN HODGSON STORM (1791-1861) Fisherman m.1814 Ann Ridley (1791-1874),
                  who was born at Staithes.

   Elizabeth
   Thomas Wickham
   Thomas, died in infancy, 1817.
   Thomas (1818-33)
   Mary Ann (1822-)
=1845 Isaac Storm, Fisherman. (p..)
   Alice (1821-1853)
=1844 James Storm Harrison, M.Mariner
   Ann (1823-)
=1843 John Pinkney, M.Mariner
   Margaret (1826-)
   Tindale Avery, M.Mariner
   JOHN HODGSON STORM (1828-1867), M.Mariner
   Isabella (1831-after 1881)

JOHN HODGSON STORM (1828-1867), M.Mariner m.

   William (c.1853-)

William and Elizabeth

John (1769-1845), who continued to live in Langentry, was known as "Auld Stormy". He kept a beer house which was notorious for the brewing of particularly strong ale. His father-in-law, John Mills, was a sailor. Sons Nathan and Isaac moved away, to Teesside, and Thomas was lost at sea. William (1798-1885) owned the brig *Lomar*, from which he was well known as "Lomar Will". He also owned the *Naiad* and the *Abbotsford* and his sons-in-law John Shaw and Edward Granger commanded them. He is a typical fisherman in the Sutcliffe study entitled *A Bit of News*, but in 1844 he appears to have been master of the sloop *Blucher*, owned by Robert Campion of Whitby. The *Lomar* was lost in 1859, and with her William's son John, the master, and brother Thomas, mate. With the coming of steam John Shaw became a tugmaster at Hartlepool. One of his daughters, Ann Storm Shaw (1875-1965), was the grandmother of Mark Adlard of Seaton Carew, author of the novel *The Greenlander*, a story set in the Arctic whale fishing out of Whitby. Edward Granger left the sailing ships and became Chief Officer of the S.S.Mildred, owned and built in 1879 by Turnbulls of Whitby. She left New York and foundered with all hands in 1880. Lomar Will was the official Minstrel of the Fylingdales friendly society known as the Ancient Shepherds, an institution that brought together representatives of all facets of local life; the Shepherds "walk" to church was an annual event of importance.

John Storm (1800-67) was distinguished from others of the name by the nickname "Attaliah Jack", which came from the brig of which he was long master. She was owned by his father-in-law, Jonathan Skerry, who had prospered and become the owner of some half-dozen such vessels. The Skerry-Storm links were strong: William Pearson, M.Mariner, father of Mrs.Jacob Storm of Leeside, was apprenticed to Jonathan in 1816. Attaliah Jack's son, James Skerry Storm, was master of one, and his son-in-law, Isaac Storm Harrison, commanded another. James Skerry (1799-1876), M.Mariner, Jonathan's surviving son, took over the fleet, but in his time the competition from steamers was beginning to be felt and the Bay shipowning interest was in decline. Increasingly the local men became masters of steamers based elsewhere. James Skerry Storm was lost in the brigantine *Wrights* in 1877.

JOHN (1769-1845), Fisherman　　　　　　　m.1798 Mary Mills (1773-1847),
　　　　　　　　　　　　　　　　　　　　　　dau. of John and Mary,
　　　　　　　　　　　　　　　　　　　　　　nee Peacock.

    WILLIAM (1798-1885), Fisherman and Shipowner
    JOHN (1800-1867), M.Mariner
    George (1802-)
    Jonathan (1804-)
    JONATHAN ("NATHAN") (1805-1868). (p...)
    Mary (1807-1811)
    ISAAC (1810-), M.Mariner. (p.110)
    THOMAS (1813-1859), Mariner (p.112)
    Mary (1814-)

WILLIAM ("LOMAR WILL")　　　　　　　m.1824 Ann Bedlington (1794-1868),
    (1798-1885), Fisherman　　　　　　　dau. of Richard and
    and Shipowner.　　　　　　　　　　　Elizabeth.

    Mary (1824-1849)
    John (1827-1859), M.Mariner.
    =Elizabeth Storm, dau. of Thomas and Jane. (p.115)
        (ch'n in 1861: Ann E. (6) and William T. (2))
    Ann (1833-)
=1854 John Shaw, M.Mariner, at Scarborough.
    Elizabeth (1836-1908)
=1858 Edward Granger, M.Mariner, son of Thomas and Catherine.

JOHN (1800-c.1867), M.Mariner　　　　　　m.1828 Elizabeth Skerry (1805-),
　　　　　　　　　　　　　　　　　　　　　　dau. of Jonathan
　　　　　　　　　　　　　　　　　　　　　　(M.Mariner and Shipowner)
　　　　　　　　　　　　　　　　　　　　　　and Mary

    Mary (1829-1906)
=1851 Isaac Storm Harrison (1828-1891), M.Mariner
    George (1831-1858), M.Mariner
    JAMES SKERRY (1837-1877), M.Mariner

JAMES SKERRY (1837-1877), M.Mariner　　　　　m. Elizabeth Tyerman

    Mary
    =1.. ....
    =2. Joseph Lythe
    GEORGE, who was born at sea; M.Mariner
    JONATHAN SKERRY (p.111)

William and Elizabeth

The information about the birth of George Storm at sea came from Arthur, his son, who lived in Middlesbrough. Arthur believed that his parents owned vessels at one time, but that the times were too hard for the sailing craft. James Jobling junior, son of Eleanor and James, remembered being taken on Sunday after church to see George his grandfather, and hearing stories of his life at sea "from cabin boy to skipper". Once when George was very young he was paid off at the end of a long voyage to Argentina with á and felt "like a millionaire". His granddaughter, Edith (Mrs.Doran) recounted how he handed down the story of James Skerry Storm on a Baltic trip rescuing a Russian noblemam from a sinking yacht and being rewarded by him with a jewelled cross.

From this period a movement into work other than seafaring is evident. In another generation Harold George Atkinson Storm (whose names came from uncles killed in WWI) was still in shipping, but as the office manager of the Headlam steamship business in Whitby. This was the successor to the company of Rowland & Marwood. The company also managed many ships under the title of International Lines Ltd. Great numbers of Whitby and Bay men were employed by these and other local owners - so many that men sought a living carting to and from Whitby station the kit of crews leaving to join a ship or returning from a voyage. Jacob Storm of *Leeside* was Superintendent; he was also John Rowland's cousin- once-removed, and his wife bore the same relationship to Christopher Marwood. There is insufficient room for detail here, but the exploration of relationships and occupations in Whitby reveals connections almost as close as those in Bay, which is what might be expected from the way both places were confined between moor and sea and lived off shipping-related employment. Good further illustration is provided by the Headlam case: William Headlam started in the business as a clerk (previous family occupations having been jet-ornament making and tailoring), and not only was William Headlam junior a descendant of Jane Storm on page 181, but John Rowland can be traced from her brother Issac, as will be seen further on in Chapter 8. The business and professional significance of such connections is a matter for more than a little speculation. In 1991 the estate of William Headlan junior, of Raithwaite Hall near Whitby, was valued at £7 million.

James Skerry served at sea and also with the Green Howards at Dunkirk in 1940 in WWII. His son Gordon was one of the last of the family to serve at sea.

GEORGE, M.Mariner   m.1888 Eleanor Breckon

    JOHN (1889-1970), Post Office Engineer   m.1914 ....
    Eleanor
    = James Jobling
    Arthur (-1982)
    = Nancy
    George, killed in WW1, aged 19.
    Edith
    = Valentine Pearson of Carlin How
    Doris
    = John Warnock
    JAMES SKERRY

JOHN (1889-1970), Post Office Engineer   m.1914 ....

    Lillian
    = John Moore, British Rail Ganger Platelayer
HAROLD GEORGE ATKINSON, Office Manager
    Edith   ) dau. Mrs.Susan Winter
    = Eric Hardy Doran, Photographer)
    William, Coldstream Guards in WW2
    =Alma Stephenson

HAROLD GEORGE ATKINSON (1920-75)   m.1944 Eva Pearson (1923-)
    Shipping Office Manager

TREVOR, B.Sc. (1948-); Operational Research, Nuclear Electric
    (Julie Elaine (1952-)
= 1972 (Brian Haigh

TREVOR, B.Sc. (1948-),   m. 1975 Alison Mary Howick,
    Operational Research,   Schoolteacher
      Nuclear Electric;
        Bristol

    Michael Philip (1977-)
    Peter Matthew (1980-)

JAMES SKERRY   m. Ada Smithson (-1986)

    Donald
    James Alan   ) dau. Gail
    =   ?   )
    Irene
    = Peter Sharpe, Det.Inspector and Coroner's Officer
    GORDON, Marine Engineer

William and Elizabeth

Maurice Edmund - who was also at Dunkirk - recorded some reminiscences of his father, Jonathan Skerry, who accompanied his parents to sea when he was very young. They had two vessels and their trade was usually in Baltic timber. In Robin Hood's Bay the family owned a house on the cliff from which a line could be lowered to the sea, and one day, Jonathan recalled, his mother heard a creaking sound and just had time to rush out with him when the cliff crumbled and the house fell into the sea. The family moved to Whitby. It seems that mother, Elizabeth, was quite able in her young days to take charge of a vessel, and she lived long enough - into her nineties - for Maurice Edmund to remember her as a "very upright, stately, independent lady". Her story about the destruction of the house is evidence of a long-term process, the village having lost until recent times rather more than ninety feet of land per century, on average. The road down into the village was eventually too near the sea, and fell away, to be replaced around 1790 by the New Road which leads inland and reaches the upper part of the village by means of the famous three-in-one ascent Bay Bank.

Nathan Storm, clerk, appears in the 1847 directory of Middlesbrough. Afterwards he became a shipchandler and had money in ships. He lived on The Terrace, West Hartlepool.

In 1833 Capt.Isaac Storm in parnership with a Jarrow shipbuilder bought the brig *Tula* in which John Biscoe had voyaged and explored in the Antarctic sea. In 1856 the family was at West Hartlepool, where all the children were born, ansd Isaac was keeping a beerhouse. No evidence of descendants has been encountered.

JACOB (1837-1926). Master mariner, Marine Superintendent, Local Historian and genealogist. He was the only son of Andrew and Rebecca of Wavecrest who survived to marry. 'Uncle Jake' to many in his time, he is still referred to as 'Cap'n Jake' The photograph was taken by his daughter Rebecca Mercy, shortly before his death. At about the same time the present writer was taken to *Leeside* from Tynemouth to see and be seen by Jacob, his great-grandfather.

ISABEL STORM (1838-1923) wife of Jacob of Leeside, and daughter of William Pearson, Master Mariner. Her portrait is by Sutcliffe, who dated it 1892, when she was fifty-four.

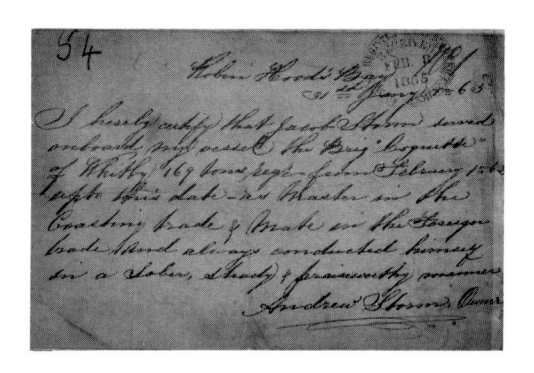

JACOB'S REFERENCE from his father, Andrew.

GORDON, Marine Engineer   m. Ann Dixon

  Nicola Louise
  Neil (1967-)

Continued from page 107:

JONATHAN SKERRY   m. Hannah

  Thomas Henry Baden (1900-c.1960)
  =   ?
  MAURICE EDMUND

MAURICE EDMUND   m. ?
  Hull

  EDMUND GEORGE
  Marjorie
  = ?

EDMUND GEORGE   m. ?
  Rotherham

  Kevin
  David
  Kathryn
  Marie

Continued from page 107:

JONATHAN ("NATHAN") (1805-68) m.1835 Dinah Cook (born Stanghow,
  M.Mariner   1810) at W.Acklam.

  Isaac Scarth (1844-)

Continued from page 107:

ISAAC (1800-), M.Mariner   m.1838 Rebecca Ann Binnie, born
               c.1822 at Scarborough.

  Ann Elizabeth (1840-)
  Jane (1842-)
  Binnie (1844-)
  May (1846-)
  Rebecca, died in infancy, 1847/8
  Rebecca (1848-)
  Margaret (1850-)
  Isaac (1855-)

William and Elizabeth

Thomas was mate of his brother William's ill-fated *Lomar*. Benjamin was apprenticed to a tailor, and married in Hull the daughter of J.Robinson who worked in the Hull Packet Office. Thomas and Martha were married at North Ormesby. Two daughters are known: Elizabeth Jane who died in 1941, and Mrs. Edith Ann Prentice of York (1882-1961).

"Victualler" for Nathaniel could mean a supplier of food to ships: he was cousin, nephew or father-in-law to seven owner-masters, and cousin-removed to numerous others, which should have been good for business. On the other hand if the term means he was an innkeeper, an agreement of 1750 about a malt kiln, involving him and a maltster, might clinch the matter. There are descendants of daughters Esther and Dorothy, and Alan Neesam of Scruton, Northallerton supplied the information in 1988 that he and many others descend from both, by way of lines that include the Fylingdales names Chester and Estill (Eskdale).

Matthew and Elizabeth were married on the same day as Isaac and Mary (p.185). Matthew was the owner of one of the larger fishing craft, and in 1787 he bought a new one, the *Three Brothers*, which probably cost him upwards of £600. When she was registered in Whitby the Customs official entered Matthew as "gent". For many years he paid the highest parish rates in Fisherhead, and the impression is gained that he was a fisherman of substance. When he was 90, he was succeeded in ownership by his sons, led by Isaac, who was the son named as the payer of the parish rate levied by agreement on boats and ships as well as houses in Fylingdales. This assessment was known in brief as the "ship sess".

There was great continuity of the fishing in this family, whereas in others if there were sons some were lost at sea, or turned to other employment, mainly seafaring. Among Matthew and Elizabeth's direct descendants were those fishermen who were still active in Bay in the present century.

Although William (1756-1827) is usually described as a fisherman, he was attracted to the shipping. In 1786 he returned from a voyage to the Arctic as second mate of Richard Moorsom's whaler *Lively*. Perhaps the earnings on this venture helped to pay for the *Three Brothers*. Then William is found with an interest in the brigantines *Polly* and *Juno*. Others with shares in these vessels from time to time were connected with supply of coal to the alum works and with the Wear, which implies there was trading on the coast. A notable participating name is Cropton, in both Fylingdales and Sunderland, in the coal business. If James Storm, father of Frances, is brought in, there is an interesting, enterprising group here, for he also was master of a fishing vessel. (p.183) That shipping ventures were in the air is evident from the acquisition by Bay men of 25 vessels - nearly all brigantines - at various times during the first two decades of the eighteenth century. There were as many as 16 of these trading in 1820, and pointing the way to a great expansion as the century wore on.

Part of the expansion is to the credit of Mercy and Thomas Harrison, about whom there is much in Jacob Storm's memoirs, for they were his grandparents. The parish register says Mercy was the daughter of William and Ann Storm (p.173), but her place here is confirmed by an inscription on her father's headstone in Old St.Stephen's churchyard. This begins, "By storms at sea two sons I lost, which sore distressed me, because I could not have their bones, to anchor here with me", and goes on to mention his granddaughter,

Continued from page 107:

THOMAS (1813-1859), Mariner,   m.1845 Jane Granger (1809-1875),
       lost in the brig <u>Lomar</u>   dau. of Ben. (Fisherman)
                                                and Isabella, nee Tindale.

        Benjamin (1847-   ) a son, Sydney living in 1965
=1876   Martha Ellis Robinson at Hull .
        Thomas 1849-1911, Mariner
=1877   Martha Storm (1844-98), dau. of John, M.Mariner, (p.129)
                          and Martha

Continued from page 103:

NATHANIEL, Victualler and   m.1725 Elizabeth Johnson
           Householder (1702-1749)   at Malton
        Esther (1727-1794)
=1728   William Newton, M.Mariner
        Dorothy (1729-1794)
=1752   Philip Moody, M.Mariner
        Nathaniel (-1734)

Continued from page 103:

MATTHEW, Master Fisherman (1714-1804)   m.1742 Elizabeth Storm (1723-
                                                              1797) dau. of
                                                              Bartholomew and Mercy. (p.87)

        Ann (1745-1829)
=1767   WILLIAM STORM (p.173)
        Mary (1747-1752)
        Mercy (1754-1773)
        WILLIAM (1756-1827), Mariner, Fisherman and Shipowner.
        ISAAC (1758-1824), Master Fisherman. (p.127)
        Elizabeth (1761-1763)

WILLIAM, fisherman (1756-1827)   m.1781 Frances Storm (1757-1839)
        Mariner, Fisherman and Shipowner   dau. of James, Master
                                                            Fisherman, and Elizabeth.
                                                                  (p.180)

        WILLIAM (1783-1851), M.Mariner
        EDWARD (1785-1808), M.Mariner. (p.121)
        Mercy (1786-1880), Shipowner
=1812   Thomas Harrison (1787-1860), Master Fisherman and Shipowner
        JAMES (1790-1855), M.Mariner. (p.123)
        Bartholomew (1793-1795)
        Bartholomew (1795-1808)
        John (1799-1801)

Damaris, child of Thomas and Mercy. Thomas and Mercy's achievement was to make enough out of fishing to buy the *Brothers* with Jacob's father in 1840, and the *Harrisons* in 1843, both being new vessels. The family company of parents and five shipmaster sons - ultimately Mercy Harrison and Sons - became a major part of the local shipping scene.

Another member of the group around the *Juno* and the *Polly* was Sampson Thompson, father-in-law of William (1783-1851), and Parish Clerk as well as innkeeper. It was in his capacity as shipowner that Sampson took on William's younger brother James as an apprentice to the sea in 1805, paying him £10 a year for six years, and three shillings a week subsistence when the ship was laid up in winter, as was the practice. Sampson's son John duly took over the King's Head. The subsequent popularity of the name "Sampson", which is still in use, suggests he was a respected figure.

According to Jacob Storm of *Leeside* the *Juno* "traded around a bit". The brothers William and James became respectively master and mate of her. In 1815 in Ostend they were asked if they would take a passenger to Harwich, and when they agreed the person who came to join them was Louis Philippe, the King of France, on his way into exile. A chest was left aboard the *Juno* which was found to contain weapons, some of which remained long in James's family. Unfortunately William was discovered to have included smuggling among his operations - "disagreement with the government over imports" was Jacob Storm's definition - and his *Juno* was confiscated. In 1828 she came into the Thames from the continent, with William her master, but in 1830 she had gone to Scarborough registration. Before this misfortune James had become owner of his own *John and James* with John Smith for partner. William died in the Seamen's Hospital in Whitby in 1851, after seeing, as Jacob put it, "the inside of Durham Gaol".

Thomas Coggin, husband of William and Hannah's daughter Frances, was the son of John, a militia sergeant who settled in Bay and joined the company of investors in shipping. The new brig *John Coggin* joined the local fleet in 1840 and she was worked until Frances sold her in 1882. In 1861 Frances' son, John Coggin, M.Mariner, was lost in the Black Sea; his widow married a Nonconformist clergyman, the Rev. Charles Brighouse.

The Levitts were shipmasters who came from Kent, settled, and bought interests in the village's shipping; the traditional "maid's garlands" that were displayed in Old St.Stephen's were carried at the funeral of Jane of this family in 1859.

Bartholomew (1820-47) was lost in the North Atlantic when the *North Britain*, of which he was master, went down with all hands.

In 1827 Sampson Storm registered the brig *Squirrel*. He went on to acquire a substantial interest in several vessels ranging up to 318 tons, and this sort of holding was maintained when he retired from the sea and kept the *Fleece* in Church Street, Whitby, to which he had moved some time after 1832. His son John commanded his barque *Royal Rose* for a time. Sampson was a member of the board that enquired into the Whitby lifeboat disaster of 1861, of which there is a moving memorial in St.Mary's church, bearing some of the opening words of the Rev.W.Keane's letter to "The Times": "We have had a fearful storm today at Whitby...." Sampson was a trustee of the Whitby and Robin Hood's Bay Steam Packet Co. which operated the *Goliah*, *Hilda* and *Esk* between 1853 and 1867. There were salvage and towing activities and a passenger service to Hartlepool. Many familiar Bay names are among the shareholders. After Sampson's death in 1865 his son John does not appear in the list of Robin Hood's Bay shipowners when the fleet was at its largest with 91 vessels insured in the village in 1867. He had died in Shanghai in 1866.

WILLIAM, M.Mariner (1783-1851)　　　m.1803 Hannah Thompson (c.1781-1827) dau. of Sampson, Innkeeper and Parish Clerk

       SAMPSON (1803-1865), M.Mariner
       Frances (1806-1891)
= 1829　Thomas Coggin, M.Mariner
       JOHN (1808-1844), M.Mariner
       Elizabeth (1810-)
       =William Levitt, M.Mariner
       William (1813-)
       Bartholomew, M.Mariner (1820-1847))　A son, Joseph Middleton
       =Alice Middleton　　　　　　　　　) died in infancy, 1844

SAMPSON, (1803-1865) M.Mariner,　　　m.1825 Mary Stephenson (1803-1883)
   Shipowner, and Innkeeper
      in Whitby

       Hannah (1826-c.1833)
       Elizabeth (1828-1859)
=1846　Thomas Harrison, M.Mariner (1821-1872)
       Mary (1828-1851)
=1846　Francis Robinson (-1876), M.Mariner and Shipowner
       William (1830-)
       Hannah (1833-)
=1853　1.William Jameson, (-1865), M.Mariner, son of Wm., Pilot.
=1872　=2.George Galilee, Sailmaker and Shipowner
       Frances (1835-1884)
=1855　William Edward Kirby, M.Mariner.
       John (1837-1866), M.Mariner. Died at Shanghai.
       Rebecca Mary (1839-c.1844)
       Jane (1841-1879)
       Rebecca (1845-1882)　) Issue in
       =Thomas Piper, M.Mariner) London

JOHN, M.Mariner (1808-1844)　　　m.1829 Mary Harrison dau. of John (farmer) and Mary of South House, Fylingdales.

       Hannah (1830-)
       = ... Sleightholm
       John (1835-)
       =Mary Foxton (1840-)
       WILLIAM (1837-1914), M.Mariner
       SAMPSON (1841-1895), Sailmaker
       Mary (1844-)

William and Elizabeth

Sampson's son-in-law, William Jameson, was one of the masters of the Steam Packet Co. and father of William Storm Jameson who was master of the *Saxon Prince*, the first steamer of Sir James Knott's prestigious Prince Line. (p.96). Voyages in this ship are mentioned in *Journey from the North*, the highly acclaimed autobiography of the master's daughter, (Margaret) Storm Jameson, Hon.D.Litt., novelist (1891-1986). The *Saxon Prince* was sunk by the German cruiser *Moewe* in 1916, and her master returned from captivity in 1918 to find his son Harold of the Royal Flying Corps had been killed after winning the M.C., the D.C.M. and the French *Medaille Militaire*: this from a boy whom his sister had seen pleading tearfully not to be sent back to sea a few years before. William Storm Jameson's neighbour in Park Terrace, Whitby, was the diligent historian of local shipping Richard Weatherill, who expanded the documentary record with anecdotes obviously derived from first-hand experiences of sailors.

Thomas Harrison (1821-72) belonged to the long-standing Bay family. He died at Arendal in Norway while he was master of the brig *Spectator*. He and Elizabeth had a son, and a grandson called Sampson Storm Harrison who lost his life in an explosion aboard the S.S.*Abaris* in 1906 and was buried at Yokohama.

Francis Robinson's career as a shipowner began in 1852, after Mary's death. His most notable purchase was the brig *Robinsons*, new from a Sunderland yard, in 1865; the Quaker sailmaker George Galilee was a shareholder, and ultimately Francis' executor. There is a memorial inscription to Mary in the north chancel block of St.Mary's churchyard, Whitby.

Wm.Edward Kirby was the son of a Whitby schoolmaster, George Young Kirby, a name which suggests a connection with the Independent minister the Rev.George Young, who kept a school as well as being the author of the valuable history of Whitby. The Kirby family lived for a time in South Shields and Frances died at Newcastle upon Tyne.

Latterly Sampson and Mary, and daughter Jane, lived in Esk Terrace, Whitby, part of the residential development facing the the upper harbour where the sailing fleet used to tie up in winter. As many as a third of the houses would be occupied by shipmasters. After Jane's death Mary went to Clarence Place.

John (1808-44) and Mary went to Whitby and all their children married there.

WHITBY TOWN is an ancient town
Near a wide and sandy shore
And ships have sailed from the little port
A thousand years or more.
Tom Stamp

WHITBY HARBOUR It was this part of the Esk, above the bridge, that scores of sailing vessels used to be laid up for the winter. In February the work of preparing for sea began and at the beginning of March the fleet moved out.

William and Elizabeth

William (1837-1914) lived in Windsor Terrace, Whitby, overlooking the Endeavour Wharf, but for the intervention of the railway station. Windsor Terrace suffered much damage when German warships shelled the town in 1914, the year of William's death.

Sampson (1841-95) worked as a sailmaker in Whitby, but he left for Hartlepool after 1881, there being more work in steamers by that time. His family grew up there, and Sampson became foreman in a shipbuilding yard. There is little further information. His son Charles went through the South African War unscathed, but William was badly injured in the German bombardment of Hartlepool on 16th December, 1914; John's son Arthur, then aged seven, was slightly injured in the same raid. The youngest of the family, Arthur (c.1883-1906), went to sea, and at the age of 23 he was washed overboard from the S.S.*Resolution* near Pernambuco.

John (1868-1923) was employed in the Whitby jet-working industry, until that declined, and then he walked 56 miles to Hartlepool in two days and found work in a shipyard, working on steamships as a plater's helper at a guinea a week. He became foreman. His son Sampson served in the Army in WWII and was subsequently Deputy Town Clerk of the old Hartlepool County Borough. Another son, Arthur, became a foreman of welders, working for Cammel Laird, Swan Hunter, Vickers Armstrong and Palmer's. He worked on the battleships *Prince of Wales* and *Anson*, the aircraft carrier *Ark Royal*, the cruiser *Edinburgh* (from which the wreck of which the gold was recovered in 1981), the cruiser *Dorsetshire* of the *Bismarck* action in WWII, and the nuclear submarine *Warspite*. He lived at Wallsend on Tyne, where he had family.

WILLIAM, M.Mariner (1837-1914)　　　　m.1858 Hannah Tomlinson (1835-
　　　　　　　　　　　　　　　　　　　　　　　1913) dau. of John,
　　　　　　　　　　　　　　　　　　　　　　　　　Shipwright.

　　　　John (1859-1899), Confectioner, Whitby.
　　　　Mary Eleanor (1861-1913)
　　　　Hannah J. (1866-)
　　　　Frances c.(1869-)

SAMPSON, sailmaker (1841-1895)　　　　m.1861 Jane Allison (1842-1901)
　　　　　　　　　　　　　　　　　　　　　　　dau. of Thomas, jet-
　　　　　　　　　　　　　　　　　　　　　　　worker, and Elizabeth
　　　　　　　　　　　　　　　　　　　　　　　　(nee Trueman).

　　　　Mary Elizabeth (1861-)
　　　　Jane Ann (c.1862-)
=1888　Thomas Pennock
　　　　Thomas Allison (c.1865-1923) A son, Thomas,
=1886　Harriet Eliza Collis   ) and five daughters.
　　　　JOHN (1868-1923), Jetworker and Shipyard Foreman
　　　　Charles, jet turner (c.1870-1940)
　　　　Sampson (c.1871-)
　　　　William (c.1871-)
　　　　Dora (1872-1874)
　　　　Emma (1875-1876)
　　　　Eliza (1877-1879)
　　　　Lillie (c1879-)
　　　　Arthur (c.1833-1906), Mariner

JOHN (1868-1923), Jet-worker　　　　m.1889 Teresa Ann Scales, Midwife
　　　and Shipyard Foreman;
　　　　　　Hartlepool

　　　　JOHN (1894-1962)
　　　　Arthur (1907-1983), Foreman Welder; a dau., Mrs, Marjorie
=1933　Amy Odell   )   Smillie, Wallsend on Tyne.
　　　　Sampson (1896-1907
　　　　Sampson (1916-72), Local Government Officer
=1943　Marie Jean Hutchinson
　　　　Lillian   )
　　　　Edith   )
　　　　Ada   ) no further record
　　　　Theresa Ann)
　　　　Elizabeth)
　　　　Anne, died aged 17.

William and Elizabeth

Edward (1785-1808), second son of William and Frances (p.112), was lost at sea when fishing with his brother Bartle.

Edward (1807-52) was lost in the brig *Gazelle*.

Richard Russell was Chief Officer of the S.S.*Jane* when he was accidentally killed at Ibrail, Constantinople, in 1881. Captain Wm.Storm Russell, son of Richard and Sarah Jane, was master of the *Redgate* which was trapped at Shanghai in 1937 when the authorities threw a boom across the Whangpo to prevent the invading Japanese from moving upriver. The Japanese forced the boom and the *Redgate* was able to make a precarious exit after five months. The Storm Russell name went into a fifth generation in 1972 with the birth in Canada of Christopher David Storm Russell.

Edward (1838-83) was lost with all hands in the brig *Emily*.

Jane Ann Law was the granddaughter of James Law, popularly referred to now as "the Staintondale smuggler", who was fatally shot in 1823, in Staintondale, just outside Fylingdales, to the south. There had been much smuggling in the neighbourhood, and much informing, and the shooting followed accusations and threats made during a night of drinking in Scarborough. There was so much feeling in the locality that a move to have the case tried out of the county had to be checked by the appointment of a jury of West Riding men. William Mead was found guilty of manslaughter.

Stranton became West Hartlepool, where John Storm (1841-) was Harbour Master.

JOHN (1894-1962)   m.1919 Margaret Smithson
    Hartlepool   m.2nd 1927 Alice Holroyd, nee Herron.

    John   )
    =Elizabeth Wildberg) dau's Margaret, Doreen and Pauline
        Eliza Theodora
        =Harry Hunter   son, Harry
        Theresa Ann
        =Albert Wardrop) Australia; ch'n Barbara and Kenneth.
        Sampson
        =Elsie Hoey) dau. Lynne

Continued from page 113:

EDWARD (1785-1808) Mariner and   m.1806 Mary Tindale (1785-)
    Fisherman   dau. Ben (M.Mariner) and
                                         Elizabeth (nee Smith).
EDWARD (1807-52), M.Mariner   Mary married William
                                           Wright in 1810.

EDWARD (1807-52), M.Mariner   m.1833 Elizabeth Cooper (c.1813-)
                                           dau. Boyes, fisherman, and
                                                 Sarah.

        Frances
        =Anthony Newto) Issue.
        EDWARD (1838-1883), M.Mariner
        JOHN (1841-), M.Mariner .
=1865 Mary Ann Ward
        BOYES (1843-)
        Mary Ann (1846-)
        =Philip Newton (1841-)
        William (1849-)
        Sarah Jane 1852-1934)
        =Richard Russell (-1881), Mariner

EDWARD (1838-1883), M.Mariner   m.1867 Jane Ann Law (-1874)
                                          dau. of James Law, Eskdaleside.
                                          m.2nd 1877 Elizabeth Pearson,
                                              nee, Moorsom

        Sarah Elizabeth (1869-)
        =JOHN STORM (1869-1960) (p.164)
        Lucy Mary (1873-1966)
        =Thomas Johnson Barnard (1870-1908)

JOHN (1841-), M.Mariner; Hartlepool   m.1865 Mary Ann Ward at Stranton
                                                   (West Hartlepool)

BOYES (1843-)   m. Isabella Anson
    William Henry

James (1790-1855), third son of William and Frances (p.112) was a leading shipowner in the village. After purchase of the *John and James* in 1827 (p.101), he went on to buy several vessels, eventually in various partnerships with his son and three sons-in-law, each of whom also entered the market on his own account. There was a great complexity of intertwined interests, typical of what was to happen throughout the community, but the principal combination that arose from this household was Matthew Storm and Co., led by Mercy's husband. James left properties in Sunny Place to his daughters, which accounts for the three sons-in-law occupying adjacent houses in 1861.

William and Frances Steel's daughter Mary married the Rev.William Dalton, Congregational Minister at Bay for thirty years, and a historian of the village. Two other daughters married shipmasters, one of whom was Nathan Hewson, a descendant of one of the oldest families and owner of several vessels. Two sons of the Steels became masters of steamers; one of them, James Storm Steel (1845- 1894) died at Buenos Aires

In 1849, at the age of 29, John Harrison Storm was master of his father's brig *John and James*. By 1867, the peak year for shipping, when the village's fleet was worth £112,350 for insurance by the Bay "Club" (disregarding vessels covered elsewhere), he had two vessels of his own and four in which he was the major shareholder. In 1851 he was living in the New Road, the way cut through the village in 1792 after the cliff road had become unsafe. By 1861 he was living above the village at Seafield House, one of the shipmasters who were beginning to give the settlement the shape and character familiar today, and portended by Isaac Storm's Prospect House of a century earlier. Eventually he moved to Whitby, where he lived at 1,Esk Terrace. On his death the *Whitby Gazette* recalled that in his younger days "Bay was reputed to be the richest town for its size on the English coast, and among its residents were many opulent shipowners and well-to-do sea-going captains who had a substantial interest in the vessels they commanded". A photograph of John Harrison Storm has survived, on a *carte de visite* produced by F.M.Sutcliffe.

Thomas Pyman was master for a time of John's *Brazilian Packet*, but the Pymans went into steam a little later and became prominent in Whitby, Cardiff and London shipping. There is more about this family - but still regrettably little - in *Call to Arms* (1971) by Gen.Sir Harold Pyman.

John Lawson, husband of John's daughter Rebecca, was nephew of Emma Alice Lawson, wife of Thomas Turnbull of the Mount, Whitby, shipowner and principal shipbuilding pioneer of the port. The Lawsons were one of the numerous old Catholic families of Egton.

At the age of 24, William (1847-1920) was master of his father's *Donna*. Two years later he married the daughter of a Danish sailmaker. His eldest son, John Harrison, was born at Elsinore. Still only 26, in 1873 William sailed to Port Natal in his father's last vessel, the barque *Teazer*, taking 65 days from the English Channel, the fastest passage of the time. A ship that had sailed on the same tide dropped anchor only half-an-hour later. This achievement does not appear in Richard Weatherill's useful *Ancient Port of Whitby and its Shipping* of 1907, which only reports an incident off Whitby in 1875 and the end of the *Teazer* in the Azores in 1880.

Continued from page 113:

JAMES, M.Mariner (1790-1855)   m.1815 Damaris Harrison, dau. of
                                      John, Mariner, and Rebecca,
                                              nee Cooper.

         Mercy (1816-1890)
=1840 Matthew Storm (1816-1890). (p.135)
         JOHN HARRISON (1819-1898), M.Mariner and Shipowner
         Frances (1822-1904)
=1844 William Harrison Steel, (-1881), M.Mariner) Issue
         James William (1827-1832)
         Rebecca (1831-1908)
=1853 William Bedlington, M.Mariner Issue

JOHN HARRISON STORM (1819-1898),   m.1843 Hannah Newton (1820-1876),
                                 dau. of William, Farmer, and Jane, nee Frank
                                 M.Mariner and Shipowner, Bay and Whitby

         Damaris (1843-1931)
         Thomas Marwood Rose (1840-1924)
         Jane (1844-1892)
         WILLIAM (1847-1920), M.Mariner
         Hannah (1850-1886)
=1877 J.W.Collier, M.Mariner, son of J.W.Collier of Messrs Collier
                      and Thompson, Shipbrokers, Newcastle.
                      The marriage was at Bromley, Kent.

         Elizabeth (c.1852-55)
         Rebecca (1854-1914)
         =John Lawson (1855-1924)
         Elizabeth (1856-1910)
         James (1859-1881), Mariner
         Frances (1862-1953)
         =James H.Vince, M.A., of Ulpha, Cumbria.
         Alice Newton (1865-1931)

WILLIAM, M.Mariner (1847-1920).   m.1873 Laura Cecilia
         Shipping agent, founder of   Bornholm of
         Storm and Co., and   Elsinore,
         Danish Vice-Consul at Durban.   Denmark.

         John Harrison (1875-1900).
         CARL LUDVIG (1877-1937), Company Director
         WILLIAM (1880-1942), Company Director. (p.127)
         JAMES (1882-1945), Company Director. (p.127)
         Hannah (1884-1928)
         =Alec Eustace Green
         Laura
         =E.Henry Ballard

William and Elizabeth

The occurrence in 1875 concerning the *Teazer* was significant. William was bringing her inside the piers with the aid of a tug when she began to drift outside the west pier; he slipped the tow but could not sail off and the vessel ran ashore. Although the repairs were covered by insurance, a wider problem remained. To compete with steamers the sailing vessels had to extend the working year into winter months. As Jacob of *Leeside* remembered, the *John Bowes*, the Tyne's first iron-built screw collier, had carried 650 tons of coal to the Thames in 1852 and reached home again in five days, whereas the sailing vessels made about ten trips a year between spring and winter. Losses rose and insurance premiums with them. Robin Hood's Bay had been nothing if not enterprising and had its own two ship insurance associations or "Clubs", but they became difficult to operate. Steam tugs could help vessels in and out of harbour in bad weather, but had to be paid for. These events and circumstances caused John Harrison Storm to withdraw from business.

Port Natal appealed to William and in 1879 he took employment as a shipping agent and settled there. A year later he started his own business. He also acted for 35 years as Danish Consul, and frequently served as nautical adviser to the Court of Marine Enquiries. The business concern came to comprise agency, shipchandling and stevedoring, with offices in Durban, Johannesburg, Cape Town, Port Elizabeth and East London. It was reorganised as Storm and Co. in 1907, and in 1928 it became Storm and Co. (Pty) Ltd., under William's surviving sons.

William's younger brother, James, had been sent away to school, but he came back to the ships, only to be lost in the Atlantic when the steamer *Saxon Monarch*, of which he was Second Officer, went down with all hands.

John Harrison Storm (1906-1979): founded the South African stevedoring company Jack Storm and Co.(Pty); sometime Commodore, Royal Natal Yacht Club.

Peter John and Anthony David are involved with their step-brother Michael in M.J.H.Storm and Co.

CARL LUDVIG, Company Director.　　　　　m. Helena May, dau of
　　　　　　　　　　　　　　　　　　　　　Henry Ballard, C.M.G.,
　　　　　　　　　　　　　　　　　　　　　Port Captain, Durban.
　　Natalie May (1904-59)
　　JOHN HARRISON (1906-1979), Company Director
　　HENRY ALFRED (1907-1964), Farmer
　　WILLIAM LLOYD (1918-1976)

JOHN HARRISON (1906-1979),　　　　　　m.(1) Mrs Gladys Hardaker
　　Company Director, Durban　　　　　　　(2) Florence Anne Stafford
　　　　　　　　　　　　　　　　　　　　　　　(1923-1985)
　　MICHAEL JOHN HARRISON (1938-)
　　PETER JOHN (1946-)
　　ANTHONY DAVID (1948-)
　　Ann Elizabeth (1950-)
　　Sally Joy (1951-)

MICHAEL JOHN HARRISON (1938-)　　　m.1966 Gabrielle Josephine
Managing Director M.J.H.Storm & Co.　　　　　　Murray
　　　(Transport)
　　Justin John Harrison (1970-)
　　Simon Anthony (1972-)

PETER JOHN (1946-)　　　　　m.1970 Rosemary Patricia Dean (1945-)
　　John Anthony (1971-)
　　Matthew Lyall (1973-)

ANTHONY DAVID (1948-)　　　　　m. Lee Pieterse (1955-)
　　Carl Anthony (1977-)
　　Brad David (1980-)
　　Anton John (1984-)

HENRY ALFRED (1907-64),　　　　　m. 1. Doreen Ardnesen
　　Farmer, Natal.　　　　　　　　　　2. ...... Ferguson
　　Charles Anthony (1942-)
　　Hilton Colin (1946-), Farmer (dairying and horses).
　　Pauline May (1951-)

WILLIAM LLOYD (1918-76)　　　　　m. Cecile Ruth Swales (sister of Edwin
　　　　　　　　　　　　　　　　　　　　Swales, V.C. (WWII)
　　Jane May (1947-)
　　David Lloyd (1950-)
　　Susan Elizabeth (1953-)

Continued from page 123:
WILLIAM (1880-1942)　　　　　　　m. Clara Petch (1883-1957)
　　Laura Alma (1912-)　　　　　　adopted daughter and son.
　　=Lombard Swann (-1979))
　　Sheila Damaris (1914-1990) two sons and
　　=James Mackormack (-1974) a daughter.
　　Charles William (1919-1984) two adopted
　　= 1.Norah Van Vloten(1923-1953) children
　　= 2.Joan (1918-1982)

William and Elizabeth

James (1881-1945): Managing Director, Storm & Co., from 1942.

Frank (1922-): Chairman, Storm and Co. from 1947, following WWII service with the South African Artillery in the North African and Italian campaigns.

The fishing tradition continued longer and more strongly in the line of Isaac, third son of the patriarch Matthew (1714-1804) and his wife Elizabeth Storm.(p.113) Nevertheless the trend towards seafaring and shipowning soon becomes evident. It was Isaac who took over the fishing vessel *Three Brothers* . The later part of the century was a time of great and profitable activity on the part of Bay fishermen: the Scarborough historian Thomas Hinderwell remarked that while the fishermen of his town claimed five-man boats could not be made to pay, the Bay men had been busy and successful in the seventeen-nineties. Nevertheless there were many more seafarers than fishermen in the village at the time when, say, Isaac was born. In 1818 there were only four boats listed as rateable by the parish, and Isaac Storm, Martin Granger, John Hewson and Moorsom Bedlington - all names of the familiar kind - were the payers.

Isaac's charge of a Storm boat can be followed until 1818, when the "sess" ceased to be paid to the parish. Three sons, John, Thomas and Reuben, continued to fish, but John's son became a shipmaster, as did Matthew, and Thomas had no- one to take his place in a boat after his son Stephen died young. Reuben outlived his brothers and it was with two households in his line that the fishing survived into the twentieth century.

George and Elizabeth Granger lived in Fisherhead, and in June, 1841 their four-year-old granddaughter Elizabeth Hewson was staying with them. Her father was Nathan Hewson, M.Mariner. Children left in the care of relatives are a regular feature of the Census in Bay, because wives frequently accompanied their husbands to sea, or went to the ports to join them. In 1841, for instance, the young Jacob Storm of the memoirs was at the house of his grandparents, Thomas and Rebecca Harrison, while his parents were away with their schooner *Brothers* .

Lydia's husband William Harrison was lost at sea in 1833 with his brother-in- law Thomas Storm, and another Thomas Storm, son of John Hodgson Storm. (p.105) Their daughter Lydia married John Stubbs, a third-generation stonemason in the village. (See also the marriage of Mary, daughter of William and Mercy on p.163)

RICHARD STORM (1864-1953) eldest son of Jacob and Isabel, gave up the sea after a few voyages with his father as his steward, and took to farming but three of his sons and a son-in-law were ship masters.

WILFRED STORM (1891-1929) on a visit to Leeside on leave during WWI after qualifying as Master. Trading out of South Wales led him to settle in Herefordshire.

CAPTAIN WILLIAM STORM grandson of Andrew (1830-86) and Damaris; lost with his ship, the S.S. *Widestone*, in WWII Atlantic convoy in 1942.

CAPTAIN JACOB STORM Jnr, (1870-1946) survived enemy action in WWI and then came ashore to enjoy life at Crossgates, the house on the Bank Top which his brother James had built for him just before the war.

The future **CAPTAIN RICHARD STORM** (1902-1989) as a junior officer about 1922. he was to survive two torpedoings in WWII.

ANDREW STORM (1830-1886) married his cousin Damaris Storm, daughter of Andrew and Rebecca of *Wavecrest*. He was master of the brig *Magnet*, lost in 1886

Continued from page 123:

JAMES (1881-1945), Managing   m.1921 Elsa Melita Dorothy Stevens
    Director, Durban   (1895-1976)

    Frank (1922-), Company Chairman
    Shirley (1923-81)
    =Donald Kenneth Stayt (1922-92), Journalist and Columnist;
        ch'n Judith Wyatt, Wendy Nola and Robin John.
    Monica (1927-)
    =Etienne Rocco de Villiers, B.A. (1922-), Teacher;
        ch'n Annette Jane, Daphne Lynn and Louise Joan.

FRANK (1922-) Chairman,   m.1952 Llona Maureen Wijnberg
    Storm & Co., Durban   (1929-)

    Denise (1953-), Music Teacher
=1975 Howard Trevor Uberstein (1954-), Company Director;
        ch'n Steven and Catherine; Australia.
    Gillian (1954-))ch'n Nicola and Harold Gavin.
=1977 Harold Mark Drinn)
WILLIAM NEIL (1956-), Telecommunications Engineer
    Erica, B.A. (1959-)
=1981 Joseph Allan Earl-Spurr, B.Sc. (1956-), Quantity Surveyor;
        ch'n James and Craig Richard; Australia.

WILLIAM NEIL (1956-)   m.1981 Merrill Ann Budgen
    Telecommunications Engineer

    Lee Roy (1981-)
    Jo-Ann (1984-)

Continued from page 113.

ISAAC (1758-1824), Master   m.1785 Elizabeth Hodgson (1758-
    Fisherman   1838), dau. of John and Lydia

    Elizabeth (1786-1863)
=1813 George Granger (1785-1865), Fisherman.
    ISAAC (1786-after 1861), Fisher
    JOHN (1789-1864), Fisher
    MATTHEW (1791-1823), M.Mariner. (p.135)
    Thomas (1793-1795)
    THOMAS (1794-1833), Fisher. (p.135)
    Lydia Hodgson (1795-1875)
=1823 William Harrison, M.Mariner and Fisherman; lost at sea, 1833.
    REUBEN (1797-1882), Master Fisherman. (p.137)

ISAAC (1786-1861+),   m.1818 Isabella Harrison (1787-), dau. of
    Fisherman   Thomas and Anne, nee Bedlington.

    Oliver (1812-1882), Fisherman

William and Elizabeth

The movement away from the fishing is increasingly apparent with the family of John and Mary. Mary Anderson herself was the daughter of a sailor.

James Hall was the son of a cordwainer born in York. His brother Charles continued the craft in the village. In 1867 James was master of the *Bounty* owned by a company led by George Russell, a Fylingdales master mariner who did not come from the usual seafaring circle but was a successful shipowner. The Russells more often worked on the land or at the alum works, where George's father-in-law, Abraham Streeting, a Kent man, was servant to the owner. Several of Abraham's descendants had notable careers. One of them, Captain John Arthur Streeting, won Lloyds' Silver Medal for saving his ship, the *Antiope*, when she was torpedoed in WWI. Another, Captain Thomas Streeting, in 1972 at the age of 94 was believed to be the last surviving holder of a "square-rigged" Extra Master's Certificate.

A few of the numerous Zachariah Grangers were joiners. Occasionally one or other of them is alternatively described as a sailor, which may indicate service as a ship's carpenter. In 1821 when the present Old St.Stephen's was being rebuilt the Zachariah appearing here was one of the contractors. Sometimes his occupation was given as wright or cartwright. Undoubtedly he had something to do with the great three-decker pulpit which is a much more dominant feature of the unusual church than the altar. His son of the same name took up the work, but later in life became postmaster and a shopkeeper in Bay. The marriage of a daughter to Thomas Thurlow, a draper of Loftus, accounts for the presence of the widowed Martha, a visitor, in that place in the 1871 Census.

William Cockerill has not been traced, largely because there were so many of that name. The family was remarkably numerous in Hackness and there were several branches in Whitby and Fylingdales, usually connected with farming and alum- making, but members entered shipping circles in Scarborough and Sunderland.

It was Jacob of Leeside's belief that William Pearson's family came from Ebberston, a parish almost adjoining Fylingdales high on the moor. He was interested in the family because his wife was another of William's daughters. A connection with the land persisted, until John, William's cousin-once removed, lost his property in Staintondale on account of smuggling.

John Storm (1841-89), master of the S.S. *Kathleen*, died at Rio de Janeiro, of yellow fever, and his son, William Pearson Storm, was lost in the brig *Granite* off the Tees. Unusually, the *Granite* was not local: the master was of Hartlepool but formerly of Bay, and the mate, John Steel, was a Bay man also.

Capt.Arthur Gibson, master with the Turnbull fleet, descended from Bay sailing-ship owners and masters, among them Harrison Allison and Hansell Gibson who appear with the lists of locally-insured vessels. (Appendix 1) Their *Medora* was the source of the name of a cottage in the village. Arthur Gibson's own house was *Trongate*, after a ship of which he was master.

Charles Taylor, M.Mariner, was of a Coastguard family settled in Bay. His son Thomas Andrew (1878-1967), M.Mariner, was widely known as host of the Victoria Hotel. Richard Storm Gibson, M.Mariner, grandson of Richardson and Charlotte Ann Storm, resumed the association with the hotel after a lapse of years. Zachariah Granger Storm was lost by enemy action near the end of WWI, when his daughter Elizabeth was a few days old. His name appears on the parish's war memorial. Lena, his widow, married Capt.Ernest Carter, who was appointed to a post ashore at Cape Town by Ellerman Lines, and settled there.

JOHN (1789-1864), Fisherman   m.1812 Mary Anderson (c.1788-1850),
dau. of William and Mary,
nee Bedlington

         Elizabeth (1788-1850)
=1843   William Cooper, Mariner
         JOHN (1815-53), M.Mariner
         WILLIAM (1818-96), Fisher. (p.133)
         ISAAC (c.1820-1888), Fisher. (p.133)
         Mary (1823-)
=1847   Benjamin Avery, Mariner
         THOMAS (1827-1905), M.Mariner. (p.133)
         Martha (1831-)
         =James Hall, M.Mariner

JOHN (1815-1853), M.Mariner   m.1837 Martha Grainger (1812-98),
dau. of Zachariah, Joiner,
and Ann, nee Prodam.

         Mary Ann (1838-)
=1861   William Cockerill, Mariner, at Whitby St.Mary's.
         JOHN (1841-89), M.Mariner
         Martha (1844-1928)
         =THOMAS STORM (1849-1911). (p.113)
         Elizabeth (1847-)
         = 1.Thomas Thurlow
         = 2.David Moug, Coastguard, Runswick, widower of Jane,
                                   dau. of Andrew and Jane Granger.

JOHN (1841-1889), M.Mariner   m. Elizabeth Pearson (1840-1922),
dau. of William (M.Mariner) and
Isabella, nee Robinson.

         JOHN (1867-), M.Mariner
         William Pearson (1871-1888)
         ISAAC (1869-1949), M.Mariner. (p.131)
         Elizabeth Granger (1880-)
         EDWARD (1873-1931), M.Mariner. (p.131)
         Richardson (1876-1931), M.Mariner
=1903   Charlotte Ann Taylor (1877-1971), dau. of Charles, M.Mariner.
            Daughter Hannah Mercy m.Arthur Gibson, M.Mariner.
         Zacharian Granger (1883-1918), M.Mariner (Extra Master).
         =Lena Rebecca Taylor, dau. of Charles, M.Mariner
            Daughter Elizabeth, Mrs.Stoke, of Capetown.

William and Elizabeth

The seafaring career of Isaac (1870-1949) had begun aboard the Storm-owned *Black Prince* at a time when a vessel had to be worked hard if she was to pay her way. There is an interesting chapter in *It's a Strange Game*, the unpublished memoirs of Capt.Bertie Ryan of Cardiff, concerning a voyage in 1925 as Second Officer of the S.S. *Redgate*, of which Isaac (1869-1949) was master. A picture emerges of a very tall, grave man, good at his job, dedicated to the interests of his owners - Turnbulls of Whitby - and otherwise devoted only to his family. Their home was the house *Highbury*, renamed *Wibury* when it became the Women's Institute's meeting place and Elizabeth Edith took the old name to another house in the village. Harry, her brother, became the Superintendent of the Whitby steamship company Rowland and Marwood and its branches. He served his time to marine engineering with Vickers Armstrong. Robin Hood's Bay had nothing and Whitby little to offer an intending engineer: the steamers that were built beside the Esk were usually towed to one of the ports of the North East to have engines fitted. Harry married the daughter of the Fylingthorpe schoolmaster. In 1944 he was Master of the Whitby Lion Lodge of Freemasons, of which father Isaac had been a member.

Charles Vivian: a chief planning officer in local government..

Edward (1873-1931) was master of the S.S. *Birdoswald* when she was torpedoed in 1916, and he spent two years in enemy hands. His father-in-law, Miles Burrows, was a contemporary and shipmate of Jacob Storm of Leeside. (p.68) For many years he was master of the brig *United*, but with the changing times he went, like so many others, into steam. He hailed from Holbrook in Suffolk, which explains the house The *Holbrooks* in Mount Pleasant, Bay. Leonard, who held the Extra Master Mariner's certificate, worked abroad for many years with Shell and retired to Whitby, while his sisters went to Scarborough.

JOHN (1867-),　　　　　　　　　　m. 1.Maude Cooper (1872-1909); no issue;
M.Mariner　　　　　　　　　　　　2.Agnes Stainthorpe, nee Randall,
　　　　　　　　　　　　　　　　　　dau. of a Coastguard at Bay.

    Muriel)
    Agnes) deceased
    JOHN)

JOHN m.
    John, living in Leeds in 1990, with a son, John (c.1975-)

Continued from page 129:

ISAAC (1869-1949), M.Mariner;　　　　　m.1892 Anne Lydia Harrison,
    baptised at Whitby Wesleyan　　　　　dau. of John, M.Mariner,
    Chapel　　　　　　　　　　　　　　and Eliza who came
　　　　　　　　　　　　　　　　　　　　from Essex

    HARRY (1897-1978), Marine Engineer
    Lizzie Edith (1901-1987)
    =Stanley V.Bye, Senior Partner, Chartered Accountants,
    Cleveland.

HARRY, A.M.I.Mar.E. (1897-1978), Marine　　　m.Viva Wilkinson
    Engineer and Superintendent; Whitby.

    CHARLES VIVIAN (1933-), Architect and Town Planner

CHARLES VIVIAN (1933-)　　　　　　　m.1956 Kathleen Agnes Ann Pinkney,
    Dip.Arch., Diploma in Civic　　　　　dau. John, M.Mariner, and
    Design, A.R.I.B.A., Fellow　　　　　　Kathleen, M.B.E.
    of the Royal Town Planning
    Institute; Edinburgh, Newcastle
    and London.

    Ann Fenella (1961-)
    =K.R.Straker, Ponteland, Northumberland
    Edward

Continued from page 129:

EDWARD (1873-1931), M.Mariner　　　　　m.1899 Rachel Burrows (1870-),
　　　　　　　　　　　　　　　　　　　　dau. of Miles (M.Mariner)
　　　　　　　　　　　　　　　　　　　　and Jane. (p...)

    LEONARD (1901-92), M.Mariner
    Freda (1904-), Hospital Matron.
    Nora (1908)
    =H.Waind, Farmer

LEONARD (1901-92), M.Mariner　　　　　m. Martha Eunice Addison of Jarrow.
    EDWARD IAN, Company Director

William and Elizabeth

Edward Ian: Director of Scottish Agricultural Industries.

As the size of the local fleet grew, it is remarkable how seldom the owners had to go outside the cousinage to find qualified masters; there was plenty of opportunity for younger men. Sons even of those who had clung to the fishing were being automatically apprenticed to the sea. One of the youngest appointments was that of William, son of William and Jane, who became master of the brig *Gem* at 21, but the outcome was unfortunate: He worked her successfully for two years, but in December, 1863 - a month that produced some foul weather - he and his crew were lost without trace between Hartlepool and London. She had been bought by Matthew Storm and Co., a business consisting of James Storm's sons-in-law (p.125), with the addition, for this particular venture, of young William's uncle, Thomas.

Isaac (1820-80) is among those sometimes identified as a fisherman, but also occasionally as a sailor. He died at sea on a fishing voyage. His brother Thomas (1827-1905) served his time to the sea, joined Matthew Storm and Co. to buy the *Gem*, and then went on to acquire the *Hartlepool* with his son Thomas in 1856. She was a new vessel, and was registered where she was built, in Sunderland. After a long service - which earned Thomas senior the nickname "Hartlepool Tom" - her fate was to be driven ashore in a sudden violent storm in October 1880, near Port Mulgrave, north of Whitby, and become a total wreck. Thomas junior, aged 27, was master at the time. When the local fleet was at its largest he had begun to serve his time to the sea with Andrew Storm (1810-97), and it was Andrew's son Jacob, master of the brig *Hallyards*, who at South Shields in 1871 certified that Thomas had "served his time faithfully and always conducted himself in a sober and steady manner". His future now lay in the steamers, from one of which he came to be generally known as "Roma Tom". In Bay he lived at *Roma House*.

EDWARD IAN, B.Sc., D.M.S.,   m.(1) Ann Wiley (1938-80);
    Company Director;   (2) 1981, Ann Barnes
    Scotland.

    Richard Andrew (1965-)
    Louise (1967-)
    John Michael (1970-)

Continued from page 129:

WILLIAM (1818-96), Fisherman   m. 1837 Jane Avery (c.1815-93),
    dau. of Thomas
    (Fisherman) and Jane

    Mary Jane (1838-)
    = ... Watson
    William (1840-64), M.Mariner
    Thomas Avery (c.1846-48)

Continued from page 129:

ISAAC (c.1820-88), Sailor   m.1845 Mary Ann Storm (1819-93),
    and Fisher   dau. of John Hodgson
    M.Mariner) and Ann.

    Thomas (1877-)
    Alice (1853-c.1860) ⎫ Twins?
    Mary Ann (1853-) ⎭
    Mary Ann (1859-)

Continued from page 129:

THOMAS (1827-1905), M.Mariner   m.1851 Rebecca Harrison
    (c.1830-1907), dau. of William
    (M.Mariner and Fisherman)
    and Lydia Hodgson, nee Storm.

    Thomas (1853-1939)
=1886   Sarah E.Crosby
    William Harrison (1855-1916)
    =Rebecca Storm (c.1858-1914). (p.165)
    Mary (c.1858-1909)
= c.1881 THOMAS STORM (1867-1941), Shoemaker. (p.137)
    Lydia (c.1861-1943)
    JOHN (1863-1939), M.Mariner
    Rebecca (1867-) a son, George Arthur, died in infancy
=1897   Thomas Burn

William and Elizabeth

As shipping out of South Wales increased, Whitby companies established offices there, and sailors from the district settled in Cardiff. John Storm (1863-1939) was one of these. He was for many years master of Turnbull ships. In 1929 during a voyage to the Plate in their *Saltersgate*, he made a model of a barque which was placed in the reception area of company offices. Hannah his wife was the daughter of Matthew Cooper, a fisherman who is best remembered as a Coxswain of the Bay lifeboat. Their son, Matthew, served his time to marine engineering, worked as an engineer on Turnbull ships, became chief superintendent and then a director of the company. In 1963 he received the O.B.E. for services to shipping. He was referring to narrowness of opportunity when he made the remark to a kinsman - one of the company captains - that the best thing his father did was to get out of Robin Hood's Bay. His son, Peter, served with the New Zealand Shipping Co.,Ltd. and joined Turnbulls as Chief Officer before coming ashore to take charge of the personnel department. In 1980 he became a director.

A continuing Cardiff connection of the this family is the business founded by William Harrison Storm, butcher, and carried on by his son John, who has a son, Neil.

Edward Martin Granger's O.B.E. was awarded following an action in WWII. His first and second names came from his great-grandfather who was the Bay blacksmith Edward Martin. The Martins, who combined their craft with farming over several generations, arrived in the village in the latter part of the eighteenth century. Edward Martin Granger's father, Captain Thomas Granger, had such concern for the appearance and condition of his ship that he was known as "Chipping Hammer Tom". A great-nephew, Capt.James Granger, continued the Granger line of shipmasters in Bay.

The third son of Isaac (1758-1824) was Matthew (1791-1823), who was lost with all hands. Margaret Trueman his wife was cousin of Christopher, one of those who gave their lives in the Bay lifeboat tragedy of 1843. One son, George, died in London (but was buried at Old St.Stephen's), and the eldest was the Matthew who married a daughter of James Storm and formed Matthew Storm and Co. with his brothers-in-law. (p.123) This concern owned seven vessels in 1867. In 1861 Matthew and Mercy were living in the house James had left them, in Sunny Place, and in 1871 their address was Storms' Yard.

The family of Thomas, fisherman and son of Isaac the boat-owner, was very much a victim of the sea. Thomas was drowned on a fishing expedition on New Year's Eve, 1833, his son Stephen was drowned in Gravesend Reach from James Storm's brig *Ariadne*, and John his son-in-law was master of Will Storm's unfortunate *Lomar*. (p.106) Jane remarried, taking the fisherman Andrew Granger for husband in 1838. Eight years later Andrew and two brothers William and John were lost, returning from the fishing grounds. Jacob Storm of *Leeside* said he could remember the impression made on him by the sadness of the day when their deaths became known, because the loss was so great and the men, sons of Edward Granger and Abiah, nee Storm, were related to most of the village. Remarkably, the contest with the sea went on despite repeated tragedies, and the numbers involved seemed only to increase.

JOHN (1863-1939), M.Mariner   m.1892 Hannah Cooper (-1970),
                                           dau. of Matthew, Fisherman
                             and Coxswain of the Bay Lifeboat.

    Rebecca Jane (1893-1983)
    =Edward Martin Granger, O.B.E., M.Mariner.
    John (1895-)
    Hannah Watson (1900-)
    MATTHEW COOPER, O.B.E., (1903-66), Marine Engineer, etc.
    Thomas (1904-)
    William Harrison (1908-)

MATTHEW COOPER, O.B.E., (1903-66)   m. Sally Theaker (-1992),
    Superintendent Marine Engineer   dau.of Mark, M.Mariner,
      and Company Director;   of Staithes.
         Maidenhead.

    PETER, Shipping Company Director

PETER, Shipping Company Director,   m. Ann Phyllis Herman
    living near Duras, Lot-et-Garonne, in 1992

    Matthew Paul (1978-)
    John (1980-)

Continued from page 127:

MATTHEW (1791-1823), M.Mariner   m.1816 Margaret Trueman
                                    (1790-before 1841), dau. of
                                    George, Fisherman, and
                                    Mary, nee Estill.

      Matthew (1817-1890), M.Mariner and Shipowner
=1840 Mercy Storm (1816-), dau. of James and Damaris. (p123)
      George (1819-49), Mariner

Continued from page127:

THOMAS (1794-1833), Fisherman   m.1830 Jane Cooper (1807-),
                                   dau. of Boyce and Sarah.

    Elizabeth (1831-1876)
    =John Storm (1827-59), M.Mariner. (p.106)
    Stephen (1833-52)

William and Elizabeth

Reuben (1798-1882), last son of Isaac, was a notable survivor, attaining the age of 90. Abigail his wife was a sister of John Smith who had partnered James Storm in the purchase of the *John and James*. In his time most of the Bay fishing was of the three-man coble kind. The steam trawl was invented on the Tyne and the railways could distribute great quantities of fish countrywide. The households of his sons Isaac and Thomas Smith represented the last of what had once been typical of the "fishing village" of Robin Hood's Bay, putting aside their brother Reuben's choice of a seafaring career and their sister Sarah's marriage to a shipmaster - and a "foreigner" at that, Thomas Vey being the son of a coastguard who stayed in Bay. Remarkably, Isaac died at 97 and Thomas Smith at 95. The family of Richard Bulmer. husband of Jane, was probably not classed as "foreign" as the first of them to appear, Francis, had married in the village in 1815 and again c.1820. All were joiners and housebuilders, and they made strong links by marriage within the community.

The family of Isaac offers wider evidence of the breaking of the mould. Susannah married the farmer, Robert Ripley, and their son remained in that occupation, at Ravenscar. There were seven children and fifteen grandchildren. Known desendants are of the family of Mrs.Mary Parker of Windy Ridge, Egton Bridge, who was brought up at Ravenscar. Abigail and Jane married outside the parish and Matthew went to Teesside. There is a well-known photograph by Frank Sutcliffe of Isaac and his crew with their coble on the beach at Bay: they are Reuben, Thomas and Matthew.

Isaac (1853-1938), the second son, had gone away to become a teacher by the time the beach scene was recorded, and spent much of his working life as master of a village school at Fillingham in Lincolnshire. The attraction of the sea still lingered: no-one went back to the fishing, but Alfred became a shipmaster with the Elder Dempster shipping company.

Ethelbert went through WWI in the Army, and was influenced by the work of the Church Army; the experience led him towards the church and theological college, and he was ordained in 1922. He held a curacy at Marsden near Huddersfield and became Vicar of Charnock Richard in Lancashire. His family illustrates the completeness of a change of occupational direction. Michael was a State Registered Nurse and Principal Officer in the prison service, for which work he received the Imperial Service Medal before making a new career with the National Trust. John retired to Spain in 1983. He served in submarines in the Far East in WWII.

Continued from page 127:
REUBEN (1797-1882), Master　　　　　m.1821 Abigail Smith (1799-),
　　　Fisherman　　　　　　　　　　　dau. of Thomas and Jane,
　　　　　　　　　　　　　　　　　　nee Granger.
　　　　Jane (1822-1904)
=1848　Richard Bulmer
　　　　ISAAC (1824-c1921), Master Fisherman
　　　　REUBEN (1826-88), M.Mariner. (p.141)
　　　　Abigail (1821-55)
　　　　Elizabeth (1830-65)
　　　　THOMAS SMITH (1833-1928), Master Fisherman. (p.141)
　　　　Sarah(1835-1909)
=1861　Thomas George Vey (-1901), M.Mariner
　　　　Lydia (1837-)
=1860　John Watson

ISAAC (1824-c.1921), Master　　　　　m.1850 Jane Readman alias
　　　Fisherman　　　　　　　　　　　Pinkney (1824-1875).
　　　　Abigail (1850-)
=1877　Benjamin Walley , Miner, of Sandsend.
　　　　Thomas (1851-before 1867)
　　　　ISAAC (1853-1938), Schoolmaster
　　　　Reuben (c.1854-)
　　　　THOMAS (1867-1941), Shoemaker. (p.139)
　　　　Jane (1860-)
=1884　Albert Hanson, Cartwright, at Whitby.
　　　　Susannah (1862-1940)
=1888　Robert Ripley, (-1941), Farmer
　　　　MATTHEW (1862-1944), Sailor. (p.139)

ISAAC 1853-1938), Schoolmaster　　　　m.Mary Elizabeth (-1890)
　　　　Thomas (-1960), Blacksmith)　　dau. Winifred
　　　　= ?　　　　　　　　　　　)
　　　　Alfred (1879-1966), M.Mariner) dau. Monica (-1932) .
　　　　=Jane .... (-1957)　　　)
　　　　Harold (-1954)
　　　　ETHELBERT (1882-1945), Anglican Priest; born Huddersfield.
　　　　Mary Elizabeth (1884-), Schoolteacher.
　　　　Charles (1894- Lived at Hebburn on Tyne.
　　　　=Anne

ETHELBERT (1882-1945), Vicar of　　　　m.Anne Beaumont
　　　　Charnock Richard, Lancs.　　　　　(1882-1973)
　　　　John Rodney Beaumont, B.A. (1920-), Headmaster, Staffs;
　　　　=Janet Hunter　　　　　　　retired to Spain;
　　　　daughters: Adrienne, Jonquil and Hilary.
　　　　Mary Elizabeth died in infancy)) Twins
　　　　Josephine Alfreda (1925-)　　)
　　　　= 1.Reginald Summerill (1913-74)
　　　　= 2.Allan Turrall
　　　　Peter Ethelbert Randall, (1926-), Schoolteacher
　　　　=Audrey Parker
　　　　Michael James Alexander (1933-)) Oxfordshire;
　　　　Pamela Bye　　　　　　　)
　　　　　　daughters: Michelle, Gisella and Kirsteen.

Yet another Thomas had to be distinguished, this time as "Shoemakker Tom", because his wife Mary's father and brother were respectively Hartlepool Tom and Roma Tom. Thomas and Mary lived at Ravensworth Cottage. Lydia Rebecca married a sailor, Richard Peene Pennock, who was lost overboard from the S.S.*Camellia* on a voyage from the Tyne to Hamburg in the winter of 1909, and John was killed in a boat-drill accident aboard the S.S.*Hawsker* in Hull docks. Abigail continued the demonstration of local longevity by reaching the age of 93. but she was the last with "Storm" for a surname to live down in the old village.

Matthew took his family to Hartlepool when he went "deep sea". Hannah Marlow before marriage was housekeeper to the Rev.Jermyn Cooper, Vicar of Fylingdales. As her parents had died young the vicarage was virtually her home. The children were born after the departure from the village. Their son, George Marlow, was a ship's carpenter for 17 years and came ashore with the end of WWII. He recalled that his mother had brothers who emigrated some time before 1890 and settled in Kalamazoo, Michigan, where they had families.

In 1992 Alan (1932-) was chosen to join the band of craftsmen engaged in the restoration of the historic frigate H.M.S.*Trincomalee* at Hartlepool.

Continued from page 137:

THOMAS (1867-1941), Shoemaker   m. Mary Storm (1858-1909), dau.
                                                     of Thomas, M.Mariner, and Rebecca.
     Lydia Rebecca (1882-1957)
     =Richard Peene Pennock (1878-1909), Sailor.
     Mary Jane (1884-1970)
     William Thomas (1885-1977)
     =Hannah Marsay of Hawsker
     Abigail Smith (1890-1983)
     John (1891-1915)

Continued from page 137:

MATTHEW (1862-1944), Sailor,   m.1891 Hannah Marlow of
     Bay and Hartlepool   Grosmont

     REUBEN (1891-), Marine Engineer
     Edith Hannah
     Melita
     GEORGE MARLOW (-1993), Shipwright

REUBEN (1891-), Marine Engineer m. ?
     Newcastle upon Tyne

     Elizabeth, Mrs.Burt of Newcastle upon Tyne.
     MALCOLM

MALCOLM   m. Heather
     Newcastle upon Tyne

     IAN
     Keith

IAN   m.

     Jacob (1992-)

GEORGE MARLOW (-1993), Shipwright m.
     Hartlepool

     Olga, Mrs.Bennet (1931-)   ; ch'n Owen and Karen.
     Alan (1932-), Shipwright   ) dau: Mrs.Victoria Clair
) Willis, Nurse, formerly
     =Maureen,Community Health   of St.James' Hospital, Visitor Leeds.
     Myra, Mrs.Sherwood (1936- , two sons: Philip, Sandhurst
                                 and Royal Engineers, and Andrew of I.C.I.

William and Elizabeth

Reuben, M.Mariner, was living in Pilot Street, W.Hartlepool, in 1853. He was lost with all hands in the brig *Bounty* in the mouth of the R.Elbe. He had made his home at Sandsend, near Whitby. His son lived at Gosforth, Newcastle upon Tyne. He commanded a steamship that was sunk near the end of WWI by a U-boat and he was lost. Some evidence has been found of the family of Martin Robert Storm, whom Thomas's widow married; it is contained mainly in sources relating to South Shields, but the link with Bay - which descendants accept - has not yet been exactly established. (Appendix 2)

For some unknown reason Thomas Smith Storm's nickname was "Argy". The writer Leo Walmsley who was brought up in Bay remembered that his most distinctive characteristic was insistence on wearing his braces outside his guernsey. There is pictorial evidence. His sons all served as coxswains of the Bay lifeboat, the tradition ending with Oliver. In 1936 William, the eldest, was the subject of an obituary in the *Whitby Gazette* which said that he was "of a noble and fearless nature", that "in him combined prepossessing appearance and kindly gentle manners", and that he was "held in the highest esteem". During his time as Coxswain over 70 people were rescued. The family was represented in Leo Walmsley's novel "Three Fevers" as the Fosdycks, long-established, proud of their craft and resentful of intruders, the Lunns, who were in reality the Duke family of fisherfolk who had come to Bay from Flamborough. The novel became the first feature film made by J.Arthur Rank, with the title *Turn of the Tide*. The Storm- Duke situation, if it really existed, was actually resolved by intermarriage when Robert Storm married Gertrude Mary Duke. *Gertrude* was the name of one of the Duke boats, built at Bay by the joiner Reuben Bulmer, son of Richard and Jane. (p.137)
In February, 1935, the Duke's *Faith* broke her back on Whitby bar. Skipper Henry Duke and his crew, including Robert Storm, were rescued while watchers on the piers saw the *vessel* sink.

Continued from page 137:

REUBEN (1826-88), M.Mariner   m.1853 at Stranton
                                     (W.Hartlepool)
                                     Mary Knaggs

    Ann Elizabeth
    THOMAS (1866-1918), M.Mariner
    Reuben Edward (-1954), Schoolmaster
    =Mary (-1953)

THOMAS (1866-1918), M.Mariner   m. Elizabeth Anne, who married
    Gosforth, Newcastle   2nd the widower Martin
    upon Tyne   Robert Storm, Mariner, of
                                     South Shields. (Appendix 2)

    Lily Victoria
    Gladys
    Sidney (or Harry)

Continued from page 137:

THOMAS SMITH, (1833-1928),   m.1856 Rebecca Moorsom (1838-1908).
    Master Fisherman   dau. of Peter (M.Mariner)
                                     and Isabella, nee Moorsom
                                     (dau. of Greenup, Mariner).

    Fanny (1858-)
    William (1860-1936), Fisherman and Lifeboat Coxswain
    Thomas (1863-c.1864)
    Thomas (1865-1936), Fisherman and Lifeboat Coxswain
    Reuben (1869-1946), Fisherman and Lifeboat Coxswain
    Rebecca (1870-1873)
    Isabella (1876-1932)
    Elizabeth (1877-1952)
    OLIVER (1878-1956), Fisherman and Lifeboat Coxswain
    Rebecca (c.1879-1968)) Parents of Mrs.Rebecca
    =William Smith   )   Storm Murrell.

OLIVER (1878-1956), Fisherman   m.Mary Ellen (1876-1961)
    and Lifeboat Coxswain

    Oliver (1901-1937)   )   Daughter Olive and a son who
    =Greta Watson   )   died in infancy
    ROBERT WATSON (-1976), Fisherman and Sailor

ROBERT WATSON (-1976), Fisherman and Sailor   m. Gertrude Mary Duke
    PETER (1935-1988)

PETER (1935-1988), Station Officer,   m. 1963 Marian Angela Cooper
    Greater Manchester Fire Brigade

    Keith (1970-)

Jacob and Ruth

There is a reference in the parish books to the fishermen's aisle in the old church. The implications of this are not at all clear, but the allocation of pews to Jacob (1680-1750) and others in 1710 when the church had been rebuilt may cast some light on where they were. The eighth pew on the north side of the body of the building was assigned to the houses of George Linnel, Richard Wilson, Jacob Storm, John Helme and John Johnson, for which they paid 2s.6d.

Fron the churchyard of Old St.Stephen's:

> Here lies the body of Jacob son of Jacob and Ruth
> Storm who died May the 8th 1737 aged 24 years:
> Though boreas blasts and neptunes waves: have
> tost me to and fro: yet now I am by Gods decree:
> in harbour here below: Where I do safe at anchor
> ride: with Several of our Fleet: yet once again I
> must set sail: our admiral Christ to meet.

In September, 1767, Andrew left Whitby for Yarmouth in an open boat, carrying twelve webs of British-made cloth. He was perhaps combining a little trade with his annual voyage to the Yarmouth herring fishing.

CAPTAIN RAYMOND STORM ashore after fifty years of seafaring.

CAPTAIN RAYMOND STORM sketched in Melbourne, Victoria in 1948

The writer with his Father, Raymond in Aarhus, Demark in 1939. The next port of call was in Finland and the ship cleared the Baltic just before war was declared. On the passage to Hull the Chief Engineer, who had served through WWI repeatedly assured all on board: "There will be no war", but six months later he was lost by enemy action.

RAYMOND STORM (1892-1971), still 'brassbound' at Leeside in 1912.

CAPTAIN ROBERT DUNN FRANK (1893-1943) who married Isabel, sister of Wilfred, Raymond and Richard Storm. He was lost at sea in WWII.

CHAPTER 6:

JACOB AND RUTH

The lineage proceeds from Jacob and Ruth, brother and sister-in-law of William with whose people the previous chapter was almost wholly concerned. It is unusual to find the families descending from two brothers following the same way of life, mainly in the same place, for three centuries. Jacob's line displays the same broad features as brother William's, with the exception that its fishing households disappeared earlier. This chapter therefore confirms the general picture that had been seen before; further interest lies in the individual careers and adventures of another procession of mariners.

JACOB (or JAMES) (1680-1750) m.1704 Ruth Richardson
    Householder dau. of Michael
        and Ruth.

    Jacob (1705-1709)
    ANDREW (1707-1777), Householder and Master Fisherman
    Mary (1710-1711)
    Jacob (1712-1737)
    Mary (1715-1744)
    Ruth (1718-1783)
=1738   Reuben Bedlington
    Elizabeth (1722-1779)
=1742   James Peacock, son of Matthew and Jane.

ANDREW (1707-1777), m.1730 Rebecca Rickinson (1710-1772) dau.
    Householder and Master of William, Householder, and
    Fisherman Jane, nee Peacock.

    William (1733-1739)
    Rebecca (1735-1767
=1763   Thomas Hewitson
    JACOB (1739-1783), Fisherman
    WILLIAM (1742-1800), Fisherman. (p.161)
    Henry died in infancy, 1747
    Abiah (1748-1801)
=1771   Nathan Peacock
    Andrew died in infancy, 1752

Jacob and Ruth

Jacob (1739-83) was lost at sea with his brother-in-law Thomas Skerry and Jacob Peacock, a kinsman. The parish rate books show their last contributions on the 6th January, 1784, and on the 25th May, 1784, the widows Ann Storm and Esther Skerry appear.

Moorsom Bedlington was the brother of Jacob who was captured by the enemy in the French Wars and shot trying to escape.

Jacob (1766-) sold his house in Cowfield Hill to his son James in 1823 and went to Sunderland, his wife Dorothy having died. In Sunderland he lived with his son Isaac. James sold the house to his brother Jacob about ten years later and went to South Shields. Jacob junior was master of the two-year-old brig *Attaliah*, from which he was drowned in New Orleans in 1829, leaving a wife and three daughters in South Shields. The *Attaliah* was the vessel later acquired by Jonathan Skerry, to be commanded by his son-in-law, "Attliah Jack" Storm. (p107) She was still accepted at a valuation of £1200 by the Bay Ship Insurance Association in 1865.

There is some uncertainty about the early career of James (1792-1861), the foregoing Thomas's elder brother: he is easily confused with his kinsman James (1790-1855), who was also a shipmaster; one or the other served in Scoresby's whalers out of Whitby, in years when they would both have been in their early twenties. (p.123) In 1844 James let his kinsman Matthew Rickinson the grocer build a warehouse on his frontstead in Cowfield Hill, with six years of rent-free use. Matthew also had money in shipping, but the grocery grew into trading in wine, first in Whitby and then in West Hartlepool, where his grandson became a prominent pioneer of the port's shipping by selling his holdings in sail to acquire a fleet of steamers known as Rickinson and Sons.

Frances and William Johnson had a son, Jacob Storm Johnson, M.Mariner, who became a pilot on the Tyne and lived at Dunston on that river. He was killed in a railway accident in 1902.

James (1792-1861) finished his "time", married in Bay, and went to Middlesbrough around 1830. Jacob of *Leeside*, who knew the place well from his own voyages, said James became well known in the town. From there the family scattered about the North East ports. His son Jacob established himself as a butcher in the new port of Seaham Harbour, where there were two daughters, Mrs.Halliwell and Mrs.Price. Of the family of the latter, if any, nothing is known. The former settled in Brighton, her husband's work on the Brighton Line, for Robert Stephenson, having taken him there. These were the great-grandparents of the late Professor Frank Halliwell of the University of East Anglia.

Thomas (1818-) was of the Storm and Gray shipowning partnership mentioned in White's *Directory of Hartlepool* in 1847. Whellan's directory of 1856 shows Thomas and James living near each other in the same street in the town. James Gray was later owner of steamships in Whitby, several of which were built at the Whitehall yard there. He is best remembered in the town as "James Gray of *The Shrubberies*". He was an executor of Thomas's will.

JACOB, Fisherman (1739-1783)　　　　　m.Ann Storm (1736-1815), dau. of
　　　　　　　　　　　　　　　　　　　　　James, Master Fisherman,
　　　　　　　　　　　　　　　　　　　　　and Elizabeth, nee Helm.
　　　　　　　　　　　　　　　　　　　　　　　(p.183)

　　　　　Ann died in infancy, 1765
　　　　　JACOB (1766-), M.Mariner and Fisherman
　　　　　James (1769-1789)
　　　　　Rebecca died in infancy, 1773
　　　　　Rebecca (1774-1819)
=1801　　Moorsom Bedlington
　　　　　Andrew died in infancy, 1776
　　　　　ANDREW (1778-1850), Fisherman and M.Mariner. (p.151)
　　　　　Ann 1782-)
=1808　　Jonathan Mills, mariner

JACOB (1766-)　　　　　　　　　　　m.1791 Dorothy Harrison, dau. of Thomas,
　　M.Mariner and Fisherman.　　　　　　　M.Mariner and shipowner,
　　　　　　　　　　　　　　　　　　　　　and Frances Huntrods).

　　　　　JAMES (1792-1861), M.Mariner
　　　　　Mary died in infancy, 1793
　　　　　Dorothy (1794-)
=1814　　1.Thomas Cork, M.Mariner
　　　　　2.Thomas Pearson, M.Mariner
　　　　　Jacob (1796-1829), M.Mariner
=1818　　Ann Jefferson, widow, nee Jameson
　　　　　Thomas (1798-), M.Mariner and shipowner
　　　　　=Deborah Smyth, who was born in Darlington
　　　　　Isaac (1800-), M.Mariner, who went to Sunderland
　　　　　Andrew (1803-1804)
　　　　　Frances (1805-1861)
　　　　　=William Johnson, mason.

JAMES (1792-1861),　　　　　　　　　　m.1813 Jane Cooper (1788-), dau.
　　M.Mariner　　　　　　　　　　　　　　of John and Hannah.

　　　　　JAMES (1815-1906)
　　　　　Thomas (1818-1820)
　　　　　Jacob (1822-) two daughters in Seaham Harbour, where he
　　　　　=　　　　　) had a butchering business.
　　　　　Mary Jane (1824-)
　　　　　WILLIAM (1828-1873), M.Mariner. (p.149)

Jacob and Ruth

The eldest son of the Middlesbrough family, James (1815-1906), stayed in that town and worked as a shipmaster. In the 1871 Census Ann was at home with the children in Queen's Terrace, and is entered as "Sea Captain's wife". Ten years later he had become Harbour Master, a post which he held for 13 years. His wife was the daughter of a sailmaker, whose name, Baxter, was associated with Fylingdales, and continues in use among descendants in Australia. Franklands are to be found in Whitby, involved with tanning, which connects with sailmaking, and some of them did well enough to set up in banking. In 1906 James appears in the Middlesbrough directory as "James Storm Gentleman". He died in that year, his ninetieth. Jacob Storm's comments are that he was particularly noted in the town for " his sprightly demeanour in advanced years", and that he had once been master of his father-in-law's brig *Seven*. Bethalina ("Lina") and Lydia lived on for some time in the Queen's Terrace house, but in 1926 Bethalina was at Great Ayton.

Marshall Pearson, James' son-in-law, was son and successor of Wm.Pearson of Leeds, a noted manufacturer of shoemaking machinery. In 1884 he joined forces with the Leicester manufacturer Charles Bennion, and the firm of Bennion and Pearson was the beginning of the B.U.S.M. Co., Ltd., the world's largest makers of shoemaking machinery and footwear materials. Marshall Pearson's daughter, Elizabeth Storm Pearson, lived in Leicester.

Edward and William Ridley Storm went to Australia and prospered. Their brother Elliot Baxter joined them but did not stay.

Elliot Baxter married in Stamford, where his wife came from a family of corn and seed merchants. His daughter, Blanche Lydia, lived to 97. Her husband, Alfred Willmer Pocock, Architect, practised in Burma.

Edward was a jeweller and was traced by means of the Goldsmiths' records in London. He was listed in the Post Office directory of New South Wales in 1883 as a watchmaker, but he was also a successful dealer in property. The Baxter name continues with his grandson in Australia. Of his sons, Cecil was killed in France in WWI, and Wiiliam Milton, brought to England by the war, married there and returned to live in Adelaide.

JAMES (1815-1906), M.Mariner   m.Ann Baxter (1821-1891)
    and Harbour Master,   dau. of Elliot (1799-1883),
    Middlesbrough   Sailmaker, and Bethelina, nee Frankland (1800-83)

    ELLIOT BAXTER (1845-1905), Pharmacist
    Bethelina (-1926); died aged 79
    James) twins, died in infancy, 1851
    William)
    Ann (1853-8)
    James (1856-1876)
    Isaac
    Jacob
    Lydia (c.1861-after 1906)
    Sarah E. (c.1863-   )
    Jane   ) three children, including Elizabeth Storm and Senior Waterhouse
    =Marshall Pearson)
    EDWARD, Jeweller
    WILLIAM RIDLEY (1860-1908), Chartered Accountant.
                                                                      (p.149)

ELLIOT BAXTER (1845-1905),   m.Janet Duncan Hart (-1925)
    Pharmacist; Worcester   of Stamford, Lincs.
    and S.Wales

    Blanche Lydia (1875-   )) a daughter, Ursula,
    =A.Willmer Pocock, Architect) Mrs.Glanville Goodin
    Elliot Percy (1877-1927)
    =Minnie ..... (-1912)
    Herbert Ridley (1881-1963), Pharmacist, married, and
    lived at Worthing.
    Hilda Anne (1882-   )
    Margaret Olive, went to the U.S.A.
    Muriel Norah
    =Thomas Eastwood

EDWARD, Jeweller, and property   m.1881 Caroline Mary Hyacinth
    dealer in New South Wales   Burg (of German descent)

    Edward James daughter Valerie married Thomas Hughes,
    =Ginny Walker   Schoolmaster
    William Milton, married and lived in Adelaide.
    Cecil, lost in France in WWI
    Clifford Leslie daughters Marina Storm and Audrey Storm.
    =Kathleen Monahan
    WALTER STANLEY
    Lydia, unmarried.
    Edith
    =Alan Johnson
    Ethel Ellen   ) sons Robert, Bernard and Herbert.
    =Herbert Stanley William)
    A daughter who died aged 4.

Jacob and Ruth

In Middlesbrough William Ridley was a "Commercial Clerk" in 1881; in Australia he practised as a Chartered Accountant in Sydney. His son Eric, of Cremorne, New South Wales, went to the Dutch East Indies and dealt in coffee, copra, and other commodities, in Java. A frequent world traveller and visitor to Britain, he stayed in Robin Hood's Bay annually, but decided that he would make the journey for the last time in 1992, in his 97th year. One interest is the Australian Natural Health Society, of which he is a foundation member, and another is researching the Australian branches of the family, to very good effect. This family is once again represented in England by his nephew, James Cerdic, who was able to re-establish contact as a result of visiting the Robin Hood's Bay Museum in 1990.

The last of the household of James (1792-1861) was William (1828-1873), M.Mariner. He was another who went to Hartlepool, but after 1851 he moved up to Sunderland, where he lived in Millfield. In 1872 he willed that his young children be entrusted to Kathleen Alderson Taylor of Gilesgate, Durham. In the following year he was lost when the S.S.*Heaton Hall* of which he was master foundered. His daughter Amy was in the nursing profession, and lived latterly in Scarborough, reaching her hundredth year there. William is the first member of the family known to have been master in steam. It was Jacob of *Leeside's* belief that he had a son, William, who was an artist in Sunderland.

To maintain the order of seniority, it is necessary now to go back to Andrew son of Jacob (1739-1783) and Ann, and trace the descent of him and his wife Hannah Pearson. Andrew worked as a fisherman and sailor and from time to time as master of the

WALTER STANLEY,　　　　　　　　　m.Eleanor M.E.Humphries
    Australia

    EDWARD BAXTER (1934-), Farmer
    Joy Elizabeth   a daughter, Linda.
    =Christopher Welsh

EDWARD BAXTER (1934-), Farmer in　　　m. 1960, Lorraine Snell.
    Australia

    Two daughters and two sons

Continued from page 147:

WILLIAM RIDLEY (1860-1908), Chartered　　m. Beatrice Sayers Mayle
    Accountant in Sydney

    CERDIC (1894-1957)
    Hilda   a son, John Raymond.
    = ... Burrell)
    Eric (1896-), living in Cremorne, N.S.W.; an annual
        visitor to Robin Hood's Bay to 1992.
    =Blanche Amelia Jackson
    Marjorie   ) a son, Eric, and a daughter, Joan.
    =Roy Norman

CERDIC (1894-1957),　　　　　　m. c.1915 Ellen Vignoles (1891-1961),
    Mariner, Australia　　　　　　Singer

    JAMES CERDIC (1917-), R.A.F. and Local Government
    Marjorie May (1920-)
=1949   Norman Wilkins
    Eileen (1923-1928)

JAMES CERDIC (1917-), served in　　m.1941 Jean Tessier (1921-86), born
    R.A.F., and in Local Government　　St.Johns, Newfoundland
    in England; Bristol

    Patricia Lorraine (1946-)
    Kathryn Mary (1954-)

Continued from page 145:

WILLIAM (1828-1873), M.Mariner,　　　　m.
    Sunderland

    Amy (1865-1965), Nurse, died at Scarborough in her hundredth year.
    Ernest
    Nora (1871-)) twins
    Ida (1871-))

Polly. (p.112) A note by Jacob of *Leeside* concerns the Pearson family, to which both his grandmother, Hannah, and his wife, Isabel, belonged. It reads: "It is a fact that the Pearsons came from Ebberston. My wife's great-great-great-grandfather left there and served his time to sea from Whitby. His son, Francis, born in 1717, was also a sailor, and the third Francis went to South Shields and became a builder of ships. The bank manager of his descendants there still has his canvas-backed ship Bible. The brother of the third Francis was Richard, whose daughter became the wife of Andrew Storm; they [i.e. Richard and his wife, Margaret Eskdale) were my great-grandparents. Richard had a small farm in Fylingdales and a public house in Thorpe: a nephew John was a comfortable farmer in Staintondale till he challenged the government over imports, and lost his holdings. Hannah Pearson was a niece of Ingram Eskdale the Whitby shipbuilder, who built many vessels, sloops to ships, on his own account and with his relative Peter Cato, at the Whitehall Yard. Ingram's brother George, a master mariner himself, had no fewer that seven sons and sons-in-law masters, one of them being John who was for a time Secretary of the Bay Club [i.e. Marine Insurance Association], and another, Hunter, Elder Brother of Trinity House, Hull. The Eskdales can be traced to Broxa in the 16th century, in the Hackness register. They had a great liking for the name Ingram. Their surname is spelt in the registers in about a dozen different ways; we have it Estill".

It should be added to this that Hunter Estill was several times Warden of Trinity House, Hull, and that in 1982 there was a seventh-generation Estill shipmaster.

The memoirs of his son Jacob are informative about Andrew (1810-97) and Rebecca, as far as the sea is concerned, and there is also enough of other matters to show the sort of people they and many of those around them were, and what they did. Rebecca was the daughter of the fisherman Thomas Harrison, who became a shipowner, and he was no doubt assisted in this by Mercy, who came from the enterprising, shipowning family of William and Frances Storm. (p.112) She had before her the example of the leading shipowner her brother James. After the death of Thomas Harrison, her husband and business partner, Mercy carried on the family concern under the title of Mercy Harrison and Sons.

With Andrew a typical progression in a working life can be followed. In 1841 at Census time he was away with Rebecca in the schooner Brothers (95 tons) which he shared with his father-in-law. At the next Census he was absent again, this time with his own schooner, Crosby (110). Ten years later he was trading with the brig Coquette (169), and in 1871 Rebecca in his absence was listed as "shipowner's wife", the vessel concerned being the barque Hallyards (313), commanded by son Jacob. Andrew retained an interest in the brig Black Prince but by 1881 he had followed the traditional path of the older men and in semi- retirement was a fisherman, an occupation ensuring a palatable alternative to the novelty of imported stale fish which his son deplored. (p.23)

There are portraits of Andrew and Rebecca, by Sir Hubert von Herkomer, A.R.A. Rebecca sat in her typical dress of the coast, with frilled bonnet, andon being offered a sitter's fee she cannily stated a preference for "little pictures". These remain in the family, as do portraits by Sutcliffe. Andrew and Rebecca's house was Wavecrest in Cowfield Hill, six rooms of which Rebecca was letting to visitors "without attendance" in 1901. They lived to celebrate their diamond wedding. When Rebecca died at 90 in 1904 she had 26 great-grandchildren. Of eight customary "bearers" at her funeral at Old St.Stephen's five were master mariners.

Continued from page 145:

ANDREW (1778-1850), M.Mariner and Fisherman   m.1802 Hannah Pearson (1778-1858), dau. of Richard and Margaret, nee Estill.

    Richard (1804-25)
    Ann (1806-)
    =Edward Granger
    ANDREW (1810-97), M.Mariner
    Jacob (1812-32)
    Margaret (1816-95
    =1.William Pearson, Mariner
    =2.George Rogers

ANDREW (1810-97), M.Mariner, Shipowner and Fisherman   m.1834 Rebecca Harrison (1813-1904), dau. of Thomas and Mercy (nee Storm), Shipowners

Damaris Harrison
=ANDREW STORM (1830-1886), M.Mariner. (p.165)
JACOB (1837-1926), M.Mariner, Shipowner and Marine Superintendent
Hannah Mercy (1840-49)
Andrew (1843-68)
Fanny (1845-)
=1869 Richard Knightley Smith, M.Mariner, Shipowner and Marine Superintendent.
Thomas Harrison (1847-52)
Hannah Mercy (1849-)   chn.   Charlotte Ann, Thomas,
=Charles Taylor, M.Mariner   Lena Rebecca, Florence Storm,
Thomas (1852-72)   Charles Wenlock.

    Richard Knightley Smith came from Middlesex and served his time to sea under Isaac Bedlington in the brig *Vanguard*. Like Jacob his brother-in-law he was Superintendent of the Rowland and Marwood ships of Whitby. He left an estate valued at £32,000, which shows how profitable a career in ships could be at one time, and how shrewd he had been to move his money into steam when sail was in decline. In 1901 of the 35 shipmasters listed in the village he was the only one still a shipowner. His home was Ings House. William Andrew, his son, who inherited the house, was postmaster, and also creator of a valuable photographic record of the village. Another son, Thomas, was proprietor of the Robin Hood's Bay gasworks, believed to be the smallest in Yorkshire. William Andrew and Thomas together owned one of Bay's last large cobles, a motor-powered, 42-footer called *Dora Ann*, skippered by Henry Duke and worked out of Bridlington. Dr.Richard Knightley Smith, son of William Andrew, was commissioned in the Green Howards in WWI and lost a leg at Passchendaele. After the war he studied at St.Bartholomew's and in due course became a consultant in London.

Jacob and Ruth

The Robinsons of the Mill came from Scalby parish, which adjoins Fylingdales. They were originally at the mill in Scalby village, near Scarborough. Jacob of *Leeside* believed that the Robinsons of North Shields, owners of the Stag Line of steamers, who hailed from the North Riding, were of this family, and he searched for memorial inscriptions in that town, but without finding conclusive proof.

Isabella Robinson of Bay Mill was one of ten daughters, who tightened by marriage the strong bonds among local families and interests. They include the Thompsons (farmers, carriers and the King's Head), Milburns (shipmasters and owners, one of whom was Lloyd's Agent at Whitby), Irelands (alum works, shipping and the Bay shipping insurance association known as "the Indemnity" or "Granger's and Ireland's), Martins (blacksmiths), Crosbys (farmers and butchers), Gillings (seafarers) and Huttons (farmers, of "Penny Hedge" fame). (The "Penny Hedge" is a ceremony at Whitby, recalling annually a local legendary penance concerning the killing of a monk, supposedly in the twelfth century.)

James Storm Bedlington was nephew of Matthew, M.Mariner, shipowner and Secretary of the Robin Hood's Bay Shipping Insurance Association, for whom there is a memorial window in the modern parish church. He was an adviser to the Turnbulls of Whitby, who launched the S.S.*Matthew Bedlington* at their Whitehall Yard in 1882. James and Rachel's son was William Storm Bedlington, M.Mariner, whose widow, Mary Elizabeth ("Bessie"), lived into her 104th year. Her brother, Reginald Frankland White, and his son, Peter, solicitors of the Buchanan and White partnership in Whitby, served as Seneschals of the Manor of Fylingdales, presiding over the Court Leet at the Bay Hotel. Bessie and Will Bedlington were parents of Robert William Bedlington, M.C., and James Storm Bedlington, who kept the name in Bay until 1992.

The Taylor family's history in Bay began when Henry, father of Charles, was stationed there as a Coastguard. Like so many settlers in the village he came from a place on the coast, in this case Eastbourne.

Florence Storm Taylor (Mrs Albert Garcia): There is an account by Leo Walmsley in *The Sound of the Sea* of her singing in a concert at Bay. (See "Garcia" in *The Oxford Companion to Music*.)

LAURA, 274 tons. owned for eight years by Jacob, his father Andrew and his brother-in-law Richard Knightly Smith who was her master.

MAGGIE, 305 tons. Jacob sailed as her master in 1872. "The voyage went well, the only trouble was the dispute between the crew and the rats to determine who should have the provisions."

HALLYARDS, 313 tons. "While I was her master she helped me to weather storms which overwhelmed many of her contemporaries . . .with the invaluable experience that only an unhandy vessel can give a master."

These three vessels signify the attempt in the 1870's to compete with steamers, being larger than those owned earlier in the century.

Jacob and Ruth

Jacob: (1837-1926): Master Mariner, owner of sailing vessels, Marine Superintendent and local historian. In 1926 the *Shields Gazette* outlined his career and called him "a fine type of British master mariner". Isabel's maternal grandmother, Ann Richardson, was the sister of William, the sailor who was pressed into the Navy and whose letters were quoted by Jacob in his memoirs. (p.19)

Richard made a few voyages as his father's steward but preferred to work ashore, and learnt farming at Pond Farm, Fylingdales, under John Pickering, a relative of Martha Jane ("Pattie"), his future wife. He farmed on his own account at Littlebeck, Sleights, Hawsker and Stainsacre.

Stephen Robinson Thompson was great-grandson of Sampson (c.1744-1828), Parish Clerk of Fylingdales. The name continues with Cedric Thompson Frank of Whitby, son of Isabel and Robert Dunn Frank, M.Mariner. Frank is a farming name in Fylingdales and the Dunn family has a long association with the fishing and seafaring village of Staithes north of Whitby. In midwinter, 1943, Capt.Robert Dunn Frank was fatally injured aboard the *Baxtergate* by an unusually violent sea off Iceland during an Atlantic convoy. His eldest son, Godfrey Storm Frank (1922- 1993), M.Mariner, of Whitby, received the King's Commendation for Brave Conduct when he was a Cadet aboard the *Pacific Reliance* in WWII, in 1940. Master for many years in Indian ships, he qualified in 1980 at Trinity House as a Deep Sea and Coastal Pilot, in which service he ended his time at sea. Other children of this family are Robert Dunn junior, and Adrian Storm, of Whitby, and Mrs.Marion Isabel Atkins of York. Their great-grandfather on the paternal side, Pattison Frank, M.Mariner, was a shipowner, and master of both the *Goliah* and the *Esk* of the Whitby and Robin Hood's Bay Steam Packet Company around 1860. (p.113)

"Sampson" recurs with the next family, that of Wilfred, this time through descent from Tamar Thompson and her husband, Peter Clark, the Bay baker (c.1777- 1849).
The last contact of Wilfred with his family was an exchange of greetings with his younger brother Richard in the Red Sea, as their ships passed. Shortly after this Wilfred became ill, died, and was buried at Suez. His son, Gordon, was lost in the Navy in 1940.

JACOB (1837-1926), M.Mariner,   m.1861 Isabel Pearson (1838-1923),
Shipowner and Marine   dau. of William, M.Mariner,
Superintendent   and Isabella (nee Robinson
     of Bay Mill).

       Rachel Robinson (1862-1914)
=1885 James Storm Bedlington (1859-88), M.Mariner.
       RICHARD (1864-1953), Farmer
       JAMES WILLIAM (1867-1948), Joiner. (p.159)
       JACOB (1870-1946), M.Mariner. (p.159)
       Eleanor (1871-1942)
       THOMAS HARRISON (1876-), Commercial Representative.(p.161)
       Rebecca Mercy (1881-1961)

RICHARD (1864-1953), Farmer   m.1890 Martha Jane (1865-1925),
     Dau. of Stephen Robinson
     Thompson, Farmer, of
     Fylingdales.

       WILFRED (1891-1929), M.Mariner
       RAYMOND (1892-1971), M.Mariner
       Isabel (1893-1956)
=1920 Robert Dunn Frank (1893-1943), M.Mariner.
       Marion
       =William Smithies
       RICHARD (1902-1989), M.Mariner. (p.159)

WILFRED (1891-1929), M.Mariner   m.1916 Angelina,
     dau. of Sampson
     and Elizabeth Clark of Bay.

       Gordon (-1940), lost in WWII, Royal Navy.
       Dorothy (-1963)
       =Leonard Leach, Golf Professional

Raymond served his time with Messrs. Rowland and Marwood of Whitby, whose S.S. *Kildale*, commanded by Captain Milner, was his first ship. His first voyage, in 1909, was from Cardiff to Durban, Montevideo and back. This was the year when Robert Tate Gaskin, the Whitby historian, recorded that there were 62 steamships registered at the port. Raymond moved into the Prince Line, and spent part of WWI bringing horses from Texas to Bordeaux, for use by the Army. In a Mediterranean voyage his ship, the *Egyptian Prince*, was shelled and sunk, but all the crew were allowed to get away in the boats. In 1922 he and Janet moved from Whitby to Tyneside to make more days at home from the "weekly" boats possible. Between the wars he was first master of cargo and passenger vessels frequenting ports around the North Sea. One of his ships was the S.S. *General Havelock*, in which pre-war passegers had been able to have a cabin from Scarborough to London for eleven shillings. Those "in the know" could travel on the starboard side on the southward voyage, and the port side on return, for views of the shore. Another was the *Dunstanborough* which may still be remembered at Newcastle Quayside not only by former passengers, but as "the apple boat" for the cargoes she used to bring from Ghent. Later Raymond made many Atlantic, Baltic and Black Sea voyages, and traded with Spain throughout the Civil War. His ship left Finland under the eyes of the *Scharnhorst* just before WWII was declared. He made 23 voyages in convoy between Tyne and Thames in 1941, supplying the Ford works at Dagenham, which had gone into wartime production. Writing for the company the General Manager said, "We wish to place on record our keen appreciation of the service rendered by you and your ship's company in bringing supplies to this plant throughout the year. It says much for the fundamental courage of all concerned that you have "delivered the goods" in spite of the many and varied hazards of war and adverse weather conditions". On the 24th voyage he was wounded in an E-boat attack and his ship was sunk. He returned to sea, to serve in the Malta convoys, the Mediterranean campaign - supplying the Desert Army in command of the heavy-lift ship *Empire Harmony* - and the Italian campaign. After the war he traded in iron ore in Canada and North and West Africa, and finally in general cargoes in the Far East and Australasia. He spent thirteen years of retirement in Mears Ashby, Northamptonshire, where the bells were rung on 14th November, 1992, in celebration of Janet's 100th birthday.

Jessie: born at *Harbour View*, Whitby; served in Land Army in WWII, and thereafter in institutional management. Alan: born in Tynemouth and served in the R.N.V.R. in WWII.

William Rifle Forster, was not a Bay man, but of the fraternity of Tyneside shipmasters: he served Ropners of West Hartlepool and Runcimans of Newcastle, companies familiar to many Bay men. He started as cabin-boy in sail, on a voyage to Chile via Cape Horn, and qualified as master via the fo'c'stle. Commissioned in the Royal Naval Reserve in WWI, his first command was in minesweepers. Between the wars he served the Soviet government as an Ice Pilot, pioneering the Kara Sea route in command of collier convoys. In WWII he was voluntary Chief Air Raid Warden of the County Borough of Tynemouth. Afterwards he was Mayor.

Rachel: author of *In Search of Heaven on Earth*, 1991 (Bloomsbury Reference), a study of contemporary cults and their origins, and *The Exorcists*, 1993 (Harper Collins).

Roy, who was born in North Shields, served in the Royal Marines and was commissioned in the Royal Northumberland Fusiliers in WWII. After university he joined the Sudan Agricultural Service. On return he went into industrial consultancy, and founded

RAYMOND (1892-1971), M.Mariner   m.1918 Janet Chapman (1892-),
dau. of Joseph and Agnes
of Whitby.

    Jessie (1921- 1993)
    ALAN (1922-)
    ROY (1926-)

ALAN, (1922-),   m.1951 Berta Ovidia Forster. B.Com.,
M.A., B.Com., Ph.D.   (1923-), dau. of William R.
Forster, M.Mariner, and Berta
(nee Olsen, dau. of Martin of
Bergen, Norway.

    Andrew B.A., H.N.D. in Nautical Studies (1957-); Systems
        Development Manager.
=1983 Emma Caroline Eldergill, M.A., Systems Programmer;
        dau. Imogen Mary Eldergill-Storm
    Marion, M.B., Ch.B. (Edin.) (1958-), Psychiatrist.
=1987 Brian David Todd, F.R.C.S.(Edin.), F.R.C.Orth., Consultant
        Orthopaedic Surgeon; ch'n. Kate Storm, Alastair
        Storm and Alison Storm.
    Rachel Margaret, M.A.(Oxon.), (1961-) Author, Journalist;
=1988 Michael Prescott, M.A.(Oxon.), (1961-), <u>Sunday Times</u>
        Political Correspondent; son: Isaac Michael Storm

ROY, M.A.(Oxon.), (1926-)   m.1971 Anne Elizabeth Millar of
    Senior Partner of Storm   Sydney, N.S.W.,
    Management Services,   dau. of Flying Officer
    Swindon.   Thomas Roberts, B.Econ.,
        R.A.A.F., and Elizabeth
        Grace Millar.

    Robert William Millar (1972-), Scholar of Downing College Cambridge.
    James Alexander Millar (1974-)
    Andrew Lachlan Millar (1979-)
    Elizabeth Katherine Edwina Millar (1984-)

Storm Management Services in Swindon in 1975. Thomas Roberts Millar, a Royal Australian Air Force pilot, was shot down over Italy in WWII.

Richard spent much of his sea-going career with the King Line. In WWII he survived two torpedoings. The ship he commanded, the *Fort Slave*, was allocated for special transport work in August, 1943, which involved him in the notorious Arctic convoy duty to Murmansk. He was destined to take the same vessel into the Normandy landings in 1944.

The unusual name "Greenup", which is frequently linked with the Moorsom surname, often arouses some curiosity. It is traceable to a carpenter in Whitby, Thomas Greenop, in the early eighteenth century, when shipbuilding drew men of his craft to the town. Moorsoms, and other "core" families, have used the name since that time. Greenup Moorsom Storm exhibited at the Royal Academy, the Royal West of England Academy and the Walker Gallery, Liverpool.

James William Storm succeeded his cousin Thomas Knightley Smith as proprietor of the Bay gasworks. He was also a church organist and a maker of violins. His daughter and son-in-law, John and Nancy Sargeant, were known to many as hosts of the Grosvenor Hotel at Bay.

Jacob (1870-1946) was master of Messrs.Rowland and Marwood's *Blue Cross* which called at New Orleans in 1900 in time to pick up some of the crew of the same company's *Roma* which had been driven ashore by the historic hurricane at Galveston. The real purpose of her call was to load mules for South Africa, to be used in the war with the Boers. When the mules were discharged the ship was attached to the warship *Powerful* as a supply ship, and the crew were able to watch her big guns being dismantled for transport up-country to assist in the relief of Ladysmith. When the *Blue Cross* returned she loaded coal at Cardiff to bunker the *Powerful* at Hong Kong, where the Navy was helping to deal with the Boxer rebellion. Shortly after this she took on a cargo of cement at the Black Sea port of Novorossisk and carried it to Vladivostock for use in the fortifications there. The next operation arranged by the owners was to load coal in Japan to bunker the Japanese fleet, which proceeded to demolish the Russian forts at Vladivostock. In WWI Jacob was master of the *Beemah* when she was sunk off Lands End in 1915 by a U-boat. Four men were trapped below and lost. Several survivors were picked up by a vessel which went on to the Mediterranean, only to be sunk with all hands. One of those who returned to Whitby was an apprentice, Lance Chapman, brother of Janet.(p.157) In WWII he was master of a ship which took part in the Dunkirk rescue operation. (An uncle, Capt.Jack Wedgwood, was Harbour Master at Whitby between the wars. The North Ridng Wedgwoods stem from a seventeenth century branch of the Staffordshire pottery family.)

Jacob Francis ("Fran"): family historian in Bay and Whitby.

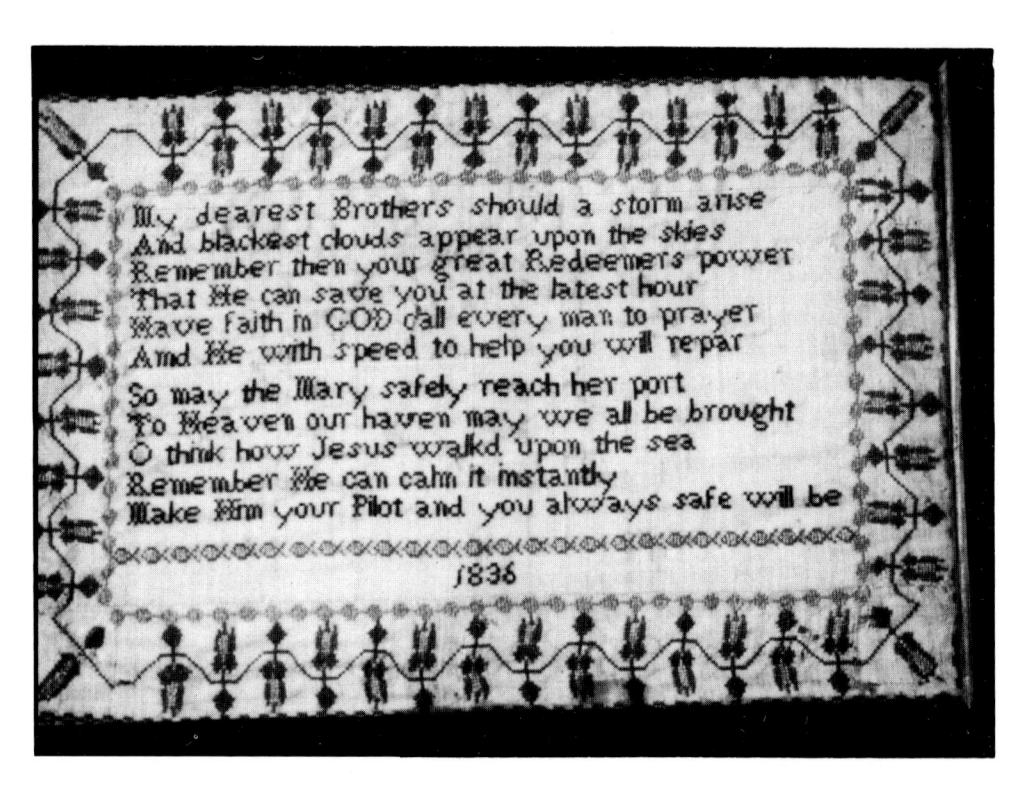

> My dearest Brothers should a storm arise
> And blackest clouds appear upon the skies
> Remember then your great Redeemers power
> That He can save you at the latest hour
> Have faith in GOD call every man to prayer
> And He with speed to help you will repar
> So may the Mary safely reach her port
> To Heaven our haven may we all be brought
> O think how Jesus walkd upon the sea
> Remember He can calm it instantly
> Make Him your Pilot and you always safe will be
>
> 1836

MARTHA'S SAMPLER Martha, future wife of the Congregational minister, Thomas Phillips, was about thirteen when she made this. Two of the shipmaster brothers whom she addressed were lost within two years.

ANN STORM SHAW'S SAMPLER was worked to commemorate her grandfather, Lomar Will Storm, who died a year later, aged 87.

Continued from page 155:

RICHARD (1902-1989), M.Mariner   m.1940 Katherine Beaven
    Petersfield and Whitby

    RICHARD (1945-)

RICHARD (1945-);   m.1968 Judi Victoria Louise Tastevin
    South Africa

    Nicola Caroline (1969-)
    Richard Simon (1970-); Royal Air Force (Mountain Rescue)

Continued from page 152:

JAMES WILLIAM (1867-1948),   m.1899 Ethel Anne Moorsom (1880-
    Joiner   1964), dau. of Greenup,
                                                              M.Mariner.

    Andrew (1900-)
    =
    Greenup Moorsom (1901-), Artist) ch'n. Mrs Anne Fenton
=1928 Constance Muriel Bramald   ) and Mrs.Gloria Bagge.
    Anne Jefferson   ) ch'n.   Mrs.Anne Baker and
    =John Sargeant   )   Mrs Jill Taylor
    Eleanor   ) ch'n.   John Tennent, B.E.M., Captain,
    =William Tennent)   Regular Army, and Entomologist;
                                            Mrs.Susan Crompton, Teacher.

Continued from page 155:

JACOB (1870-1946), M.Mariner   m.1913 Eliza Herbert Mills (1886-
                                                      1964), dau. of John,
                                                  M.Mariner, and Sarah Selina
                                                  of Nookfield House, Bay.

    Eileen Isabel (1914-)
=1938 Thomas Knightley-Smith (1908-), Solicitor
    Geoffrey (1916-56), M.Mariner) dau. Ingrid
    =Florence Lucy Walker   )
    ARNOLD (1918-), Bank Manager
    Jacob Francis (1920-)

Jacob and Ruth

The autobiography of Arnold, *In a Teacup*, appeared in 1989. It tells of a career principally in banking but also of many interests, including an active involvement in farming. The narrative reveals both directly and incidentally much of interest and value concerning family, Bay and Whitby. In WWII he was wounded in the Dunkirk operation when serving with the Green Howards and invalided out of the army. The nautical tradition was maintained with his commodoreship of the Whitby Yacht Club in 1981. Like several forebears he served as Master of the Whitby Lion Lodge of Freemasons.

The Haslop family came to Whitby early in this century when Isaac, who worked for the Missions to Seamen, took over the Whitby Mission. One of his daughters married McKenzie Horne, whose family owned the *Whitby Gazette* and published many valuable works on Whitby and district.

Jennifer May and George Ward: hosts of the Manor House Hotel, Holy Island, Northumberland. Their son, Richard Storm, is a boat-owning fisherman and Coastguard on the island.

William (1742-1800) was the second surviving son of Andrew and Rebecca. (p.143) There is a group of names here highly representative of the village, and also of the fishing. The work took its toll: William was drowned with Michael Granger in 1800 and three of the six sons of Edward and Abiah Granger were lost on their way back from the fishing ground in October, 1810. Only one son of Edward and Abiah had male issue. This was Andrew, grandfather of Dr.Richard Granger, who practised as a surgeon in Bridge Street, Whitby, well within living memory.

ARNOLD (1918-), Bank Manager   m.1947 Grace Margaret Haslop

    PETER MICHAEL (1949-)
    Jennifer Margaret) ch'n. Paul Douglas and Catherine
    =John Douglas Cope)   Margaret

PETER MICHAEL (1949-)   m. 1. Stephanie Cloete of S.Africa
                             2.
    Ellen Margaret (1976-)
    Joseph David (1982-)

Continued from page 155:

THOMAS HARRISON (1876-);   m. Elsie May, dau. of Capt. and
    Northumberland   Mrs Jefferson who with two
                                   of their children were lost
                                   off the Hook of Holland.
    WILLIAM JEFFERSON (-1982)
    Thomas Harrison (1909-)   ch'n. Mrs.Dorothy Gillian
=1941 Dora Edith Beattie   Webster and Mrs.Jennifer
                                   May Ward.
    Rachel (-1992)
    =William Proudlock, Rothbury.

WILLIAM JEFFERSON (-1982),   m. Eileen McQueen
    Land Agent, Northumberland.

    WILLIAM JEFFERSON (1939-)
    Michael Farren (1943-) dau's: Susan Maud (1981-) and
    =Susan Sykes   Rachel Susan (1985-).

WILLIAM JEFFERSON (1939-)   m.1939 Margaret Norman

    Richard Jefferson (1971-)
    Lynda Anne (1972-)

Continued from page 143:

WILLIAM (1742-1800), Fisherman   m.1770 Margaret Skerry, dau. of
                                        Jonathan (householder)
                                        and Dorothy.
    ANDREW (1770-1810), Fisherman and Sailor
    Rebecca died in infancy, 1771
    Dorothy " " "
    Rebecca (1775-1835)
=1799 John Hewinson (1774-1833), Fisherman.
    Mary (1775-1780)
    Abiah (1778-1827)
=1800 Edward Grainger (1775-1864) Fisherman
    Mary (1781-1783)

Jacob and Ruth

The awakening of a seafaring interest appears in the next generation, with Andrew (1770-1810), who is another of those with a varied career in boats and ships. In his family there also appears evidence of the lure of the Whitby whaling industry: his son-in-law John Trueman may have been the "giant of a man, a former harpooner", who taught Jacob of *Leeside* some of the rudiments of seamanship when he was a boy. (p.19)

The *Providence Protector*, a Scarborough-built yawl, was registered, and worked for many years, by William (1801-85) and George Harrison. George Harrison lived up the hill near Old St.Stephen's, and although there is a connection between the Bay Harrisons and those from elsewhere in the parish, the ususal close family link that brought people together in their work is not obvious until the Storm marriages of two of his sons are observed. There was, however, a close vocational link that went further than the sharing of the *Providence Protector*, because George Harrison was handler of fish catches and a carrier.

William's wife, Mercy, was of the *King's Head* household of John and Martha Thompson. Walter White visited the inn in 1858 and recorded the conversation that took place while Martha prepared a meal. In his *A Month in Yorkshire* he wrote of the village, "It is a strange place, with alleys which are stairs for side streets...Everything is on a slope......Some of the shops are curiosities in their appearance and display of wares; yet there are traders in Bay Town who could buy up two or three of your fashionable shopkeepers in the watering places".

William Cubitt came from Bacton on the Norfolk coast. He and Isabella went to Middlesbrough. There were were several children, one of whom was Andrew Storm Cubitt, born at Linthorpe, who had a daughter born at Wood Green, London, in 1905. William Cubitt was lost near Lands End in the steamer *Harriet Shiel* and Isabella was living in Bacton House on Mount Pleasant in 1901. In 1909 she was offering six of its rooms to summer visitors.

William Nellist was the son of the Fylingdales farmer David. He put his seafaring experience to account by founding a marine school at South Shields which achieved some fame particularly among mariners from the North East who prepared for their certificates there. It was known widely simply as "Nellist's". William and Martha's son John taught at the municipal marine school in South Shields, but left to establish the Nellist Nautical College in his house opposite the Town Hall. From about 1924 "Nellist's" operated at Newcastle upon Tyne, in Summerhill Terrace.

The Stubbs were a family of masons in Bay for three generations. The first to arrive was John, who had married Ann Fewster in Hackness parish in 1780. Their great-grandson, Thomas, who married Mary Storm, first made a career at sea, and then came ashore to take over the bakehouse and shop in Bay. Thomas and Mary's son Thomas (1877-1956) was a junior officer of the *Roma* with Capt.William Storm at Galveston in 1900. (p.165) As master he served with the Chapman company of

ANDREW (1770-1810)　　　　　　　　m.1793 Isabella Bedlington,
　　　Fisherman and Sailor　　　　　　　dau. of Thomas and Rebecca

　　　　　Margaret (1794-1848)
=1812　1.George Granger, fishermen
=1820　2.John Trueman, Whaling Harpooner
　　　　　Sarah (1797-1838)
　　　　　WILLIAM (1801-1885), Fisherman

WILLIAM (1801-1885), Fisherman　　　　m.1830 Mercy Thompson
　　　　　　　　　　　　　　　　　　　(1809-1898) dau. of
　　　　　　　　　　　　　　　　　　　Johhn and Martha
　　　　　　　　　　　　　　　　　　　of the King's Head, Bay.

　　　　　ANDREW (1830-1886), M.Mariner
　　　　　JOHN (1832-1919). (p.171)
　　　　　Isabella (1835-)
　　　　　=William Cubitt (-1886), M.Mariner; went to M'bro.
　　　　　Sarah (1838-1936)
　　　　　Martha (1839-)
=1864　William Nellist, M.Mariner, son of David, Farmer, and Mary.
　　　　　Mary Ann died in infancy, 1843.
　　　　　Mary (1850-)　　　　　　) ch'n William, Mary Hannah,
=1872　Thomas Stubbs, M.Mariner)　Thomas, John and Martha

Newcastle and Sir William German of Cardiff. In 1911 he commanded the *Castlegarth* at Tripoli during the Turco-Italian war and when the city was bombarded he took 1,307 refugees to Malta with provisions for 15. Robert Watson Storm (p.141) was a member of his ship's company. In 1924 for the rescue of the crew of the foundering *Ethel M.Barlett* in an Atlantic gale he received inscribed binoculars from the Newfoundland government. His ship was the *Caldy Light*. Ill health brought him ashore in 1929, and a year or two later he bought the Heather Motor Service, of affectionate memory, which under his management operated buses between Fylingthorpe, Bay and Whitby until 1946.

Thomas's sister, Mary Hannah, married Thomas Fewster, and their son was the Andrew Storm Fewster to whose memory a tree in Bay bears a plaque. The Fewsters are an ancient family in Fylingdales. In 1786 John Fewster was concerned with the making up of a road fit for carriages across the moor from Whitby to Scarborough, through Fylingdales. The earlier road had gone via Bay and along the shore, tide permitting, towards Stoupe Brow, where it was dangerously steep.

Capt.W.E.Stubbs, grandson of Thomas and Mary, embarked 1,800 British evacuees in the S.S.*Saltersgate* at Cannes when France fell in 1940. He was awarded the O.B.E. and also received a letter of appreciation from a number of evacuees, one of them being the author Somerset Maugham.

Andrew (1830-86) married the sister of his cousin, childhood companion and occasional shipmate, Jacob of *Leeside*. He was master of the 248-ton brig *Magnet* when she was lost near Sizewell on the Suffolk coast on 27th December, 1886. The date is significant, this being a time of year when formerly the shipping would have been laid up for the winter. The story runs that while relatives were considering how the news should be broken to Damaris she read of the loss in a newspaper, and never fully recovered from the shock.

George Church was another of those who came to Bay in the Coastguard service and stayed there. The sons of George and Mary Ann almost inevitably became sailors. These were Capt.Laurie S.Church and Capt.Alfred Church, O.B.E., who was master of the Bibby liners *Monarch of Bermuda* and *Queen of Bermuda*. He was on troopship service in WWII.

William Leadson Gillings was son of Edward Gillings (1843-1907), M.Mariner, and grandson of the Edward Gillings, Mariner, who was lost in 1843 in the Bay lifeboat when she was returning with the crew of the brig *Ann* and capsized. The wife of the first Edward Gillings was one of the many daughters of William and Elizabeth Robinson of the Bay Mill; another sister married William Leadson who followed at the mill. A son of William Leadson and Fanny Gillings was the late Ronald Storm Gillings of Bay, who served on the Village Trust and made an important photographic record of the place. His nephew, Richard John Gillings, B.A., Canon of Chester, Rural Dean of Birkenhead and sometime member of the General Synod, holds binoculars inscribed , "From the President of the United States to Captain Edward Gillings, Senior of the British S.S.*Ranmoor* in recognition of his humane rescue of the Captain and Crew of the American schooner *Elwood Harlow* February 1895". The American vessel was burdened with ice and foundering in a heavy gale. The father of Canon Richard Gillings is Major John Albert (Jack) Gillings, M.B.E., B.Sc., of Scalby. The Storm Gillings name went into another generation with Heather Storm (Mrs.George Paul), daughter of Gwen and Ronald Storm Gillings, and her sons are Euan Douglas and Alistair Storm.

Capt. William ("Roma Will") Storm of the Galveston tidal wave incident was Chief Officer of the S.S.*Sharon* at the time of his marriage at King's Lynn. He lived at *Lynfield* in Station Road. At Galveston in 1900 his *Roma* was swept inland about a mile, and over three railway bridges. Although 12,000 lives were lost in the disaster the ship's company came through unscathed, but there was a remarkable salvage operation which involved digging a channel back to the sea. The name of the ship was derived from that of her company, Rowland and Marwood. Her Chief Oficer was Thomas Andrew Taylor, son-in-law of the master and son of Hannah Mercy Storm and Charles Taylor, M.Mariner. One of the apprentices aboard her was another relative, William Storm Harrison, who until he was picked up by the company's S.S.*Blue Cross* spent the time burning bodies at five dollars a day.

Thomas Andrew Taylor went to sea at 15, in Whitby vessels. He gained his master's certificate at 23 and spent much of the rest of his thirty years at sea with Cardiff-based ships. In WWI he survived the loss of his ship by enemy action. On leaving the sea he returned to Bay to take over the Victoria Hotel, former guests of which remember his daily ceremony of hoisting the flag in the grounds - a custom of masters of Whitby ships when ashore. His brother-in-law, Richard Knightley Storm, J.P. (known as "Knightley"), was in business nearby at the Central Stores, the "Top Shop"; his daughter Irene has a granddaughter, Catherine Storm Jowett.

ANDREW (1830-1886) M.Mariner   m.1856 Damaris Harrison Storm
                                   (1835-1921) dau. of Andrew
                                   and Rebecca. (p.151)

    WILLIAM (1857-1950), M.Mariner
    Rebecca Harrison (1858-)
    =William Harrison Storm (p133)
    Mary Ann (1862-)
    =George Church, Coastguard
    Thomas Harrison (1863-1887)
    Andrew (1866-1898)
    =Mary Jane Barnard, dau. of John.
    JOHN (1869-), M.Mariner. (p.167)
    Fanny (1871-)
    =William Leadson Gillings, son of Edward, M.Mariner.
    JACOB (1874-). Shopkeeper. (p.167)

WILLIAM (1857-1950), M.Mariner,   m.1882 (at King's Lynn) Hannah
    of Lynfield, Bay   Mary Crosby, dau. of
                                   Stephen, farmer and
                                   butcher, Fylingdales.

    Elizabeth Law
=1907 Thomas Andrew Taylor, M.Mariner and hotel proprietor;
                  chn. William, Mollie, Charles and Gwen.
    William Andrew (1888-93)
    Richard Knightley, J.P. (1891-1955)   )dau. Mrs Irene
=1917 Melita Hutton (1890-1969); born at Bay Mill Watson of Bay

    These occupations emphasise a trend, already illustrated by William Andrew Smith, the postmaster. (p.152) In 1885 the attractive railway line from Whitby to Scarborough over Ravenscar was opened, an opportune development as tourist traffic grew. In November, 1884, a number of Scarborough gentlemen who had heard about the beauty of the new route were allowed by the contractor to view it from open trucks. They took refreshment in Bay, at Mrs.Crosby's *New Inn*, and expressed breathless admiration of the scenery through which they had passed. This was reported by the *Whitby Gazette*, which in the next year observed that the village was set to make its fortune. Seasonal increase of a population already substantial was good for local businesses and brought others into being. Many were in the hands of people who would once have become sailors, and aspired to hold shares in ships. John Storm (1869-1960), brother of "Roma Will", abandoned a seafaring career - at the insistence it is said of his fiancee - to run the post office and shop at Thorpe, and his brother Jacob had the "Bottom Shop" down Bay Bank; the *King's Head* became a temperance hotel, presided over by a brother-in-law, George Church. The estate agent was Jacob Bedlington and Matthew Bedlington had the local pharmacy. As has already been noticed (e.g. on p.162), more business still was done by many of the wives of steamer masters, who used their homes as seasonal guest houses. These were often remarkably spacious, according to their advertisements. The parents of the future Prime Minister, Sir Harold Wilson, for several years hired rooms from the Thorpe Storms for their annual holiday. Mr.Wilson wrote many years later, recalling days at Bay and how much the family had enjoyed them.

Andrew Storm (1902-1990) continued with the family business at Thorpe, and was also Inspector in the North Riding Special Constabulary. His brother, William, resumed the connection with the sea and was lost in WWII, when he was master of the S.S.*Widestone*. She was bound from Milford Haven to Newfoundland in convoy, with coal. An explosion was heard by the convoy during the night of 6th November, 1942, and in the morning the *Widestone* was not to be seen. There had been no signs of submarines and there were no survivors.

Michael John: formerly a Staff Inspector with the Inner London Education Authority; President of the Geographical Association, 1988-90; member of the Government Working Group for Geography in the National Curriculum; author and lecturer on educational affairs.

The Mills connection goes back to 1798, but the family was in Fylingdales over a century before that. Capt.J.W.Mills initially worked for his father Isaac, M.Mariner. His grandfather, Isaac, of Nook House, was a man of property in Bay as well as a shipowner. J.W.Mills went into Turnbull steamers at Whitby as boatswain, and stayed with the company for twenty years as master and nearly as long as Superintendent. He was awarded the O.B.E. fpr services to shipping in 1942. His son Isaac was Chief Officer of the *Stonegate* which was captured and sunk by the *Deutschland* in the Atlantic in October, 1939. The *Stonegate's* master, Captain F.G.Randall of Bay, and his crew, were well treated by the German commander, Captain Wenneked, and eventually put ashore at the Norwegian port of Tromso. J.W.Mills' uncle, John Mills, M.Mariner, was the builder of Nookfield House at Bay.

Continued from page 165:

JOHN (1869-1960), Mariner and   m.Sarah Elizabeth Storm, dau.
     Shopkeeper, Fylingthorpe   of Edward and Jane. (p.121)

     Edward
     WILLIAM (-1942), M.Mariner
     Andrew (1902 -1990)
     =Gladys Mary Stevenson
     John
     =Ella Burnett
     Lillian   daughters: Deirdre Storm (-1976),
=1925   Sidney Herbert Mills Teacher; Pamela Wray (Mrs.Beeforth of
                               Middlewood Farm, Fylingdales);
                               Delphine Gillian, S.R.N. (trained at
                               Royal Victoria Infirmary, Newcastle).

WILLIAM (-1942), M.Mariner,   m.Nora Taylor (-1982)
     Hull

     Shirley (1932-
     =   Abbott) Lancashire
     MICHAEL JOHN, B.A. (1935-), Inspector of Schools

MICHAEL JOHN, B.A. (1935-)   m.Jacqueline Newham, Schoolteacher
     Inspector of Schools;
        Berkshire

     Helen Elizabeth (1956-)   dau's Laura Frances Storm and
     =Michael Rigby   Grace Helen Storm; Gloucs.
     JOHN WILLIAM (1959-
     ANDREW JAMES (1962-

JOHN WILLIAM (1959-)   m.1987 Valerie Hamilton

     Anna Elizabeth (1989-)
     Thomas Michael (1991-)

ANDREW JAMES ((1962-)   m.1987 Denise Ridgley

     James Andrew (1991-)

Continued from page 165:

JACOB (1874-),   m. Mary Jane, widow of brother Andrew (p.165)
     Shopkeeper, Bay

     (Andrew (-1982)   )
     (1.Marjorie, dau. of Capt.J.W.Mills, O.B.E.) dau. Helen
     (2.
     John, living at Scarborough in 1982

Jacob and Ruth

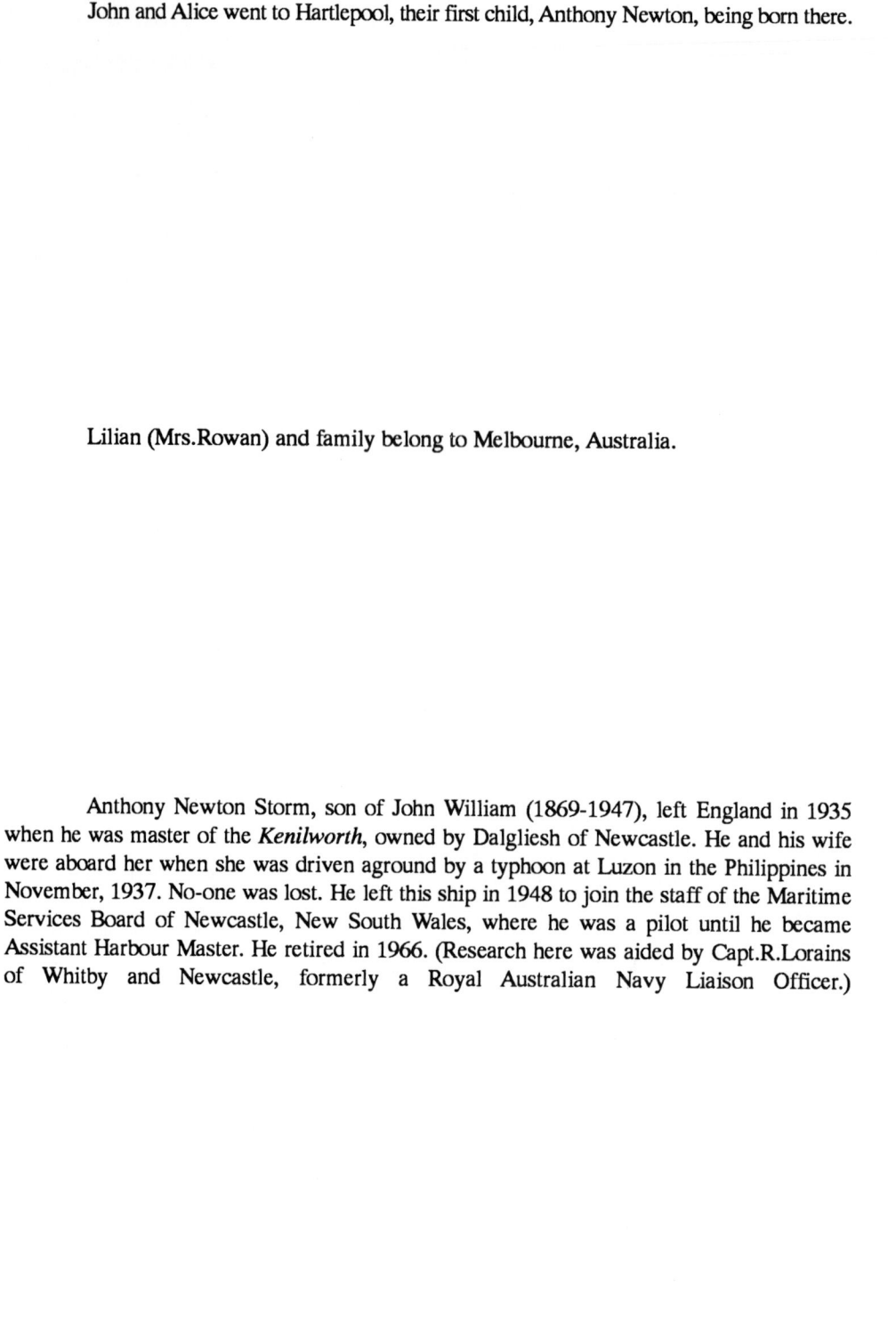

John and Alice went to Hartlepool, their first child, Anthony Newton, being born there.

Lilian (Mrs.Rowan) and family belong to Melbourne, Australia.

Anthony Newton Storm, son of John William (1869-1947), left England in 1935 when he was master of the *Kenilworth*, owned by Dalgliesh of Newcastle. He and his wife were aboard her when she was driven aground by a typhoon at Luzon in the Philippines in November, 1937. No-one was lost. He left this ship in 1948 to join the staff of the Maritime Services Board of Newcastle, New South Wales, where he was a pilot until he became Assistant Harbour Master. He retired in 1966. (Research here was aided by Capt.R.Lorains of Whitby and Newcastle, formerly a Royal Australian Navy Liaison Officer.)

Continued from page 163:

JOHN (1832-1919), M.Mariner   m.1858 Alice, dau. of Anthony Moody
    Hartlepool   Newton, M.Mariner, and
     Alice, nee Estill.

    ANTHONY NEWTON (c.1860-1898)
    JOHN WILLIAM (1869-1947). M.Mariner
    Mary Alice   children John, Eliza, Mary,
    =James Needham, coal exporter   Miriam and James.
    Rachel Crosby

ANTHONY NEWTON (c.1860-1898),   m. Ada Patterson
    M.Mariner; Hartlepool

    Lilian   ch'n James, Mary, Ursula
    =J.S.Rowan, Barrister-at-law and   John Adrian; Australia.

JOHN WILLIAM (1869-1947), M.Mariner   m.Kate Sweeney (1874-1914)
    Hartlepool

    ANTHONY NEWTON, M.Mariner
    Kathleen
    John

ANTHONY NEWTON, M.Mariner, Pilot,   m. Maisie Ellis of West
    and Assistant Harbour Master   Hartlepool
    at Newcastle, N.S.W.

    Ingrid

John may have made a second marriage, to Mary Sharp of Egton, in 1740. A Mary Storm died in 1761 in Fylingdales.

Matthew (1705-42) was taken by the press-gang before his son William was baptised, and probably before he was born. He was taken ill aboard H.M.S.*Marlborough* and transferred to the Gibraltar hospital where he was entered "D.D." (1.e. discharged dead) in 1742. Elizabeth, his kinswoman and widow married John Peacock, sometime master of the *Brotherly Love* of Whitby.

CHAPTER 7:

Matthew and Martha

This branch has come to be identified by the names of the couple about whom most is known, and who are indeed highly representative of the community's way of life, an attachment to Congregationalism being one aspect of this. Matthew is particularly notable in that although a fisherman he made the transition to shipowner. He was the great-grandson of John whose household appears first, and intermarriage made him also the great-grandson of Francis and Jane. (p.83).

JOHN (c.1670-1742), Householder and Fisherman   m.Jane Moorsom (1674-1739), dau. of Robert and Elisse

       Robert (1695-1717)
       Ellis (1697-1724)
       Martin (1702-20)
       MATTHEW (1705-44). Sailor; pressed into Royal Navy.
       Jane (1708-)
=1738   Robert Conn
       Anne (1711-1719)
       JACOB (1712-1742), Mariner. (p.177)
       Isaac (1716-1749), Householder   daughters Ann and Mary
=1734   Hilda Archer   baptised in 1735; Ann
                                died in 1737.
       Robert (1721-1731)
       JOHN (1700-1737), Fisherman. (p.177)

MATTHEW (1705-1744), Sailor   m.1732 Elizabeth Storm (1711-1776), dau. of Francis and Jane. (p.83)

       Robert died in infancy, 1733
       Ann (1734-1795)
= 1783   Philemon Montague, M.Mariner
       Jane (1737-)
       Isaac died in infancy, 1739.
       Matthew (1740-)
       WILLIAM (1743-1824), Fisherman

Matthew and Martha

The parentage of William and Ann illustrates how complex local relationships were: each had a Matthew Storm and an Elizabeth Storm for father and mother. There is a nucleus of seafaring and shipowning people in their household. Sampson Thompson, Robert Richardson, John Pearson and William Todd were among the owners of the fleet - mainly brigantines of about 90 tons - coming into being at the beginning of the nineteenth century. Customs work brought Hezekiah Godden to Bay: his surname is usually found in Kent, Rye being one relevant location. He stayed on to join local men in shipowning ventures which led eventually to the purchase of the new brig *Goddens* from a South Shields yard in 1841. His partner was his son-in-law, James Steel. The son of Elizabeth and Hezekiah went farming, but the grandson - the third Hezekiah - was lost in the brig *Maria* of which he was master. This was in a great storm in March, 1874, one remembered by Jacob Storm as having given him "a rough three days" in his favourite, the *Black Prince*.

Matthew and Martha achieved the change from fishing to shipowning, with the co-operation of seafaring sons. In the year of their marriage they were paying a token rent of a shilling a year for one of the ancient 1,000-year freeholds. Martha was the daughter of the Fylingdales farmer William Coulthirst (or "Coultas"), and a brother, William, was a master mariner, commander of the transport *Majestic* in 1807, in which year he wrote from Funchal making Martha his executrix and telling her to see the alum works manager John Ridley (of *Plantation House*, the future Fylingdales vicarage) if she needed advice. He also enquired whether another transport master, Israel Allison of Bay, and his son, were still prisoners-of-war. Within a year Capt.William Coultas had died of fever in the West Indies. The war was long over when Matthew and Martha became shipowners, and it is only through the distinctive name of Coultas Storm in the Whitby shipping register that the direction of their aspirations is first detectable. In 1826 he and his brother William became the young owners of the brig *Mary*, initiating yet another "Matthew Storm and Co.". (p.122) This concern owned six or seven vessels much of the time over the next forty-odd years.

In 1840 a purchase that should have given much pleasure was a new vessel from Sunderland named after Matthew's parents, *William and Ann*, but the same year brought the loss of Andrew with all his crew, and the drowning of William in The Halfway Reach of the Thames. William's body was brought back to Bay for burial. These events give much poignancy to the sampler worked by their sister Martha, The other surviving sister, Ann, married a shipmaster, Thomas Harrison, brother of the local fish merchant and only remotely connected to the Bay Harrisons.

The young Martha married Thomas Phillips, the Congregational minister who came to Bay from Chepstow via the Pickering seminary, and gave thirty-two years of remarkable service to the community. The Congregational Church in Fisherhead, and the Congregational Hall, provided another focus for community life, along with the Methodist Chapel. These alternatives to the remotely-situated St.Stephen's were to be a challenge to the new parish priest, the Rev.Robert Jermyn Cooper, a little man of great authority and abiding influence who arrived in 1859 and responded to the situation with the building of the new St.Stephen's nearer the main centres of population within eleven years. Through Martha, Thomas Phillips became a joint owner of the *Nymph* with his brother-in-law, Edward, and when sail declined he made himself familiar with the law, to help those around him who stood to lose much money. This interest may have infuenced the choice of profession of his son, Thomas Louis, the solicitor who acted for Jacob Storm in the purchase of the site of *Leeside*. An obituary of the Rev.Thomas Phillips descibed him as "a

WILLIAM (1743-1824), Master Fisherman   m.1767 Ann Storm (1745-1829),
                                                              dau. of Matthew and
                                                              Elizabeth (p.113)

        Elizabeth (1768-78)
        Margaret (1770-1826)
1=1792   Sampson Thompson, Innkeeper and Parish Clerk
2=1802   Robert Richardson, M.Mariner
3=1816   John Pearson, Mariner
        Ann (1772-1856)
=1792   William Todd, M.Mariner
        Mercy (1774-1782)
        Isabella (1776-)
        MATTHEW (1778-1861), Fisherman, Shipowner and Householder.
        Elizabeth (1781-after 1832), Shipowner
=1804   Hezekiah Godden, Shipowner, formerly of H.M.Customs.
        Mercy (1786-1880), Shipowner
=1812   Thomas Harrison, Fisherman and Shipowner

MATTHEW (1778-1861), Fisherman,   m.1799 Martha Coulthirst
    Shipowner and Householder   (1778-1848), dau. of
                                                              William, Farmer, and Ann.

        Ann died in infancy, 1800
        William (1801-1840), M.Mariner and Shipowner
        COULTAS (1804-1871), M.Mariner and Shipowner
        Matthew (1804-)
        Ann (1805-7)
        Ann (1808-1883)
      =Thomas Harrison, M.Mariner and Shipowner
        ANDREW (1810-1840), M.Mariner and Shipowner. (p.175)
        Edward   (1813-1816)
        EDWARD   (1817-1980), M.Mariner and Shipowner. (p.177)
        Martha   (1822-1903)   son Thomas Louis Phillips,
      =Rev.Thomas Phillips (1822-1880) Solicitor, and two other children.

favourite at Yorkshire gatherings". His granddaughter, Nan Phillips, was an Elder of the United Reformed Church and spent 38 years of retirement involved in the life of the village until her death at 93 in 1981.

Esther Skerry was the daughter of the master mariner and shipowner Jonathan, who lived in Bloomswell. His son James continued in the same line, having four or five vessels. One of them, the brig *Crown*, was commanded by Jonathan Skerry Storm. Coultas bought the brig *Ocean*, took over the family's *Nymph* and employed his sons Jonathan Skerry and William Coultas as masters of the two vessels. A visitor to Bay in 1904 wrote in the Whitby Gazette of a meeting with William Coultas' widow Mercy, who lived in the villa *Norcliffe* on Mount Pleasant, surrounded by souvenirs of voyages with her husband, but reconciled at last to finding contentment in the mowing of a lawn. A valued possession was a painting of the *Nymph*. Her brother-in-law had taken the vessel away in August, 1871, encountered bad weather as he approached the Baltic and been washed overboard in the Kattegat. The *Nymph* was driven on to the Paternoster Rocks on the Swedish coast, but the crew got away. This was the family said to have been in the mind of Mary Linskill, the Whitby novelist, when she wrote *Between the Heather and the Northern Sea*.

The Edward Harrison, M.Mariner, that Coultas' daughter Esther married, was one of the five Harrison brothers in shipowning business with their parents, Thomas and Mercy. A son of the family was Jonathan Skerry Harrison, Chief Officer of the Whitby S.S.*Daisy* when she was lying at Santander in April. 1881.

Andrew's vessel foundered off Lands End in a violent storm. Bodies were washed ashore, among them that of Andrew, who was buried at Redruth.

COULTAS (1804-71), M.Mariner and　　　　m.1828 Esther Skerry,
　　　　　　Shipowner　　　　　　　　　　dau. of Jonathan and Mary;
　　　　　　　　　　　　　　　　　　　　　　1837 Jane Keld

　　　　Matthew died in infancy
　　　　JONATHAN SKERRY (1830-1871), M.Mariner
　　　　Esther Skerry
=1858　Edward Harrison, M.Mariner, son of Thomas and Mercy nee Storm)
　　　　William Coultas (1835-1873), Mariner
　　　　=Mercy Hall, widow, nee Harrison, dau, John, M.Mariner
　　　　Sarah
　　　　=James Houghton, M.Mariner
　　　　Andrew (1840-1911)
　　　　Elizabeth Ann (1845-1848)

JONATHAN SKERRY (1830-1871),　　　　m.1854 Rachel Robinson, (1830-
　　　　M.Mariner　　　　　　　　　　　　1894), dau. of Robert,
　　　　　　　　　　　　　　　　　　　　　M.Mariner and Innkeeper (Mason's
　　　　　　　　　　　　　　　　　　　　　Arms) and Rachel, nee Emmerson.

　　　　Esther Skerry (1856-)
　　　　James Skerry (1860-)

Continued from page 173:

ANDREW (1810-1840), M.Mariner and　　　m.1832 at WhitbyElizabeth
　　　　Shipowner　　　　　　　　　　　　Mills, dau.of Isaac
　　　　　　　　　　　　　　　　　　　　　(M.Mariner and Ship-
　　　　　　　　　　　　　　　　　　　　　owner) and Grace.

　　　　Martha (1836-
　　　　=Richard Herbert
　　　　WILLIAM GRANGER (1837-), Innkeeper
　　　　Andrew (1839-1840)

WILLIAM GRANGER (1837-)　　　　　　m. Jane Coverdale (-1917)
　　　　Innkeeper, Hartlepool

　　　　Margaret Ann　　　dau. Jane
　　　　=Harry Allison Unthank
　　　　Jane Robinson (1873-)
　　　　= .... Broxson
　　　　William (1879-1926)
　　　　Hannah Eliza
　　　　= ...... Bolland or Bollen
　　　　Mary Elizabeth
　　　　=

Matthew and Martha

When Edward (1817-1908) was a boy of 14 he tried the notorious brew prepared by "Auld Stormy" in Langentry (p.106) and vowed never to take strong drink again. Nearly sixty years later his support was recorded in the *Whitby Gazette* for a movement to close public houses in Bay on Sundays. An account of a voyage in a brig owned by Edward illustrates the hazards of Baltic trade. She was the *Northumberland*. In April, 1871, she met drift ice in the Baltic on approaching the Gulf of Finland. The following evening she got into a mass of ice off Hango in Estonia and the bow was damaged. Despite pumping she filled and the crew got the boat away just before she sank, and had to pull ten miles through the ice to reach Hango harbour.

In 1871 Edward was living in Belmont Place at Bay, and already said to be retired. He was one who saw the future in shipping more clearly than many and had begun to invest in steam. In 1880 Edward and John Rowland were two of four representatives of majority shareholders on a committee which enquired into the management of Thomas Turnbull and Sons' Whitby fleet. Thomas Turnbull emerged with credit from this, and John Rowland went on to prominence in Whitby shipowning. Very unusually for one of his name Edward settled in Fylingthorpe, where he lived at Gordon House. He died at the age of 91 in 1908. In the following year his widow was advertising to prospective summer visitors the eight-roomed Gordon House with "good sea view" and without attendance.

A Methodist interest is discernable in Edward's family: the eldest daughter, Margaret, was baptised at the Whitby Wesleyan Chapel, and the name of her husband, Egan Harmston, appears on a foundation stone of the Wesley Hall in Church Street.

Another daughter, Martha Charlotte ("Pattie"), married Thomas Watson of Lythe who has been designated by those more familiar with F.M.Sutcliffe's work as "Whitby's other photographer". After studying photography in London Thomas Watson travelled the world for some years with his camera, until about the time a daughter, Mary, was born, in 1904. Pattie died in 1940, after which Thomas lived with Mary. A booklet about his career was published before his death in 1957, and a brochure was produced to accompany an exhibition of his work in Whitby in 1980.

Jacob married at Sunderland, on which occasion both he and Eleanor were said to be of that place. However, when Jacob was lost at sea in 1742 he was "late of Robin Hood's Bay".

Continued from page 173:

EDWARD (1817-1908), M.Mariner   m.(1) Margaret Bouge, Hartlepool.
   and Shipowner; Bay and   (2) Mary Jane (c.1836-1915)
       Fylingthorpe.   born at Cockermouth,
                                                 Cumbria.

   Margaret
   =James Egan Harmston, Draper, Whitby.
   Edward
   Mary Isabella

   Martha Charlotte (c.1870-)   ) chn. Mary and William
   =Thomas Watson of Lythe, Photographer)   Edward.
   Elizabeth Ann (c.1873-), Schoolteacher, known to have died
                        at Lythe at a great age.
   =Robert Williamson, Builder and Local Preacher.
     EDWARD (c.1875-c.1962)

EDWARD (c.1875-c.1962)   m. Edith Daniels of Newcastle upon Tyne

       Edward Egan Storm (-1984), who lived at Bristol and
                         Pinner, Middx.; Aircraft
                         Engineer at the Bristol
                         Aircraft Company, Filton..

Continued from page 171:

JACOB (1712-1742), Mariner   m,1732 Eleanor Hodgson at Sunderland

       John (1734-)
       Mary (1736-before 1740)
       Elizabeth (1738-)
       Mary (1740-)

Continued from page 171:

JOHN (1700-37), Fisherman   m.1726 Susannah Ridley (-1737)

       Elizabeth (1728-30)
       John (1729-)
       Elizabeth (c.1731-1735)
       Damaris (1731-)
       Jane (1733-)
       Ruth (1735-)
       Hannah (1736-)

The Allisons and the Huntrods were Whitby Abbey tenants in the sixteenth century in Fylingdales. Postgates appear early in the next century and Prodams a little later. Dowslands - confusable with Dowsons - were present before the century's end. These three are only a few of the names new to the parish which suggest, along with increasing numbers of entries in the register, that Fylingdales was attracting population.

S.S. ROMA which survived the Galveston tidal-wave disaster of 1900, despite being swept more than mile inland, and earned her master, William Storm of *Lynfield*, the nickname 'Roma Will'.

QUEEN OF BERMUDA commanded by Captain Alfred Church, OBE, grandson of Andrew Storm (1830-86) and Damaris.

CHAPTER 8:

Mainly Edwards

This part of the family begins properly with Edward who married Frances Allison in 1668, but the possible earlier start shown here is suggested by the popularity of "Edward" down to George John Edward (-1944). To this the title of both branch and chapter is due.

The familiar phases of the economy occur, to the extent that the continuing interest in the sea and shipping would seem to contradict the statement made in the introduction to Part 2 that this branch would introduce a break with tradition. It is after several generations that one of the Edwards makes a career in the Royal Navy, to be followed by sons, and for most of Robin Hood's Bay families this is unusual. The circumstance serves to underline the great extent to which the village was essentially one of merchant sailors.

ROBERT   m.1606 Ellena Postgate

    EDWARD (1606-)

EDWARD (1606-) m.1638 Agneta

    Hellena (1639-)
    EDWARD ?

EDWARD (-1702)   m.(1) 1668 Frances Allison
                                          (2) 1677 Ruth Dowsland

    Elizabeth (1669-)
    Anna (1672-)
    An infant died in 1677
    EDWARD (1678-1733)

Mainly Edwards

There are Richardsons in the earliest Bay records. In 1563 two were occupying cottages, and another held land which went with a cottage. Marriages with the familiar Bay names were numerous.

Robert Richardson was one of the village's early shipmasters. He is mentioned in 1734 as the seller for £134 of one of the 1,000-year leases - one that had already run for a hundred years in the family. He and Frances went to Sunderland. The Bay property is interesting because since the inception of the lease a house had been built in the garden. This was one way in which Bay acquired its compact appearance and complex street plan. Frances and Robert Richardson's son Robert followed his father's profession, as did grandson John who with Andrew Harrison, Matthew Storm and William Allison appears in a list of prisoners-of-war from Bay in the fortress of Verdun in 1811.

Frances' second husband Joseph Wright owned a vessel jointly with his brother John, and named it after their parents, *Peter and Ann*. Joseph also owned the *Company* and their elder brother Matthew had the *Brotherly Love*.

Robert Richardson was lost in Tees Bay in a heavy storm. A son, Robert (1739-1800), M.Mariner, became a shipowner in Sunderland, to which town Frances had taken him back after her remarriage. He married Isabella, daughter and heiress of Gerard Atmar, an innkeeper and man of property. The uncommon name used to be commemorated by "Atmar's Stairs", later Youll's Passage, off the High Street in Sunderland. A son, Gerard Atmar Richardson, is traceable to Plantation Enterprise in Demerara; he died in 1828, and his granddaughter, Barbara Cecily Fanning, married Lord Vivian.

Frances' sons by Joseph were Joseph and John, who became attorneys in Sunderland. Charles, John Joseph and John Wright, solicitors in the Sunderland area, and Henry Broughton Wright of Seaham Harbour, of the same profession, were all of Frances and Joseph's line. In 1856 J.J. and G.W.Wright were solicitors to the Sunderland Improvement Commissioners and the Sunderland Dock Company, and John Joseph was a Deputy Lieutenant of Durham County. The Bay connection was not severed: in 1800 Edward Richardson, M.Mariner, was loading in Sunderland, and in a letter to his wife he mentioned taking the opportunity to consult Mr.Wright about the property of their son William who had died in the Navy at Jamaica. (p.14)

Edward (1705-68) seems to have traded occasionally: in 1766 he sailed from Whitby in the *John and Isabella* with ten spruce deals for Sunderland. He may have returned with coal for the alum works. Two of his children had connections, direct or indirect, with the industry: his son Edward was master of the sloop *Heckington* owned by John Ridley, alum-works manager, who had oversight of production at both Brow and Peak, and his daughter, Isobel Knaggs by her second marriage, had a child of the same name who married John Ridley in 1783. The Knaggs' raising and selling of beef went well with the provisioning of local vessels, many of which served the alum works.

EDWARD (1678-1733) m.1702 Elizabeth Huntrods (1664-1705), dau.
    Master Fisherman   of Edward and Jane.
                          2nd 1705 Ann Prodam (1670-), dau. of
                                    Thomas and Anne

         EDWARD (1705-68)
         Jane (1707-1749)
=1732   Thomas Richardson (1706-54), Householder.
         JAMES (1708-c.1762), Master Fisherman
         ISAAC (1712-1756). (p.185)
         Frances (1713-98)
=1737   Robert Richardson (1714-39), M.Mariner: a son, Robert.
=1750   Joseph Wright (1721-88), M.Mariner and Shipowner.
         Ann (1713-19)

EDWARD (1705-68), Master   m.1731 Margaret Huntrods (1703-74),
    Fisherman   dau. of Thomas and Elizabeth.
         Isabel (1733-1796)
=1754   1.Michael Richardson (1725-1754), Householder, son of John,
                                                    Householder.
=1757   2.John Knaggs (1736-1813), Farmer and Butcher
         Elizabeth (1735-1818)
         Edward (1738-after1808), M.Mariner
         Thomas (1743-)
         Margaret (1746-)

Mainly Edwards

James (1708-62), who lived in Fisherhead like most of the boat-owners, was Overseer of the Poor of the parish in 1755. This is worth noting because parish office was seldom held by members of seafaring and fishing families, presumably because they were too frequently and too long absent to be able to perform the duties. Something has already been seen of the Skerry and Storm connections of his children (pp.103 and 107), but there were other interesting links within the community.

Edward and Thomas Granger who married James' daughters Mary and Jane were brothers. Thomas and Jane were the grandparents of Benjamin Granger, who was a co-founder of the second of Bay's two shipping insurance associations, founded when shipping was booming in the middle of the nineteenth century. Jacob of *Leeside* said of him that he was "too well known for words of mine".

Elizabeth (1741-95) lost her first husband when his ship went down. There was a son, Andrew, who owned the brigantine *Gorleston* in the early years of the eighteenth century, when the shipping began to show signs of increase. His son went to Bishopwearmouth and had money in ships, and it was a descendant, Captain Squance, formerly of the P. & O. Line, who founded the Hindoostan Shipping Company of Sunderland in 1893 with F.J.Common, son of a banker in the town. This concern was absorbed eventually into Common Bros., a familiar name in Tyne shipping, and associated with oil tankers.

Elizabeth's second husband was John Spink, a Riding Officer in the Customs who before posting to Bay had been commended for his work north of Whitby following the murder of a colleague by smugglers. Their son, John, obtained a commission in the army, gave notable service as Colonel of the 12th Foot, became a Knight of Hanover and rose to the rank of General. He died in 1877 at the age of 94. His half-brother, Marshall Spink, headed the London business Spink and Son, still associated with medals, coins and fine art. His sister Mary married first Daniel Cole, M.Mariner and owner of the brigantine *Dove*, and second Robert Danby, M.Mariner and shipbroker in Cornhill, London. Robert Danby's son, a bank official in London, used to visit Robin Hood's Bay. Another sister, Esther, had a daughter, Elizabeth Prudence, who married Rev.Thomas Jackson, Prebendary of St.Paul's, and their son was Sir Thomas Sturges Jackson, K.C.V.O., the admiral referred to on page 7. A former captain of the battleship *Colossus*, he was "Father" of the Navy at the time of his death at the age of 92 in 1934. Admiral Sir Thomas Jackson, K.C.B., a Director of Intelligence in WWI, was his son. Prebendary Jackson's father was Thomas Jackson, son of a blacksmith and smallholder of Sancton near Market Weighton in the East Riding. Having served his time to carpentry the boy was attracted to Methodism and local preaching, and is said to have preached in the Bay chapel. He became Professor of Divinity at the Richmond Theological College and in 1838-9 was President of the Methodist Conference on the centenary of the founding of the Society by the Wesley brothers.

JAMES (1708-c.1762),   m.1733 Elizabeth Helm (1712-68), dau.
        Master Fisherman   John and Mary

         Mary (1734-1818)
=1755   Edward Granger, Fisherman
         James died in infancy, 1735
         Ann (1736-1815)
=1765   JACOB STORM (1739-1783), Master Fisherman. (p.145)
         John (-1738)
         Robert (1740-)
         Elizabeth (1741-1795)
1 =1762 Andrew Harrison (-1763), M.Mariner
2 =1769 John Spink, H.M.Customs son: General Sir John Spink
         James (1742-)
         Esther (1745-1832)
=1770   Thomas Skerry, Fisherman
=1793   William Moorsom, Master Fisherman
         Jacob (1748-)
         Edward (1750-before 1783)
         Jane (1755-1837)
=1774   Thomas Granger, Fisherman
         Frances (1757-1839)
=1781   WILLIAM STORM (1756-1827), Fisherman, Mariner and
                                           and Shipowner. (p.113)

Mary Storm, widow, appears in the rate books of the parish as occupant between 1751 and 1757 of a house in Cowfield Hill. The tradition is that Edward (1747-84) left home after his mother's remarriage and took her less distinctive maiden name of Hall, perhaps because he was in breach of an apprenticeship agreement. There were twin sons of the second marriage, Reuben and John Granger. Their father was master and owner of the appropriately- named sloop *John and Mary*. Edward became master of the *Empress of Russia* (683 tons) which served as a whaler and a transport, and among the 35 able seamen aboard her was Reuben Granger. Reuben was a seaman aboard the prize *Ville de Paris* which foundered in a hurricane off the West Indies in 1782, when she was carrying French and Spanish prisoners-of-war.

Of Isaac (1745-), Jacob of *Leeside* wrote, "...a descendant of the family says he was a roper, and seeing that his maternal grandfather was a Whitby shipmaster it is probable that he served his time to that business in Whitby. He married and had issue. His daughter Anne Maria left money in trust for her brother and sister which is now in Chancery; the brother could not be found. Anne lived in Whitby until 84 years of age and died unmarried".

Hannah (1750-) married the Stainsacre farmer Robert Nicholson. Their grandson George Rowland was a joiner in Whitby who invested in shipping. His son, John, a grocer and tea dealer in Church Street, Whitby, was co-founder of the Rowland & Marwood's Steamship Co., Ltd., which operated many more vessels as International Lines, Ltd. This branch is represented locally, and has been researched by John Rowland's great-granddaughter, Sophie Weston, G.R.S.M., A.R.C.O. of Tinkler Hall, Ugglebarnby, Whitby, and Giggleswick School.

The runaway Edward (alias Hall) entered the Navy as Master. His ship the *Empress of Russia* was taken into the Navy as H.M.S.*Vigilant*, and burnt in 1779 to keep her from falling into the hands of the American rebels. Edward was for a time Master of Admiral Rodney's flagship in the West Indies. His younger son, George Rodney, is supposed to have had the admiral for a godfather, and a sponsor for entry into the Navy. Edward's last appointment was to Antigua, as Master Intendant of the Dockyard, and he died there of yellow fever. The last entry relating to him in naval records concerns pay of £200 for two years and nine months at Antigua.

Continued from page 181:

ISAAC (1712-1756)　　　　　　　　　m.1742 Mary Hall (dau. of a Whitby
　　Bay and Whitby　　　　　　　　　　　M.Mariner) who married in
　　　　　　　　　　　　　　　　　　　1757 John Granger of Bay
　　　　　　　　　　　　　　　　　　　and had twin sons, Reuben
　　　　　　　　　　　　　　　　　　　　　　and John.

    Ann (1743-)
    Isaac (1745-), Roper in Whitby, with issue.
    EDWARD (1747-84), Master Mariner and Master,R.N.
    Hannah (1750-)
    =Robert Nicholson, Farmer, Stainsacre

EDWARD (1747-84), M.Mariner and　　　m.1776 at New York Christine
　　Master,R.N.　　　　　　　　　　　　Kidd, dau. of John,
　　　　　　　　　　　　　　　　　　　Master of a W.India
　　　　　　　　　　　　　　　　　　　　　　Packet.

    EDWARD (alias Hall) (1777-1860), Captain, R.N.
    George Rodney (1781-1801), Midshipman, R.N.
    John Robert died in infancy, 1783.

Mainly Edwards

The career of Edward (1777-1860) is given at some length in O'Byrne's *Dictionary of Naval Biography*, under the name Hall:

Captain Edward Hall entered the Navy in November 1787, as a boy, onboard the Cygnet sloop, Captain Nicholls, with whom, and with Captain Manley Dixon of the Orestes and Lieut.James Hill of the Pilote he served on the Channel and Irish stations, until January 1789. Re-embarking in August 1793 on board the Juno 32, Capt.Sam Hood, he proceeded to the Mediterranean, and in January 1794 was present in that ship when she effected a remarkable escape from the inner harbour of Toulon, into which she had entered in ignorance of the previous evacuation of the place by the British; in January 1795, after having assisted at the siege of Bastia as a midshipman of the Illustrious 74, Capt.Thos.Lennox Frederick, he became attached to the Berwick 74, Captain Adam Littlejohn, under whom, who fell in the action, he was captured by the French fleet, notwithstanding a brave defence 7 March following. Being soon afterwards, however, returned to liberty, he rejoined Captain Frederick on board the Blenheim 74, and thus had an opportunity of witnessing the evacuation of Corsica, and of sharing, 14 February 1797 in the action off Cape St.Vincent. He removed immediately subsequent to the latter event, to the Victory 100, and Ville de Paris 110, successive flagships of Earl St.Vincent; before he had been long under whom he was appointed 1 May 1797, Acting Lieutenant of the Namur 98, Captain Jas. Hawkins Whitsed, stationed off the port of Cadiz, where he was confirmed on 10 June in the same year, into his former ship, the Victory, Capts.Thos.Sotheby and Wm.Cuming. During the last four years of the French Revolutionary War we find him further employed on the last mentioned, and on the Mediterranean, Channel and West India stations, in the Blenheim and Princess Royal, both flagships of his old Captain, then Rear-Admiral Frederick, and Juste 80, Capts.Sir Henry Trollope, Rich.Dacres and Sir Edm.Nagle. Having spent a few months of the short-lived peace in the Africain 38, commanded in the North Sea by Capt.Thos.Marly, Mr.Hall was subsequently appointed in December 1803, to the charge of a signal station at North Yarmouth - 3rd July, as senior, to the Zebra sloop, Captain Wm.Strandway Parkinson, employed in the Downs - 8 October 1805 to the command of the Speculator lugger, on the same station - 22 May 1806, and 18 October 1807 again as First to the Nassau 64, Capt.Nabert Campbell, and Prince of Wales 98, bearing the flag of Lord Gambier, in the former of which ships (besides commanding her boats, in conjunction with those of the Musquito, at the cutting-out and destruction of several vessels at Ebeltoft, in Jutland) he contributed to the destruction of Copenhagen - 30 Novemer 1807, to the command of the Eijderen, a Danish prize lying in the R.Medway - 20 May 1808, again to the Nassau. Captain R.Campbell, attached to the force in the North Sea - in January 1809, to the impress service at Dundee, where he remained until November 1810 - and 16 April 1811, as First, to the Tremendous 74, commanded by his friend Capt.Campbell, on the Baltic and Channel stations. He obtained a second promoted commission 12 August 1812.

EDWARD (alias Hall) (1777-1860)　　　　　　　　m.1820 Elizabeth
    Captain, R.N.
    Elizabeth Isabel
    EDWARD (1842-77), and numerous daughters; only Edward married.

EDWARD (alias Hall) (1842-1877), Solicitor　　　　m. Maria Cook

    George John Edward (-1944)) No issue
    =　　　　　　　　)
    Lucy Constance
    = ... Richardson

It was one of the *Juno's* midshipmen who raised the alarm and made possible the escape from Toulon referred to in the foregoing passage.

A note by Edward in the log of the *Nassau* on 5th September, 1807, relates to one of the above actions, and includes, "...made the signal for the *Musquito* to go in chase, sent the barge, pinnace, and cutter to cut out six [Danish] vessels in the Harbour of Ebeltoft".

George John Edward (-1944) was a visitor to *Leeside*, and took much interest in his ancestry. He was able to help with research in London at the Public Record Office, because he lived in Surrey. He used the name "Storme" for his grandfather and great-grandfather.

The experience of Robin Hood's Bay raises the broad context of family history, regarding which Sir Anthony Wagner, author of *English Genealogy*, has said:

"Since the total number of the ancestors of each of us doubles in each generation we go back (save as modified by the marriage of cousins), most ancestries, if they could be carried back on all lines for eight or ten generations, would probably traverse a surprisingly wide social range. The exceptions would be the endogamous groups.....the dwellers in the lonely valleys and the far-off settlements.....and even these closed communities are far from being genetically watertight".

Robin Hood's Bay was not "genetically watertight", but although a wide social range is to be found if it is sought outside, the community was to a notable extent self-contained and equalitarian for much of its history. A most remarkable circumstance, however, is that despite its outstanding record of seafaring, and enterprise in sail, the description "fishing village" has always been applied to it. No doubt this is an aspect of its isolation: people came to look, and saw fisherman about the shore, and knew nothing of the scores of men in faraway places and the shareholders and partners in the houses, cottages and inns carefully keeping simple accounts of the vessels in which their kin were serving. The uncovering of the misapprehension repays the investigation.

Another incongruity is that while there is repeated evidence of an interest in Nonconformity, and behind the mechanism of kinship and partnership more than a hint of the earnest endeavour associated with it, there was also an involvement in smuggling. For all that much can be discovered about it, the village remains an enigmatic place.

Narrowing the view to that of the family, several features have been remarked upon, but two seem to be outstanding. There is the obvious unusual record of intense involvement with the sea, and the other is the example provided of a whole collaborative community being characterised by its inner "core", to the extent that Storm and Robin Hood's Bay might be deemed almost synonomous.

APPENDIX 1

THE 1865 LIST OF THE ROBIN HOOD'S BAY SHIP INSURANCE ASSOCIATION

ROBIN HOOD'S BAY INSURANCE ASSOCIATION.
1865.
M. BEDLINGTON, Jun., Secretary.

No.	Owners.	Ships.	Masters.	Abode.	Value.	Sums Insured.	Tons.
1	James Skerry	Attaliah	James Storm	R. H. Bay	1200	800	197
2	Ditto	Sarah Margaret	— Brown	ditto	1600	700	214
3	Ditto	Crown	J. S. Storm	ditto	1400	800	212
4	Ditto	Eltham	Joseph Steele	ditto	1300	600	224
5	Ditto	Lady Stanley	Isaac Harrison	ditto	2200	700	333
6	James Baxter & Co.	Areta	James Baxter	ditto	1200	800	210
7	John H. Storm & Co.	Princess	John Parkes	ditto	1000	600	169
8	Ditto	Brazilian Packet	A. Orwell	ditto	1200	800	185
9	Ditto	Isabella	Richard Pinkney	ditto	500	500	105
10	John H. Storm	Rienzi	A. Allen	ditto	1400	600	188
11	Ditto	Donna	— Parkes	ditto	1600	800	226
12	Matthew Storm & Co.	Rebecca	Wm. Bedlington	ditto	1400	400	180
13	Ditto	Victor	James Arlington	ditto	1300	700	208
14	Ditto	Prince of Saxe Coburg	Reuben Storm	ditto	1000	700	163
15	Ditto	William	— Johnson	ditto	1600	500	234
16	Ditto	Ethel	William Steel	ditto	1400	500	191
17	Ditto	Runo	Robert Johnson	ditto	1300	700	192
18	Ditto	Eliza Ann	William Storm	ditto	1200	500	212
19	William Steel & Co.	Kezia	John Steel	ditto	1200	400	184
20	Wm. Bedlington & Co.	Ariadne	Matthew Storm	ditto	1000	300	154
21	Mary Moorsom	Welcome	Granger Moorsom	ditto	1200	700	202
22	M. Bedlington & Co.	Peace	John Pinkney	ditto	1000	600	157
23	Ditto	Ami	Jacob Bedlington	ditto	1100	600	163
24	Ditto	John & Jane	John Bedlington	ditto	1400	600	187
25	Ditto	Maria	John Storm	ditto	1300	700	196
26	Ditto	Ellen	Thomas Smith	ditto	1200	600	183
27	M. Bedlington, jun. & Co	Eleanor	William Harrison	ditto	1000	600	150
28	John Mills	Clara Jane	John Mills	ditto	1000	600	155
29	Isaac Mills & Co.	Frances Ann	Francis Harrison	ditto	1000	600	224
30	Ditto	Alexander	William Levitt	ditto	1200	800	212
31	John Mennell	Tanner	John Mennell, jun.	ditto	1300	800	195
32	Ditto	Eleanor	George Mennell	ditto	1400	800	233
33	I. Shadforth & Co.	Porcia	Isaac Shadforth	ditto	700	700	136
34	Mercy Harrison & Sons	Harrisons	James Harrison	ditto	700	700	116
35	Ditto	Fortitude	Storm	ditto	500	500	107
36	Ditto	Arica	Wm. Harrison	ditto	1200	800	184
37	Ditto	North of Scotland	Edward Harrison	ditto	1300	600	250
38	Ditto	Spectator	Thos. Harrison	ditto	1600	600	295
39	John Harrison	Daring	John Harrison	ditto	1000	600	151
40	Andrew Storm	Coquette	Storm	ditto	1000	600	169
41	Fanny Coggin	John Coggin	George Pinkney	ditto	1100	700	154
42	Nathan Hewson	Doune Castle	Thomas Avery	ditto	800	800	156
43	Ditto	Amelia	Nathan Hewson	ditto	1200	800	185
44	Executors Thos. Coggin.	Emily	J. Mills	ditto	1700	500	219
45	Coultous Storm & Co.	Nymph	Wm. Coultous Storm	ditto	1200	800	186
46	Coultous Storm	Ocean	A. Storm	ditto	1200	700	211
47	Edward Storm & Co.	Northumberland	Andrew Storm	ditto	1300	700	196
48	Edward Storm	Leda	— Storm	ditto	1000	500	202
49	Matthew Peacock	Voyager	Matthew Peacock, jun.	ditto	1300	700	223
50	Ditto	Orion	Peacock	ditto	1200	600	186
51	John Hoggarth	George	John Hoggarth	ditto	1000	500	175
52	Jane Sedman	Britannia	James Hunter	ditto	600	200	119
53	Edward Bedlington	Ann	Edward Bedlington	ditto	1000	600	154
54	Harrison Allison & Co.	Medora	— Marshall	ditto	1100	500	211

55	Ditto	Garland	Edw. Bedlington, jun.	ditto	1200	700	194
56	H. Gibson & Co.	Iddo	Hansel Gibson	ditto	1100	600	183
57	George Russell & Co.	Beeswing	Wm. Allen	ditto	1000	600	163
58	Ditto	John & Isabella	John Sayers	ditto	1250	650	241
59	Ditto	Bounty	James Hall	ditto	1150	550	168
60	Hannah Barnard	Raisbeck	John Barnard	ditto	1100	550	209
61	Smith Stainthorp	Derwent	William Estill	ditto	1200	600	196
62	Ditto	Isabella	John Storm	ditto	900	450	138
63	Ditto	Mermaid	Smith Stainthorp	ditto	1200	600	198
64	Ditto	Jean	Joseph Benn	ditto	800	300	196
65	Wm. Butterwick & Co.	Providence	Richard Butterwick	ditto	1000	500	158
66	Ditto	Jane White	William Butterwick	ditto	1200	600	186
67	William Baxter	Mary & Agnes	— Witten	ditto	1000	400	164
68	Ditto	Comet	— Witten	ditto	1100	400	200
69	Wm. Todd	Liberty	William Burgess	ditto	1200	400	182
70	Wm. Todd & Co.	Victoria	Zebulon Hodgson	ditto	1000	500	225
71	Matthew Todd	Ark	Matthew Todd	ditto	700	300	142
72	William Todd, jun.,	Rosa	James Todd	ditto	1200	600	213
73	Marshall Granger	Isabella Granger	Marshall Granger	ditto	900	500	145
74	Zachariah Granger	Silistria	Robert Granger	ditto	1300	500	
75	Benjamin Granger	Sharon's Rose	F. T. Robinson	ditto	1800	300	205
76	Ditto	Emma	Benjamin Tindale	ditto	1000	500	167
77	Ditto	Niger	T. Smith	ditto	1600	500	293
78	Ditto	Glenaen	B. Sample	ditto	1500	500	199
79	Ditto	Diana	R. Robinson	ditto	1200	600	191
80	Ditto	Sybil	George Leng	ditto	1050	450	194
81	William Storm	Naiad	Edward Granger	ditto	1300	700	177
82	Ditto	Abbotsford	John St.	ditto			
83	Christopher Moorsom	Sarah & Margaret	Christopher Moorsom	ditto	1200	300	199
84	Executors John Ireland.	Pearl	James Rayment	ditto	1050	500	171
85	Executors Wm. Granger.	Welthin	William Granger	ditto	1200	600	173
86	Thos. Huntrods & Co.	Isis	William Harland	ditto	1700	500	226
87	Thomas Huntrods	Oak	Daniel Chaston	ditto	900	500	196
88	Thomas Mills	Hippogriff	Wm. Mills	ditto	1450	500	235
89	Thomas Barnard	Harrisons	Thomas Barnard	ditto			
90	Stephen Crosby	Sea Nymph	Stephen Crosby	ditto	900	500	152

There were 171 vessels insured in this Club, but I have only copied those that were owned and sailed from Robin Hood's Bay, but many of the others were owned and sailed by members who had gone elsewhere to reside.

There was also Ireland and Granger's Club, but the above is sufficient to show the number and value of our fleet of ships at its most prosperous period.

Jacob Storm

APPENDIX 2

Although which line Henry George Storm belongs to has not been discovered, most of the earlier references to his descendants occur in what is now called Tyne and Wear. One connection that has come to light is the second marriage of his mariner son Martin Robert to the widow of Thomas Storm, M.Mariner, of Gosforth, Newcastle upon Tyne, who was lost when his ship was sunk by a U-boat just before the end of WW1. (p.139)

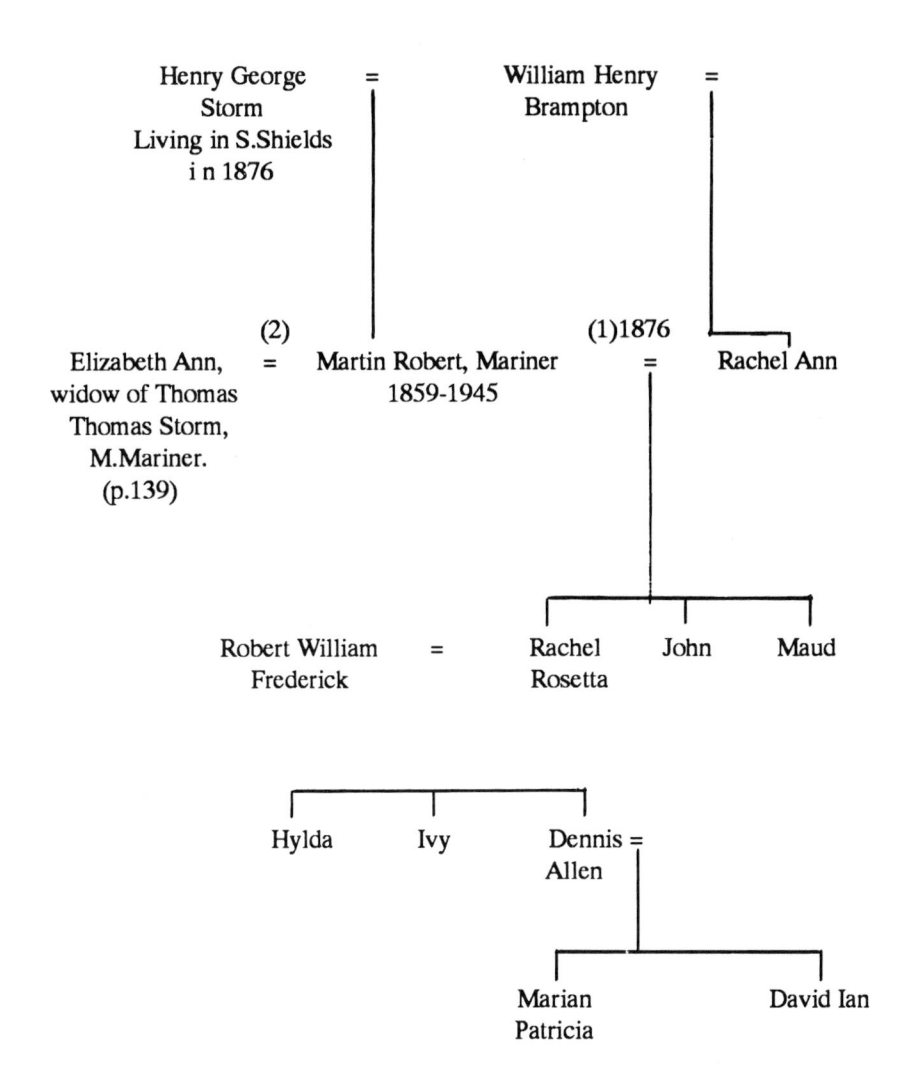

```
        Henry George      =      William Henry      =
           Storm                     Brampton
      Living in S.Shields
          in 1876


           (2)                            (1)1876
  Elizabeth Ann,    =   Martin Robert, Mariner    =    Rachel Ann
  widow of Thomas          1859-1945
  Thomas Storm,
  M.Mariner.
  (p.139)

                                   ┌──────────┬──────────┐
            Robert William    =   Rachel      John      Maud
               Frederick          Rosetta

         ┌─────────┬─────────┐
       Hylda      Ivy      Dennis  =
                           Allen
                                ┌──────────────┐
                             Marian          David Ian
                             Patricia
```

191

LIST OF MAIN SOURCES

1. A reconstitution of Fylingdales families from the parish registers and books, supplemented by registers of the neigbouring parishes.

2. The notebooks, correspondence and miscellaneous documents and transcripts in the collection of Jacob Storm (1837-1926).

3. The decennial census for Fylingdales, Whitby, Hartlepool, Middlesbrough, etc.

4. Whitby Literary and Philosophical Society's Muster Rolls.

5. Whitby ship registrations compiled under the National Maritime Museum's Port Registry Scheme.

6. Probate records of the Borthwick Institute, York, the Public Record Office and the York Registry.

7. Memorial inscriptions at Old St.Stephen's, Fylingdales, and St.Mary's Whitby.

8. Crew Lists of H.M.Ships in the Public Record Office.

9. Directories of the North Riding, Durham and Northumberland by Baines, Bulmer, Slater, Whellan, White.

10. Written and oral reminiscences, principally of many of the people mentioned in the text.